MIDDLE TEMPLE LAWYERS AND THE AMERICAN REVOLUTION

MIDDLE TEMPLE LAWYERS AND THE AMERICAN REVOLUTION

By

His Honour Eric Stockdale
and
Justice Randy J. Holland

With Forewords by

The Rt. Hon. The Lord Phillips of Worth Matravers,
Lord Chief Justice of England and Wales

and

The Honorable John G. Roberts, Jr.,
Chief Justice of the United States

THOMSON
✳
WEST

Eagan, Minnesota

material #40545152

©2007 Eric Stockdale and Randy J. Holland

ISBN 9780314976154

Title: Middle Temple Lawyers and the American Revolution
Authors: His Honour Eric Stockdale and Justice Randy J. Holland
Layout and Design: Christian Dahlager

Library of Congress Control number: 2007923643

This work was printed and bound in the United States of America on archival, acid-free paper meeting the requirements of the American Standard for Permanence of Paper for Printed Library Materials.

ABOUT THE AUTHORS

Eric Stockdale practiced as a barrister from chambers in the Temple for twenty-two years, before serving for another twenty-two as a Circuit judge in Hertfordshire. He has a Ph.D. from the London School of Economics, has qualified as a member of the California Bar, is a Bencher of the Middle Temple and a Visiting Professor at the University of Hertfordshire. Judge Stockdale's last book, partly inspired by the eighteenth-century American links with that Inn of Court, was *'Tis Treason, My Good Man! Four Revolutionary Presidents and a Piccadilly Bookshop* (Oak Knoll Press, Delaware and the British Library, 2005). He is currently one of a team of authors working on the official history of the Middle Temple, to be published in 2010.

†††

Randy J. Holland presently serves on the Delaware Supreme Court. Prior to his appointment and confirmation in 1986, Justice Holland was in private practice. He is the past national President of the American Inns of Court. Justice Holland was elected to be an Honorary Master of the Bench by Lincoln's Inn in London. He has published several books: *The Delaware Constitution: A Reference Guide* (Greenwood Press, 2002); *Delaware Supreme Court: Golden Anniversary*, 2001, co-editor; *The Delaware Constitution of 1897— The First One Hundred Years*, co-editor; and is co-editor of a law school casebook: *Appellate Practice and Procedure* (Thomson West, 2005).

"I tread the walks frequented by the ancient sages of the law; perhaps I study in the chambers where a Coke or Plowden has meditated. I am struck with veneration, and when I read their works, I almost seem to converse with them. When I view the Hall where the most important questions have been debated, where a Hampden and a Holt have opposed encroaching power and supported declining justice, in short, upon whose judgments the happiness of a nation has depended, I am filled with awe and reverence."

***

"Besides there is great variety and entertainment in the study of our profession, especially in England. Here we are not always plodding over books: Westminster Hall is a school of law where we not only hear what we have read repeated, but disputed and sifted in the most curious and learned manner, nay, frequently hear things quite new, have our doubts cleared up and our errors corrected."

***

"It would be impossible to enumerate all the benefits to be acquired in London, but it cannot be disputed that more is learned of mankind here in a month than can be in a year in any other part of the world."

JOHN DICKINSON, writing home, as a twenty-one-year-old student at the Middle Temple: 8 March, 22 April and 25 May 1754.

CONTENTS

LIST OF ILLUSTRATIONS

FOREWORD

by

The Rt. Hon. The Lord Phillips of Worth Matravers, Lord Chief Justice of England and Wales

Eton, Oxford or Cambridge, and finally one of the Inns of Court to become a barrister, learned in the law—such was the path followed by many an English gentleman in the eighteenth century. Those who read this book may be astonished to find just how many of the families of means that had made their homes in the New World made sure that their sons followed the same path, or at least the final stage of it. The uncomfortable and sometimes hazardous voyage across the Atlantic was regarded as no impediment. John Dickinson, who sailed from Philadelphia to join the Middle Temple, wrote home reporting that he had been terribly seasick for thirty-five days of his fifty-nine day voyage.

The Middle Temple was the preferred Inn of Court for the American colonists. In the course of the eighteenth century, some one-hundred-and fifty of them enrolled in that Inn. Of these the authors have selected about half in order to put together, like pieces of a mosaic, the roles that they played in the dramatic series of events that saw the English colonies translated into the United States of America.

This work does more than this, for it also portrays, through the eyes of these young colonists, the life of a student at the Middle Temple. Not all who joined the Inn, from whichever side of the Atlantic, were motivated solely by the desire to practise at the Bar. The social life of the Inn, and its proximity to Covent Garden, gave ample scope for a rather broader completion of a young man's education. Peter Manigault, from a wealthy family in South Carolina, wrote home for "a little Madeira wine and some rum" so that he could entertain with proper southern hospitality, while Charles Carroll from Maryland reported "few young gentlemen are here to be found of sound morals." These, and similar vignettes, are a delight to those conversant with today's somewhat more sober Middle Temple, as are the descriptions of the opportunities seized by the more diligent students of attending sittings in the courts created by flimsy partitions set up in the great Westminster Hall, interspersed with listening to debates in Parliament and then dining in Middle Temple Hall in the company of judges and the great lawyers of the day. In November 1769 Edward Rutledge and Thomas Heyward, from South Carolina, found themselves dining with William Blackstone, who was celebrating the completion of his great four-volume *Commentary on the Laws of England*. Rutledge and Heyward were two of the five Middle Templars who signed the Declaration of Independence. Subsequently seven members of the Middle Temple assisted in the drafting of the Constitution, which they signed.

Of these statistics most of the members of the Inn are aware. But many will not be aware, until they read this fascinating book, of the number of members of the Inn who played significant roles in the gaining of Independence and the forging of the Constitution. Many of these achieved high judicial office, but it is not with this that the book is primarily concerned. Indeed, where qualified lawyers were in short supply, it is not surprising that many who had read for the Bar at the Inns of Court received preference. Nor was there much observance of the separation of powers, and it was not unusual for senior judges to be involved in both politics and executive action. A Chief Justice of today reads with astonishment, and perhaps a tinge of envy, that to further the allied efforts against the French and the Indians, William Allen, Chief Justice of Pennsylvania, sent in 1755 a request to Barclays, his London agents, to purchase a thousand muskets and cartouche boxes and a tun of musket balls and to ship the same to Philadelphia by the first opportunity. He and his four sons, two of whom had followed him to Middle Temple, though not in sympathy with George III and his government, reluctantly felt obliged to remain loyal to the Crown when Independence was declared. Other Middle Templars concluded that the manner in which England was treating the American colonies left them no option but to seek Independence. In many cases this conclusion was only slowly and painfully reached. Once reached, however, the contribution made by members of the Middle Temple to the revolutionary cause was considerable.

The authors have concentrated on those members who came from Virginia, Pennsylvania, Maryland and South Carolina. Of these they single out as especially worthy of consideration John Dickinson, John and Edward Rutledge and Joseph Reed. What is so fascinating, however, is to see how the paths of so many criss-crossed, both in the Temple and in America—they knew each other, they married into each other's families and they ensured that, at every stage of the story, the Middle Temple was represented. Members of the Inn will be delighted with this scholarly work, which brings the threads of our history together, but it will surely appeal also to any with an interest in American history for the new light that it throws on familiar events.

FOREWORD

by

The Honorable John G. Roberts, Jr., Chief Justice of the United States

Americans proudly celebrate the courage, genius, and extraordinary vision of the patriots who pledged their lives, fortunes, and sacred honor in founding the United States of America. Our nation's founders declared independence, crafted an enduring Constitution, and created uniquely American institutions of government. In doing so, however, they were inspired and guided to a large extent by principles and ideals derived from the study of English law and legal traditions. For many of the founders, Great Britain's Middle Temple Inn of Court was a key link between English law and the ideals ultimately reflected in the Declaration of Independence and our Constitution.

Middle Temple Lawyers and the American Revolution sheds new light on that historic connection. Established before 1400 as one of Britain's famed Inns, the Middle Temple from its early days trained extraordinary individuals who were drawn to the New World. Sir Walter Raleigh, who explored the Virginia coast, was a Middle Templar, as was Sir Edwin Sandys, who obtained the Virginia Charters of 1606 and 1618 and established the first representative government at Jamestown in 1619.

As constitutional government took hold in the colonies, Americans seeking to learn law from English sources braved the Atlantic to study at the renowned Middle Temple. By the time of the American Revolution, more than 100 American-born lawyers could call themselves Middle Templars. They included five signers of the Declaration of Independence, the president of the first Continental

Congress, four of the drafters of the Articles of Confederation, and seven drafters of the Constitution. The Middle Temple influenced countless other Americans indirectly, through the writings of the famous Middle Templar, William Blackstone.

This book examines the Middle Temple's influence from three different viewpoints. First, the authors trace the participation of Middle Temple lawyers in the crucial events leading to the founding of the United States and describe the roles of famous statesmen—such as John Dickinson, John and Edward Rutledge, Peyton Randolph, and Charles Pinckney—who applied their legal skills to the cause of independence. Next, the authors examine the formative Middle Temple experiences of the American colonists who traveled to London and took up study at the Inn. That examination, drawn from the transoceanic correspondence between the young Templars and their anxious parents, offers personal and often humorous insights into the legal and social education of America's first statesmen. Finally, the authors set out biographical sketches of some of the prominent colonial families—such as the Lees, Randolphs, Rutledges, and Pinckneys—who benefited from the Middle Temple education.

Middle Temple Lawyers and the American Revolution provides a new perspective, both entertaining and scholarly, on the remarkable early American lawyers who drew upon both their London training and their colonial experiences to launch the ongoing American experiment in representative government under the rule of law. Readers will come away with a deeper appreciation of the character of the Nation's leading colonial lawyers, the role of English legal education in their lives, and the influence of the Middle Temple in shaping American institutions.

PREFACE

In his Foreword to E. Alfred Jones' classic reference book, *American Members of the Inns of Court*, 1924, Chief Justice Howard Taft, the former President of the United States, wrote: "This contains the proof of the instilling in all the communities of the Colonies of the principles of Common Law as taught in the Inns of Court and by the decisions of the English Judges. Many of the law officers of the Colonies, including Judges and Attorneys-General and district attorneys, appointed by the Crown before the Revolution, were members of either the Middle Temple, the Inner Temple, Gray's Inn, or Lincoln's Inn—far the greater number, however, being of the Middle Temple. Many among those who were thus appointed and who were in office at the time of the Revolution were Loyalists who moved to New Brunswick, Nova Scotia, and to other parts of Canada, or crossed the ocean and spent the rest of their lives in England. Though they were thus drawn elsewhere, their presence before the Revolution in the communities where they discharged their functions exercised a potent influence upon the young lawyers who had never had the benefit of the study and associations of the Inns of Court. Moreover, many Colonial lawyers, who were strong supporters of the Revolution, also had the benefit of study in the Inns of Court. When the Revolution came on, the legal atmosphere of every community was permeated with the principles and the methods of the Common Law. So it was that the lawyers of the Revolution who took part in the formation of the new Government brought to that great task a deep respect for, and a close knowledge of, the Common Law."

The years 2006-08 mark the four hundredth anniversary of the Virginia Charter, granted in 1606 after being promoted by some leading Middle Templars; of the resultant settlement at Jamestown, Virginia, in 1607; and of the grant to both Temple Inns in 1608 of the Royal Charter, which finally legitimized their claim to occupy the

Temple in London. The authors and publishers of the present work felt that the middle of those three years—the Jamestown celebration year—might be an appropriate time for a further consideration of those American lawyers, and particularly those who were members of the Middle Temple, who in the following century contributed significantly to the Revolution in different ways. Many played their part in the discussions of the principal issues, using their legal skills, on both the local and the national scene. Some took up the sword, once the pen and the reasoned argument had failed to persuade the British government to treat the residents of the American colonies as citizens with rights equal to those living in England. During and after the conflict, many of those lawyers contributed significantly to the drafting of crucial public documents, including their different State constitutions and the United States Constitution.

As Chief Justice Taft indicated, of the four Inns of Court in London, the Middle Temple in the eighteenth century succeeded in attracting more students from the American colonies than any other. It is a fairly widely known fact that five members of the Middle Temple signed the Declaration of Independence and another seven helped to draft the Constitution, but few people appreciate the full extent of their respective contributions to the Revolution.

Rather less well known are some other Middle Templars who contributed significantly to the success of the Revolution. Among them were two of General George Washington's closest aides. Joseph Reed, a highly skilled lawyer, served with the Commander-in-Chief and was then offered the first Chief Justice's post by the newly independent Pennsylvania but turned it down and later became President of the State. John Laurens, gave up his studies at the Middle Temple to join Washington's staff, and in 1781 was dispatched by him and Congress to get desperately needed help from France. On his return he fought at the battle of Yorktown and then had the great honor of negotiating the surrender of the British as Washington's representative.

Apart from Washington's young aide, another member of the Inn, Arthur Lee, was also sent to France as a representative during the hostilities. After the war, five of the first ministers sent abroad to represent the infant United States were Middle Templars: Thomas Pinckney, his brother Charles Cotesworth Pinckney and their cousin Charles Pinckney; Thomas Loughton Smith and William Vans Murray. Both C.C. Pinckney and his cousin Charles had helped to draft the Constitution in 1787, and so figure in two distinguished lists.

Three of the Presidents of Congress, who preceded the first President of the United States as the titular heads of the infant republic were Middle Templars: Peyton Randolph, Thomas McKean and Cyrus Griffin. Finally, when President Washington was selecting candidates for the first United States Supreme Court bench, he chose two Middle Templars, John Rutledge of South Carolina and John Blair of Virginia.

As Chief Justice Taft made clear, not all American members of the Inn were on the patriot side: some were loyalists while others attempted to be neutral. Nearly all started out loyal to the Crown, but the crass mishandling of the situation by George III's ministers ensured that a majority in the place where it mattered, the Congress in Philadelphia, ended up in favor of severing the links. Between 1750 and 1805, Pennsylvania had four successive Chief Justices who were members of the Middle Temple: William Allen, Benjamin Chew, Thomas McKean (who signed the Declaration of Independence) and Edward Shippen. It was almost inevitable, given their age and background, that the first two of those, while objecting to the British taxation of the colonies without representation, declined to join the Revolution.

Some families, as in all civil wars, were divided. The first President of Congress, Peyton Randolph, obviously, was a patriot, but his brother John Randolph, who had been the Royal Attorney General of Virginia, decided to return to England, leaving behind his son, Edmund, who became Washington's aide, his first Attorney General and his second

Secretary of State. Similarly, Benjamin Franklin, who had the unique distinction of signing the Declaration of Independence, the Paris Treaty of Peace with Britain and the United States Constitution, had the mortification of seeing his only son, William, remain loyal. It was, perhaps, partly the father's fault. Franklin had entered him at the Middle Temple and then, soon after the young man was called to the Bar, succeeded in getting him appointed as the last Royal governor of New Jersey. As a consolation, Franklin was able to bring up the governor's son, William Temple Franklin, as a patriot, and to appoint him, though still a teenager, as the secretary to the American Peace Commissioners in Paris. The first American elected governor of New Jersey, William Livingston, was yet another member of the Middle Temple, one of the seven who signed the Constitution.

We initially tell the story of these different Middle Templars chronologically but briefly through the run up to Independence, the subsequent war and the later drafting of the Constitution. However, the writers came to the conclusion that it might be more helpful to examine their more detailed history in different packets, even though that involves running through the same period more than once. The scheme that has been adopted is to discuss in some detail the education and other facilities that were available for the colonial students attending the Inn; then the Chief Justices of Pennsylvania; the Lees and Randolphs of Virginia; the Rutledges and Pinckneys of South Carolina; the Dulanys and Carrolls of Maryland and finally, the ambassadors (using the term loosely). In the course of those discussions we have referred to other American Middle Templars and have interposed short notes on some of the more interesting ones.

Approximately one-hundred-and-fifty Americans joined the Middle Temple during the course of the eighteenth century, with a bulge of numbers in the middle of the century. We have discussed, at varying length, over half of that number, among whom were some loyalists. The province sending the largest number of its sons to the Inn was

South Carolina, followed by Virginia, Pennsylvania and Maryland. Although such an outcome was not inevitable, those provinces between them in fact produced a significant proportion of the leaders of the Revolution, so we have concentrated on their members of the Inn. South Carolina easily comes top of the list of colonies and States making major contributions. Of the twelve Middle Temple signers of the Declaration of Independence or Constitution of the United States, no less than seven were South Carolinians. So, too, were four of the five Middle Templars sent as ambassadors to Europe by the young republic and one of the two Middle Temple aides of General Washington. The book by Jones, although not readily available, is still there for the reader who wishes to check on the American members of the Inn we have not mentioned, as well as those of the other three Inns of Court.

We have drawn heavily on the work of Jones, who in turn had drawn on the records of the Middle Temple and earlier commentaries on them. We have also made use of a number of excellent biographies and other secondary sources, notably the letters of two students, Peter Manigault and John Dickinson, published over the years by the South Carolina Historical Society and the Historical Society of Pennsylvania, respectively. Put together, those letters give a wonderful picture of the life of the American student in the Temple in the middle of the eighteenth century. In the circumstances we have quoted from their correspondence more extensively than is customary. We have also drawn on the published letters of Chief Justice Allen, which refer to his and his sons' days at the Inn; as well as on the diary of one of those sons.

The only primary sources we have used are relatively small in number and are contained in the unique archive of the Middle Temple. Apart from owing a debt to Alfred Jones and to other previous authors, editors and publishers, we are grateful for the indispensable help given by Derek Wood, C.B.E., Q.C., Master Treasurer of the

Middle Temple for 2006; Lesley Whitelaw, the Archivist of the Inn; and the staff of various libraries, including that of the Middle Temple, the British Library, the London Library, University of London Senate House Library and Cambridge University Library. We are also grateful to C. James Taylor, Editor-in-Chief of the Adams Family Papers and formerly of the Papers of Henry Laurens, for his helpful comments; and to Joan Stockdale, Mary K. Pritchett, Jeremy David Eicher, Elisabeth Madden, Ryan Koopmans, Darlene Ghavimi, Thomas A. Uebler, Tom Leighton, Treva Bohm and Christian Dahlager. The official coat of arms of the Inn on the jacket and the two illustrations of the Hall are reproduced by kind permission of the Honourable Society of the Middle Temple.

Finally, we should like to express our thanks to The Rt. Hon. The Lord Phillips of Worth Matravers, Lord Chief Justice of England and Wales, and to The Honorable John G. Roberts, Jr., Chief Justice of the United States, for finding the time to read the book and for their very kind remarks in the Forewords.

—His Honour Eric Stockdale and Justice Randy Holland

Chapter 1
FROM JAMESTOWN TO PHILADELPHIA

The four Inns of Court in London have for centuries been the bodies responsible for calling would-be barristers to the Bar of England and Wales. Two of the Inns share the Temple, an area bounded by the Strand and Fleet Street to the north, and the River Thames to the south. The other two Inns, Lincoln's and Gray's, lie a little to the north of the Temple, in a part of London that used to be in the (no longer existing) County of Middlesex. The Temple is divided between the Inner Temple to the east, and the Middle Temple to the west, the Inner being the Inn with more than half of the area and of the buildings. This book is, of course, concerned principally with the members of the Middle Temple who played a part in the American Revolution, but Inner Templars will be referred to from time to time— sometimes as the fathers of sons who joined the Middle Temple in preference to their parent's Inn.

Middle Temple Hall
courtesy of The Honourable Society of the Middle Temple

As lawyers and temples are not usually closely associated with one another, the first question that many visiting American lawyers and others ask is: "Why Temple and Templars?" Some assume, not unreasonably, that Inner and Middle must refer to the same thing, so in books one quite often finds authors referring to a member of the Inner Temple when he was in fact a member of the neighbouring Inn, the Middle Temple.

The Temple area was settled in the twelfth century by knights of the Military Order of the Temple of Solomon in Jerusalem, who built a round church there, according to their custom, based on the plan of the Holy Sepulchre in the Holy City, which they hoped to preserve for Christianity. The round church was consecrated in 1185, a rectangular chancel being added in 1240. In 1219 one of the knights of the Order, William Marshal, the first Earl of Pembroke, was buried in the church: he had been one of the nobles who had encouraged King John to grant the Magna Carta in 1215, the origin of some of the Anglo-American common law's basic rights. The knights built two halls in the Temple, as well as a range of other buildings. The wealth of the crusaders' order soon attracted a number of financial advisers and others, including some lawyers, members of a small, unorganised profession.[1]

The Order made a number of powerful enemies over the years, and was abolished in 1312. The Temple became vested in another Order, one deemed more meritorious: that of the Knights Hospitaller of St. John of Jerusalem. However, John Baker pointed out that they probably let out the Temple and never occupied it themselves, adding: "But it is equally unlikely that the Temple was let to lawyers as early as Edward II's reign [1307-1327]." He concluded that they moved into the area in some numbers later in the fourteenth century and that the Inner Temple and Middle Temple existed as legal societies by 1388, when their separate names were recorded.

Little is known about the first hall occupied by the Middle Templars, but the magnificent hall, substantially completed in 1572, is still the pride and joy of the Inn, having been skilfully repaired after bomb damage in World

3

War II. With its double hammer beam oak roof it is reckoned to be one of the finest examples of Tudor domestic architecture, and has probably never failed to impress the law students attending it, whether for dinner, mooting, lectures or revels, and whether they came from England, the American colonies or elsewhere. The same may be said of the thirty-foot table that was reputedly the gift of Queen Elizabeth I. It was built on site, before the hall was completely enclosed, from four continuous planks taken from a single oak that was floated down the Thames to Temple Pier from Windsor Great Park. It has never left the hall. On their call to the Bar, all the students, and particular those who had crossed the Atlantic to get to the Inn, will have been similarly awed by the small table on which they were required to sign their names, as its top was made from a hatch cover from the *Golden Hind*, the ship in which Sir Francis Drake had sailed around the world between 1577 and 1580.

The four Inns never insisted that all applicants for admission should intend to qualify as members of the legal profession. They all accepted that only some of their members would be called to the Bar in due course, and that many had little interest in the law. Sir Henry Chauncey, Treasurer of the Middle Temple in 1685, wrote of the four Inns: "These societies were excellent seminaries for the education of youth, some for the Bar, others for the seats of judicature, others for the government and others for affairs of state."[2] He might have added that many youths had set their sights somewhat lower.

Some of the Middle Temple members were clearly more interested in navigation and exploration, notably Walter Ralegh (whose name is often spelled Raleigh). In 1584 he received a charter enabling him to explore the east coast of the American continent with two ships, although he did not intend to make the journey himself. One of the ships had Philip Amadas, a member of the Inn, as its captain. He had not obtained permission to absent himself from the Inn and so was fined by the Masters of the Bench (or Benchers), who together with the Treasurer governed it and its members.

The small number of expedition members settled on Roanoke Island and named the whole of the land bordering the east coast "Virginia", pursuant to the permission granted by the Virgin Queen, Elizabeth I. Ralegh was anxious to continue with his explorations, as the results of his earlier ones were not encouraging, but in 1588 he was somewhat preoccupied with the Spanish Armada and the threatened invasion of England.

The next attempt to settle Virginia came about largely thanks to the efforts of different Middle Templars. Sir John Popham, who was Treasurer from 1580 to 1587, was determined to succeed where Ralegh had failed and led the efforts to found the Virginia Company with appropriate powers. Ironically, Popham, the Chief Justice of the King's Bench, had been Ralegh's judge as recently as 1603, three years before the Royal Charter was granted to the Virginia Company by James I, on 10 April 1606. The charter had been drafted by Sir Edwin Sandys, also a member of their Inn, who over the years devoted a great deal of his time to the Virginia project. Although his 1606 charter contained no provision for the colonists to have any political control, he saw to it that a charter granted in 1612 made some provision for it.

In 1618 Sandys obtained the "Great Charter" for Virginia, which guaranteed its colonists "self-government, freedom of speech, equality before the law, and trial by jury". The contribution of Sandys to the later development of the rights of the colonists was acknowledged by a twentieth century United States Solicitor General, James Beck, who wrote: "He might not too fancifully be called the 'Father of American Constitutionalism'."[3] It was unfortunate that Sandys managed to cross his monarch and to spend a period as a prisoner in the Tower of London—just as his father, an Archbishop of York, had done in the previous century.

As pointed out by Derek Wood, the Treasurer of the Inn for 2006, the year in which the 400th anniversary of the Charter was celebrated at the Middle Temple, the Virginia Company project was novel in two ways: "It was the first joint stock enterprise, and the first vehicle for exporting governance

Sir Edwin Sandys
courtesy The Virginia Historical Society, Richmond, Virginia

under the common law." He made an important point when he added: "For the Middle Temple it was the beginning of the Inn's long-standing relationship with the United States of America." Lesley Whitelaw, the Middle Temple's archivist, has drawn attention to the fact that it was not only the most successful members who were prepared to back the new venture. "Many Middle Templars and their families were among those who invested, as were a number of London livery companies, impelled by a variety of motives ranging from patriotism and adventure to profit and religion."[4]

On 19 December 1606 three little ships set sail from Blackwall pier, downstream from the Temple on the River Thames, for Virginia. The *Susan Constant*, the *Godspeed* and the *Discovery*, crewed by a handful of brave sailors, carried a hundred-and-five equally brave settlers. The smallest of the three ships was the *Discovery*, a mere twenty-ton pinnace with room for only twenty-one souls. After a very long journey via the West Indies, they eventually made land on 26 April 1607 and went ashore at the site of Jamestown on 14 May. There they met with many problems, later described by George Percy, a Middle Templar, who had been one of the settlers and became deputy governor of Virginia. Almost inevitably, some of his colleagues were more selfish than others: they were prepared to dig for gold but not for vegetables. The situation in the colony was precarious and was alleviated only once Sandys had forced the Virginia Company to ensure that a better class of immigrant predominated, comprising men prepared to settle permanently and to work hard for the community.[5]

Picks and shovels, saws and hammers were the tools that were most essential, but it was not long before the Virginia colonists realised that they also needed some law books. As Billings pointed out in his study of the early Virginia General Assembly: "After 1619, the councillors fashioned their version of criminal procedure largely on the advice they took from such books as William Staunford's *Pleas of the Crown*, Michael Dalton's *Countrey Justice*, and William Lambarde's *Eirenarcha*. Dalton, in particular, gave the clearest direction for what to do."[6] Billings illustrated that point by adding: "Dalton's careful guidance allowed the councillors to apply the English law of crimes to the colonial setting just as they read. For that reason, as much as any other, the General Assembly seldom bothered defining criminal procedures."

The most important provision of the Virginia Charter, as far as the lawyers were concerned, was the one which dealt with the governance under the common law. The settlers and any of their children born in the new colonies and plantations, the Charter stated, "shall have and enjoy all liberties, franchises and immunities to all intents and purposes as if they had been abiding and born within this our realm of England." Similar language was to appear later in the charters of the other colonies, including Maryland (1632), Maine (1639), Connecticut (1662), Carolina (1663 and 1665), Rhode Island (1663), and Massachusetts Bay (1691).[7]

Beck pointed out that that those crucial documents did more than merely provide for the application of the English rules relating, say, to contract and tort. "These charters were the beginning of constitutionalism in America and the germ of the constitution of the United States." When in the eighteenth century the British government began to treat the colonists as though they had fewer rights than their kinsmen living in England, the lawyers among them, and particularly a significant number of Middle Templars, were quick to draw attention to the rights granted by the Virginia and later charters. Not unreasonably, they repeatedly pointed out that they only wanted their legal entitlement, no more, no less.

Although the colonists took the English law with them, they did not always apply it in exactly the same way, but regarded some of the decisions and dicta as more, and others as less relevant to their situation. For example, Chief Justice Coke in *Bonham's Case* (8 Coke Rep, 114) stated that the courts had the power to nullify a law if it were "against common right and reason". Too much stress should not be placed on that dictum, "but whether it was good law or not, the important fact is that the colonists accepted it as a part of the common law."[8] Although Coke's view was not embraced in subsequent English decisions, it appealed to some colonial lawyers and was a harbinger of judicial review in America.

One of the earliest catalysts for the assertion that the colonists were entitled to all of the rights of Englishmen was the use of writs of assistance in the colonies by British authorities. Those writs were general search warrants that permitted homes to be searched without specificity. Middle Temple lawyers throughout the colonies argued that writs of assistance were contrary to the principle that an Englishman's home was his castle.

Coke's dictum was relied on in 1761, when James Otis of Massachusetts questioned legislation by the Westminster Parliament giving customs officers the power to make general searches. Otis asserted that the warrants were illegal because they infringed the rights of English subjects to protection in their own homes. He argued that Acts of Parliament, which violated the sanctity of the home, were void and violated the charter granted to Massachusetts. His submission was made to the local legislature and not to a court, so no judicial decision was involved, but politically, statements of that kind helped to raise the temperature.[9]

Prior to 1700 only a few of American-born students were admitted to any of the Inns of Court. By 1815, however, more than two hundred such students had traveled to London to study law at one of the Inns. The overwhelming majority joined the Middle Temple, and studied there between 1750 and the outbreak of war in 1775. While at the Inn the students could learn more about the rights of Englishmen that had accrued since Magna Carta, such as those acquired as a result of the conflicts between the Stuart monarchs and their Parliaments, and especially those confirmed by the Bill of Rights of 1689. "These Americans who studied at the Inns of Court returned to their homes to become leaders, not only at the bar, but in the public life of their colonies. Later they were to take the lead in transatlantic debates over the British Constitution and the rights of the colonies, and in the formation of the new Republic."[10] The outstanding American members of the Inn will be dealt with in some detail in later chapters, but it is necessary to refer to them in this chapter, as they played a part in every milestone event from the Stamp Act crisis to the ratification of the Constitution of the United States.

THE STAMP ACT CONGRESS

The Stamp Act was passed by Parliament in March 1765 but did not come into effect until 1 November 1765. The delay was to allow time for the colonies to receive notice and for the government to appoint stamp distributors. The Act imposed the first direct taxes on the colonies and required them to be paid on a number of documents, including all legal ones. Under the Act, judicial decisions on unstamped paper were invalid, effectively closing the courts that did not comply. Enforcement was placed under the jurisdiction of the Admiralty Courts, which had no provision for trial by jury. The colonists were outraged by the taxation that had been imposed without their being represented in Parliament, and by the deprivation of jury trial for anyone charged with an offence under the Act.

Two Middle Templars responded with strongly worded pamphlets. Daniel Dulany, Sr., of Maryland, challenged the British suggestion that the colonists were "virtually represented" in Parliament, in his *Considerations on the Propriety of Imposing Taxes in the British Colonies*. He maintained that as long as the colonies could not send their own representatives to Parliament, that body had no right to tax them. John Dickinson, of Pennsylvania, wrote an articulate and widely circulated pamphlet entitled *The Late Regulations Respecting the British Colonies*. The colonists decided to join together in opposing the Act. The Stamp Act Congress met in New York in October 1765; of the twenty-seven delegates five were Middle Templars. They were John Dickinson; Thomas McKean from the three Lower Counties of Pennsylvania, later Delaware; Edward Tilghman from Maryland; and John Rutledge, together with Thomas Lynch, Sr., from South Carolina. All of them but Tilghman were to meet again at the First and Second Continental Congress, and Dickinson and Rutledge were to be important delegates at the

Constitutional Convention in 1787.[11]

Thoughts and discussions of Independence were not to arise for another ten years or so. The delegates wanted justice for the colonies, but were persuaded that their opposition to the Stamp Act would strengthen the relationship with England.[12] They were determined to be respectful to the King and to Parliament. McKean wisely recommended "that the greatest precaution be used to prevent any of the Addresses being printed before they were presented, lest they might be considered as an appeal to the people rather than an application to our Sovereign and the British Parliament." Dickinson referred to George III as "the best of Kings" and "our excellent Sovereign," and advised his colleagues: "Let us behave like dutiful children who have received unmerited blows from a beloved parent. Let us complain to our parent, but let complaints speak at the same time the language of affection and veneration." However, he was also the first person to complain in a setting of this nature about the injustice of the Act, using his own famous phrase, "No taxation without representation." Dickinson's relative and close friend from the Middle Temple, Robert Goldsborough of Maryland, resented the "acts of legislative aggression by the mother country" but remained respectfully loyal throughout the debates.[13]

McKean was concerned about the suggestion that the more populous colonies should have more votes than the others. He successfully argued that each colony should have one vote only, thus giving a preview of the similar discussions that were to take place both at the First Continental Congress, and at the Constitutional Convention, in relation to representation in the Senate. Indeed, the whole Congress in 1765 proved to be a useful dummy run, not only for the Convention, but also for the intervening meetings of the Continental Congress (which after a while dropped the word Continental from its title). McKean was to be the most assiduous attendee at the Continental Congress and to serve a term as its President, so he was well qualified to compare the two bodies. He felt that the Stamp Act Congress was rather mealy-mouthed with its assertions of loyalty to the wonderful monarch and later commented: "There was less fortitude in that body than in the succeeding Congress of 1774; indeed some of the members seemed as timid as if engaged in a traitorous conspiracy."[14]

The Middle Templars led many of the discussions that took place in New York, though they did not speak with one voice. When the time came for resolutions to be drafted, Dickinson played a leading role, producing various drafts until his colleagues were satisfied with the final one, which incorporated some of their suggestions. For example, where Dickinson's draft had simply stated the proposition: "that his Majesty's liege subjects in these colonies, are as free as his subjects in Great Britain," the delegates strengthened his wording by adding that they were entitled "to all the inherent rights and liberties enjoyed by all other natural-born British subjects."[15] This amendment enabled the Middle Templar delegates to add references to the right of trial by jury, which was being subverted by the Stamp Act provision vesting jurisdiction over revenue disputes in the Vice-Admiralty courts, where no juries were permitted. The Declaration of Rights and Grievances approved by the Stamp Act Congress was accordingly largely the work of Dickinson. His experience there was also to prove useful at the Continental Congress, where he was the principal draftsman of the Articles of Confederation.

Once the delegates were content with the wording, they discussed how best to submit their Declaration in London. The lawyers indulged in the kind of semantic debate that gives lawyers a bad name, but eventually agreed that an *Address* should be prepared for the King, a *Memorial* for the House of Lords, and a *Petition* for the House of Commons. Rutledge, who was chairman of the drafting committee, thought that only the King need be addressed, but then agreed that the Commons should not be omitted, and personally drafted the covering document for the Lords.

For reasons best known to himself, Timothy Ruggles from Massachusetts, the chairman of the Congress, declined to sign the various covering documents and resented McKean's questions designed to elicit an explanation. When Ruggles refused to give his reasons, McKean stated that he owed it to his colleagues to tell them if he thought there was anything "treasonable, offensive or indecent" in their proceedings. Ruggles then infuriated McKean, and doubtless many others, by stating merely that signing was against his conscience. When McKean gave him a piece of his mind, Ruggles challenged him to a duel. However, Ruggles sensibly decided that discretion was the better part of valor and made a hasty departure before daybreak. The reason for Ruggles' strange attitude became clear in March 1776. When the British army withdrew from Boston to Nova Scotia, he accompanied it, never to return.[16]

McKean's above account of his dispute with the chairman has an unusual provenance and justifies an aside. Fifty years later ex-President John Adams, who was particularly interested in the delegates from his own colony of Massachusetts, asked McKean for his account of the Stamp Act Congress and of his clash with Ruggles. McKean could find no written account of the proceedings from which to refresh his memory before giving his own version of the events in New York. He explained to Adams: "After diligent enquiry I had not been able to procure a single copy either in manuscript or print, done in the United States, but fortunately met one, published by J. Almon in London, in 1767, with a collection of American tracts in four octavo volumes, from which I caused the present one to be printed; it may be of some use to the historian at least." We shall see later how Almon, a friend of John Wilkes, concentrated on the publication of pamphlets relating to the dispute between Britain and the colonies, including ones by Dickinson, Dulany and Arthur Lee. These pamphlets, many of them reprinted in London, were the principal means by which the colonists' English friends were kept informed about the disputes in some detail.[17]

The British government and the King also received adverse comments on the Act from various critics in England. The combined effect of all the opposition was the repeal of the Act, but unfortunately the victory for the colonies was a hollow one. Parliament immediately began to pass a raft of legislation, commonly known as the Townshend Acts and the Intolerable Acts, intended to extract further revenues from them and to punish them for disobedience. Dickinson once more took up his pen, but this time what he wrote was avidly read throughout the English-speaking world. In his *Letters from a Farmer in Pennsylvania to the Inhabitants of the British Colonies*, he repeated the basic assertions he had drafted for the Stamp Act Congress, but elaborated on them substantially, and in a style that was appealing to the general reader.

Leaving aside the repeal of the Stamp Act, there were probably three principal beneficial results of the New York Congress. The first was that the inhabitants of the disparate colonies learned they had many common interests, which meant that they could agree on a combined course of action, if only they could meet for face-to-face discussions. The second was that the delegates had been obliged to consider at some length, and in discussions, the nature of the relationship of Britain and the colonies, even if Independence was not at that stage seriously considered. The third was that some delegates underwent an experience that was to set them on the path from being mere local politicians to becoming statesmen. Among the latter were the Middle Templars Dickinson, Rutledge and McKean, who were to play important parts in the fiery times ahead.

THE CONTINENTAL CONGRESS

During the nine year interval between the Stamp Act Congress in New York and the meeting of the First Continental Congress in Philadelphia in 1774, the British government's oppressive and foolish acts, detrimental to the colonies, continued unabated. This conduct would eventually lead to a complete break, but before that occurred, the legal and intellectual justification for resistance to the fiscal and other measures imposed on the colonies, was further considered, and especially by the lawyers who had studied law and history in London and elsewhere. After the early days, when

Dalton's *Countrey Justice* had been one of the few legal texts available, the colonies had acquired a reasonable supply of law reports and textbooks, some the work of Middle Temple authors, others reporting decision of Middle Temple judges. A number of colonial lawyers, among them Peter Manigault, a Speaker of the South Carolina Commons, were able to build up a reasonable law library, started with purchases made during student days at one of the Inns and enlarged by later acquisitions, many of them from London by mail order. The law books confirmed the reasonableness of the submissions made by the colonies and the lawyers arguing their case. The contribution of well-read lawyers to the discussions before, during and after 1776, should not be under-estimated. It is worth repeating the comment of Chief Justice Taft: "When the Revolution came on, the legal atmosphere of every community was permeated with the principles and the methods of the Common Law."

In his speech on conciliation with the colonies on 22 March 1775, Edmund Burke, one of the leading supporters of their cause in the House of Commons (and himself a Middle Templar), pointed out that in no country in the world was law so generally studied as in America, adding that as many copies of William Blackstone's *Commentaries on the Common Law of England* had been sold there as in England. Burke asserted, a little extravagantly (and making it sound like a patent medicine), that the reading of Blackstone in America rendered men "acute, inquisitive, dexterous, prompt in attack, ready in defence, full of resources." Blackstone, a great law teacher and judge, was a member of the Middle Temple, and had produced a work that was to be influential in America not only before, but also for many years after the Revolution. The success of his book there was extraordinary, and had a history that contained an element of irony.

"When Robert Bell of Philadelphia had invited subscriptions in 1770, for the first American edition of Blackstone, to be published in 1771 and 1772, he had received the startling total of 1600 orders. Bell put forward a neat defence to the suggestion that he was guilty of pirating Blackstone's work,

HONORABLE
M. JUSTICE BLACKSTONE.

Sir William Blackstone

which was protected in England by the Copyright Act. He relied on what the jurist had written in the book in question, namely, than an Act could have no effect in Ireland or America unless Parliament had expressly so provided."[18]

One of the subscribers to the American edition was Thomas Marshall; although not a lawyer, he was the father of the future great Chief Justice Marshall, and they studied the work together.[19] As Chief Justice, Marshall frequently relied on Blackstone in his opinions, including his landmark one in the most famous case in American legal history, *Marbury v. Madison*, in which he cited him for the proposition that laws must furnish remedies for the violation of vested rights.

In 1774 the Continental Congress was convened in Philadelphia for its first meeting (although later it was to sit elsewhere) for the preparation of a statement of the rights that had been violated by the King and Parliament since 1763. The influence of American Middle Templars and of Blackstone was pervasive. The call for the Congress was prompted by a proposal from the Boston Committee of Correspondence for a cessation of all commerce with England until the Boston Port Act was repealed. That Act had closed the port after the celebrated Tea Party in the harbour in December 1773, which had been provoked by the duty on tea. The idea of concerted action was undoubtedly prompted by the success of the Stamp Act Congress.

The first delegate to be elected as President of the Congress was Peyton Randolph, the Speaker of the Virginia House of Burgesses and a member of the Middle Temple, who made an excellent chairman, despite the brevity of his time in the chair. After Randolph had been elected, Congress discussed the issue of voting rights. Thomas Lynch, Sr., a delegate from South Carolina, who was soon to be replaced by his Middle Templar son, Thomas, Jr., favored a weighted system based on a combination of population and property. The representatives of the smaller colonies, including Thomas McKean, once more proposed that each colony should have one vote only at the Congress, no matter what the size of its population or its other assets.

John Rutledge on this occasion had with him his brother Edward, also a Middle Templar, as a fellow member of the delegation from South Carolina. John reminded the assembled members that they had convened to consult with one another, adding: "We have no legal authority; and obedience to our determinations will only follow the reasonableness, the apparent utility and necessity of the measures we adopt. Our constituents are bound only in honor to observe our determinations."[20] The delegates eventually decided that each colony should have one vote, following the precedent of the Stamp Act Congress.

On 14 October 1774, Congress produced a Declaration and Resolves that relied on the Virginia Charter of 1606 and its successors, asserting: "That our ancestors, who first settled these colonies, were at the time of their emigration from the mother country, entitled to all the rights, liberties, and immunities of free and natural-born subjects within the realm of England." As the colonies had consistently resented interference with the right to trial by jury, Congress also insisted: "The respective colonies are entitled to the common law of England, and more especially to the great and inestimable privilege of being tried by their peers of the vicinage, according to the course of that law." In response to the pleas of Massachusetts, ably presented by John Adams, Congress voted to stop importing from the British Isles, from 1 December until the repeal of the Boston Port Act.

Congress appointed a committee, which included John Rutledge and Dickinson, "to bring in a plan for carrying into effect the non-importation, non-consumption, and non-exportation resolved on." Dickinson drafted a petition to the King, which was approved by Congress on 25 October, and ended with a plea "that your Royal authority and interposition may be used for our relief; and that a gracious answer may be given to this petition." But answer came there none. Instead, the King later expressed his determination to stamp out the rebellion in America.

The First Continental Congress concluded with a resolution that the colonies should elect delegates for a Second Congress that would meet on 10

May 1775, unless their grievances had been resolved by then. Next day Dickinson wrote: "The Colonists have now taken such grounds that Great Britain must relax, or inevitably involve herself in a Civil War." Although he favored a peaceful resolution, he was not at all optimistic. In a letter to Arthur Lee, a member both of an influential Virginian family and of the Middle Temple, Dickinson prophesied that the first act of violence on the part of the British in America would precipitate an armed conflict.[21] It did not take long for that prophecy to come true. The shots that were fired at Lexington and Concord on 19 April 1775 marked the beginning of the Revolutionary War, and soon led to a bloody battle at Bunker Hill and the start of the long siege of the British troops in Boston.

The good thing about the date of 19 April was that it was close in time to that already fixed for the Second Continental Congress, 10 May, when the leaders of the Revolution, from George Washington down to the twenty-five-year old Edward Rutledge, were due to meet in Philadelphia. The composition of the Second Congress was much the same as that of the First, but with the noteworthy addition of a man soon to be the President of Congress, John Hancock; of Benjamin Franklin; and of James Wilson, who had learned his law from Dickinson and was to be an Associate Justice of the Supreme Court of the United States. William Livingston, who was to succeed his fellow Middle Templar, William Franklin, as governor, came from New Jersey, and was asked to draft some of the official correspondence, as he was an accomplished writer.

Dickinson's next task as a draftsman was to prepare, together with the newly arrived Thomas Jefferson, the Declaration of the Causes and Necessity of Taking up Arms. This was issued by Congress on 6 July and was to be read on his arrival to his troops besieging Boston, by the delegate from Virginia chosen by Congress to command the army, with the rank of general: George Washington. The Declaration was, once more, mainly the work of Dickinson, and again contained evidence of his foresight, as in the passage: "Our cause is just. Our union is perfect. Our internal resources are great,

19

and, if necessary, foreign assistance is undoubtedly attainable." However, it also contained his reassurance for the King: "We have not raised armies and ambitious designs of separating from Great Britain, and establishing independent states."

Although John Adams and some other delegates advocated preparation for war, Dickinson persuaded Congress to send yet another petition (the "Olive Branch Petition") to the King, seeking to negotiate a peaceful settlement. Dickinson, who once more undertook the task the preparation of a draft, in which he included the assertion that the colonies were entitled to defend themselves as long as the King's representatives resorted to force to obtain compliance with disputed laws, was adopted, virtually unaltered, on 8 July 1775. Thomas Jefferson commented, "Congress gave a signal proof of their indulgence to Mr Dickinson, and of their great desire not to go too fast for any respectable part of our body." Not everyone felt that way: John Adams for one was furious at the further protestations of loyalty.[22]

When Washington left Philadelphia for his new headquarters outside Boston, he was escorted by a local militia Colonel, Joseph Reed, a Middle Templar who had become one of the city's leading lawyers. His experiences at Washington's side will be discussed in detail in another chapter, as will his later career; suffice it to say for the present that the two men worked very closely together in the early part of the war, although not agreeing on all points.

The siege of Boston was successfully concluded, after a very long winter during which American forces were built up, on 17 March 1776, when the British withdrew to Halifax, Nova Scotia. They were to return in force to New York in July but in the meantime, on 16 May, Congress requested General Washington to come to Philadelphia to discuss the next steps. He attended on 24 and 25 May, and a committee was appointed to plan military operations. On 29 May the Congress decided to notify the colonies to prepare for military action and passed a resolution "that an animated address be published to impress the minds of the people with the necessity of their now stepping forward to save their country, their freedom and property."[23] Edward Rutledge, who had by then taken over the leadership of the South Carolina contingent from his brother John, was one of the delegates requested to prepare an appropriate address.

The next initiative came from Virginia, a colony matched only by Massachusetts in its zeal for firm action to be taken. The Virginia Convention instructed its delegation, which included two members of the Lee family, to initiate the necessary steps so that Independence might be declared. On 7 June Richard Henry Lee duly moved: "That these United Colonies are, and of right ought to be, free and independent States." The opposition to Independence at that stage was led by Dickinson and Edward Rutledge, who felt that a declaration to that effect was premature, as other colonies had not yet passed on their views on the subject to their respective delegations. On 10 June they succeeded in having the vote on the motion put over to 1 July.

On 29 June Edward Rutledge wrote to John Jay, urging him to be present for the vote on 1 July. His own state of mind is clear from the passage: "A Declaration of Independence, the form of a confederation of these colonies, and a scheme for a treaty with foreign powers will be laid before the House on Monday. Whether we shall be able effectually to oppose the first and infuse wisdom into the others will depend in a great measure upon the exertions of the honest and sensible part of the members."[24]

When Congress met on 1 July, it sat as a committee of the whole house to consider the motion. A majority voted to report in favor of the resolution but South Carolina voted in the negative at the urging of Edward Rutledge, as did Pennsylvania, under the leadership of Dickinson. At Rutledge's request the matter was adjourned to the following day, as he thought his delegation might be prepared to join the majority just to ensure unanimity—which was obviously highly desirable.

As every reader is well aware, on 2 July Congress (with New York joining in later) voted unanimously for Independence and on 4 July the Declaration of Independence, largely the work of Jefferson, was also approved without dissent. He had managed to recite the various grievances, based on the King's failure to protect his own hitherto loyal subjects and his failure to accord them their rights according to law. The format that Jefferson used was remarkably close to that used by the English Parliament when drawing up the Bills of Rights in 1689: "Whereas the late King James the Second, by the assistance of divers evil counsellors, judges, and ministers employed by him, did endeavour to subvert and extirpate the protestant religion, and the laws and liberties of this kingdom." There followed a list of twelve specific grievances, coupled with the assertion: "All of which are utterly and directly contrary to the known laws and statutes, and freedom of this realm."

The unanimity of the vote for Independence had not been easily achieved and had required action by three Middle Templars in different ways. Edward Rutledge finally brought South Carolina into the affirmative camp, and signed the Declaration. His colleagues Arthur Middleton, Thomas Heyward, and Thomas Lynch, Jr., were also prepared to support the call for Independence and signed.

The fifth Middle Templar who signed was Thomas McKean, who had all along been in favor of Independence. He realized that Delaware was in danger of having a hung delegation, as his only colleague present, George Read, was going to vote against the motion. He hastily sent a galloper for their colleague, Caesar Rodney, who arrived just in time the next morning to join with McKean in bringing Delaware in on the affirmative side.

The voting of Pennsylvania, the host of the Congress, was something of a cliffhanger, as the majority of its delegation, headed by Franklin, was at first known to be opposed to Independence. Despite that, thanks to two of those opponents absenting themselves deliberately, the vote recorded by Pennsylvania was in the affirmative. John Dickinson was a leading patriot, but still felt that the time had not yet come for Independence. He did not want to vote against the motion and so stayed away when the time came. On 4 July he left the Congress to undertake military service for a while, but returned after some months.[25]

The Declaration of Independence stated, in words reminiscent of the Middle Templar Edwin Sandys, that certain unalienable rights must be respected by the Sovereign. It also asserted that the King had "taken away our charters, abolished our most valuable laws, and fundamentally altered our forms of government." It also contained a list of the basic "rights of Englishmen" that had been invaded by the King, including the denial of "the benefits of trial by jury." The denial of those fundamental rights it described as "tyranny."

The historic decision of Congress on 2 July, confirmed two days later, had been recorded in writing, but needed to be put into effect by being communicated to the citizens of the new nation. Henry Laurens, who was destined to become the President of Congress in the following year, described the scene when a copy of the Declaration was read to the people of Charleston. His elder son John was then still a student at the Middle Temple, but champing at the bit to join the patriot forces. Laurens wrote, in moving terms that echoed the views of many of his compatriots, and illustrated the kind of problems that the conflict brought in its train:

"The scene was serious, important and awful. Even at this moment I feel a tear of affection for the good old country and for the people in it, whom in general I love dearly. I say even at this moment my heart is full of the lively sensations of a dutiful son, thrust by the hand of violence out of a father's house into the wide world. What I have often with truth averred in London and Westminster, I dare still aver: not a sober man, and scarcely a single man in America wished for separation from Great Britain. I am glad you continue with Mr.[Charles] Bicknell and your brother with Mr.[William] Henderson; frugality is essential to you both. Consider I cannot supply you while the sword of Britain remains unsheathed. May God protect and guide you all, and may he still give peace and mutual friendship to the divided family of Britain, and promote the happiness, equally of the ancient root and the transplanted branches."[26]

FROM CONFEDERATION TO FEDERATION

After the approval of the Declaration of Independence on 4 July, several States adopted their own constitutions, which included bills of rights, called Declarations of Rights. Members of the Middle Temple were responsible for drafting some of the first State constitutions: they were well equipped to do so as they had a deep respect for, and keen knowledge of the English common law, and had been influenced by men like Edward Coke and William Blackstone. Virtually all of the first State constitutions contained explicit provisions dealing with the retention or limited reception of the common law, and included Declarations of Rights substantially based on common law antecedents.[27]

The primary draftsman of Delaware's first constitution was Thomas McKean, who though a member of the Middle Temple, had never made it to London.[28] However, he was steeped in the common law and was to make an excellent Chief Justice of Pennsylvania. The convention to draft the constitution met at New Castle on 27 August 1776 and adopted the resultant Declaration of Rights and Fundamental Rules of the State of Delaware on 11 September. Section 13 of that declaration provided: "That trial by jury of facts where they arise is one of the greatest securities of the lives, liberties, and estates of the people." The first Constitution of the State of Delaware was enacted on 20 September. Article 25 stated: "The common law of England, as well as so much of the statute law as has been heretofore adopted in practice in this State, shall remain in force, unless they shall be altered by a future law of the Legislature; such parts only excepted as are repugnant to the rights and privileges contained in this constitution and the declaration of rights."

Thus under the leadership of McKean, Delaware—like many other States—commenced its existence as an independent State with an unambiguous expression of its intention to perpetuate the right to trial by jury specifically, and the common law of England generally. Other States were also guided to a similar outcome by Middle Templars. For example, when South Carolina decided to have a new constitution, eleven men were appointed to draft it, of whom no less than six were Middle Templars. In Virginia, when the constitution was drafted, John Blair of the Middle Temple, one of the most distinguished local lawyers and later on the first United States Supreme Court Bench, played an important part.

Apart from assuring that essential legal rights were safeguarded, the drafters of the various constitutions almost all favored a bicameral legislature and the application of the Doctrine of Separation of Powers as general safeguards. The Continental Congress was, of course, not a legislature, but it only had one chamber. The preference of the individual States for two chambers and the Separation of Powers was to be followed in due course by the drafters of the United States Constitution, many of whom had played their part in the making of their own State's basic law.

The history of the early years of the Continental Congress, well told by Burnett, is fascinating, but this is not the place to consider them in any great detail. What was remarkable was that the institution worked at all, without a fundamental charter and with a ramshackle structure that was expected to achieve the impossible, that is, to provide an Army, properly equipped and paid, and strong enough to defeat a powerful enemy. At the same time it was expected to drum up support not only from its members States, but also from foreign allies. It relied heavily on the goodwill and hard work of the few good men who were prepared to take on personally the particular tasks that were soon to be assigned to Departments of the United States. In the interim a few rudimentary departments were set up by Congress, but they were still largely dependent on the voluntary efforts of a small number of hard-working men.

Henry Laurens, when President of Congress as successor to John Hancock, gave two graphic illustrations of the problems that he and the institution faced. The first was that it was difficult to get delegates to remain in attendance; at one stage he complained that he was left as the only representative of his State for some months. On another occasion, at the height of the war in June 1778, when he was snowed under with official correspondence, he wrote pathetically to his Middle Templar son, John, by then with Washington as one of his aides: "You asked me some time ago why I did not employ a secretary. I'll tell you: I don't know where to get a good one."[29]

The provision of arms and equipment obviously cost a great deal of money, even allowing for the fact that France, as well as entering into treaties of alliance and commerce, supplied some essentials without charge – though exactly how much was free was to be the subject of some bitter disputes. Congress had no legal way of demanding contributions from the various States: it was entirely dependent on their beneficence in response to requests. By May 1779 the persistent financial problems had reached the point where they required the attention of Congress for three days each week. Something had to be done about that, and someone mentioned Dickinson's name.

Dickinson was appointed to serve on two different three-man committees: one was responsible for reviewing all current expenses and the other was to design a plan for future expenditure. On 21 May Congress passed a resolution asking each State to pay its share of the total of forty-five million dollars required by January 1780. Since this was a sensitive request, the best penman was appointed once more to draft it. Dickinson's draft, as amended, included the following stirring words: "Rouse yourselves, therefore, that this campaign may finish the great work you have so nobly carried on for several years past. What nation ever engaged in such a contest under such a complication of disadvantages, so soon surmounted many of them, and in so short a period of time had so certain a prospect of a speedy and happy conclusion? Consider how much you have done, and how comparatively little remains to be done to crown you with success." The sting was in the tail: "Fill up your battalions, place your several quotas in the continental treasury, lend money for public uses."[30]

Like many appeals for money, this one was not entirely composed of accurate statements. Things had not gone quite as well as Dickinson suggested. Washington and his generals had very few successes in the months preceding the document and it was not accurate to say that comparatively little remained to be done. However, the document was meant to raise morale, rather to depress it any further than the request for money alone would surely do.

In 1781 the shortage of money and supplies became so grave, that Congress sent John Laurens to France as a special minister to get more help. Washington stressed to his young aide: "If France delays a timely and powerful aid in the critical posture of our affairs, it will avail us nothing, should she attempt it hereafter. Why need I run into the details, when it may be declared in a word that we are at the end of our tether, and that now or never deliverance must come."[31] Laurens returned some months later with money and supplies: how much that success was due his initiative, and how much to the longstanding efforts of Benjamin Franklin in Paris, is not that important.[32] What was important for Laurens personally was that he returned just in time to be in at the kill at Yortktown in October 1781, where he played his part in the defeat of General Earl Cornwallis, which marked the effective end of the war. He also had the great honor of negotiating the British surrender as Washington's representative. The Peace Treaty formally ending the war was still some time off: the four United States commissioners, one of whom was Henry Laurens, had a great deal of work to do first.

By the time the Treaty was signed, as a result of a shot from a British army foraging party, young Laurens was dead. And so, for all practical purposes, was the Congress that had first met in 1774, although it was to totter on for a few more years, with lamentable records of attendance, leaving it at times without a quorum. It was perhaps symptomatic of attitudes towards the Congress, that when John Hancock was elected President once more in November 1785, he stayed at home and let David

Ramsay, America's first historian and a son-in-law of Henry Laurens, preside in his stead.[33]

In order to understand how the Constitution came into existence, with the help of seven Middle Templars, it may be helpful to consider first a short account of the attempts made earlier by the Congress to secure the passage and ratification of Articles of Confederation. On 12 June 1776 Congress appointed a committee that included the reliable three Middle Templars, Dickinson, McKean and Edward Rutledge, to prepare for a form of confederation. Almost inevitably, Dickinson was once more selected to prepare the first draft. He had earlier disagreed with a proposal by Franklin for a confederation, but by June "Dickinson, it would seem, had at length been converted to the doctrine of confederation, even if he was not yet prepared to embrace the gospel of independence."[34] Dickinson's draft was amended but became the core of the eventual Articles of Confederation. By the time the committee presented it to Congress on 12 July, Dickinson was away on military service.

The Articles included the one State-one vote provision, which proved acceptable once more, but other provisions, such as that providing for a tax on slaves, were hotly disputed. As a result, the whole issue was allowed to drift until the following 27 September, when Congress reconvened at Lancaster, having left Philadelphia shortly before the occupying British troops arrived. The Articles were soon approved by Congress at Lancaster and were sent out to the States for ratification in November 1777. The ratification of all thirteen States was required for the Articles to come into effect, but the final State, Maryland, did not ratify until early 1781, by which time the whole idea had lost some of its support. Some four months later, on 10 July, McKean, one of the original committee members, was elected President of Congress. He had by then undertaken more than his fair share of committee work. This was partly because he was often the only delegate attending from Delaware, and then entitled to be seated on any committee required to have a representative from each State.[35]

The Articles of Confederation, as drafted by Dickinson, provided for the states to retain the power of the purse, and they could not be amended without the unanimous approval of all thirteen states. In essence, the Articles established "a firm league of friendship", in which "each State retains its sovereignty, freedom and independence." Accordingly, it was a league without the powers needed for an effective government.[36]

In 1784 Charles Pinckney III of South Carolina, another son-in-law of Henry Laurens, was elected to serve in the Congress of the Confederation. He had been entered in the Middle Temple when a boy, in 1773, so that the war had prevented his attendance there, but he had qualified as a lawyer in Charleston, under the tutelage of his father. His devoted service to the United States and to his home State was to be outstanding, and will be considered further later, but he is of particular interest because of the amount of thought he gave, first to the amendment of the Articles, and then to their replacement by a new Constitution.

When Pinckney arrived at the Confederation Congress in November 1784, a few days after his twenty-seventh birthday, it was not impressive as an institution: it could not even manage to be quorate for a whole month. It did not take long for Pinckney to spot the weaknesses of the whole system. He advocated change and was encouraged when Congress called for a meeting in Annapolis. On 7 February 1786 he made a lengthy speech, during which he praised the States that had been invited to attend to consider a federal plan to regulate commerce, and which "have wisely determined to make the welfare of the union their first object, reflecting that in all federal regulations something must be yielded to aid the whole, and that those who expect support must be ready to afford it."[37]

Shortly afterwards, when New Jersey refused to pay its requisition to the Congress until a dispute with New York concerning taxation had been resolved, Pinckney was deputed to take a committee to meet the New Jersey legislature. He listened carefully to the legislature's concerns and responded to each one. On 13 March he advised its members: "If New Jersey conceives herself oppressed under the present Confederation, let her, through her delegates in Congress, state the oppression she complains of, and urge the calling of a general convention of the States for the purpose of increasing the powers of the federal government and rendering it more adequate for the needs for which it was instituted." He added: "I have long been of opinion that it is the only true and radical remedy for our public defects, and shall with pleasure assent to and support any measures of that kind which may be introduced while I continue a member of that body."[38]

Pinckney later tried to get the Articles of Confederation amended by the addition of seven new articles to the original thirteen, but his proposal was not accepted by Congress. Andrew Bethea prepared a list comparing Pinckney's rejected proposals with remarkably similar provisions in the later United States Constitution. However, there is no doubt that many delegates at the Constitutional Convention shared many of Pinckney's thoughts, and brought with them, or raised in discussion, many similar proposals for change.

In September 1786 the ineffective nature of the national government under the Articles prompted Virginia to invite all the States to send delegates to a convention at Annapolis to discuss matters that might lead to suggestions for change. Dickinson was unanimously elected to the chair. However, as four States were not represented, the convention passed a resolution, on 14 September, inviting all States to send delegates to a meeting in Philadelphia in May 1787, to discuss ways "to render the constitution of the Federal Government adequate to the exigencies of the Union."[39]

In the interim, Middle Templar William Livingston, the governor of New Jersey, gave an indication of the gravity of the existing problems, writing on 17 February 1787: "I am really more distressed by the posture of our public affairs than I ever was by the most gloomy appearances during the late war. We do not exhibit the vigor that is necessary to support a republic government. Our situation is truly deplorable."[40]

The fifty-five Framers of the Constitution, most of whom arrived in May, were a remarkable lot of men. "Although John Adams and Thomas Jefferson—the two most eminent Americans in political thought that year—were abroad at the time, nevertheless there gathered at Philadelphia in 1787 such men of mark as could not well be assembled in any convention near the end of the twentieth century."[41] Jefferson, who apart from Adams was the only remaining American minister serving in Europe, famously described the men he had been unable to join, as "an assembly of demi-gods".

John Rutledge was selected to head the delegation from South Carolina, which included both young Charles Pinckney and his more experienced cousin, Brigadier General Charles Cotesworth Pinckney. All three were Middle Templars. The other four members of the Inn who attended all came from different States. Dickinson on this occasion came as a representative of Delaware. Jared Ingersoll, Jr., who had worked for President Joseph Reed of Pennsylvania, was one of the delegates from that State. John Blair represented Virginia; thanks to the Constitution he helped to draft, and to his fellow delegate, George Washington, he was able to become one of the first Associate Justices of the new Supreme Court. Finally, the pessimistic William Livingston was one of the delegates from New Jersey, although he only became a member of his delegation after the start of the proceedings.

The authority that the fifty-five men had from Congress was, on the face of it, limited to "revising the Articles of Confederation and reporting to Congress and the several legislatures such alterations and provisions therein as shall when agreed to in Congress and confirmed by the states render the federal constitution adequate to the exigencies of Government and the preservation of the Union." Roughly half the delegates were lawyers and of those, as already indicated, seven were members of the Middle Temple, all of whom were numbered among the eventual thirty-nine who signed the draft Constitution. As experienced lawyers have on rare occasions been known to do, they sensibly interpreted their instructions very liberally, and decided that, in their clients' interests, they should abandon any attempt to make "alterations" but should draft a completely new document. Charles Pinckney was one of those who quickly persuaded the other delegates to draft an entirely new framework for the national government. His cousin, Charles Cotesworth Pinckney, did not at first believe that such a root and branch approach was necessary, but he was persuaded to change his mind.

Two of Rutledge's early proposals affected the remainder of the proceedings. The first was that Washington should take the chair, a very non-controversial point. The second was that proceedings should be conducted in secret. That was rather more controversial, but was agreed to by the Convention, with the result that some of our knowledge of what occurred may be said to derive from leaks—a well-established practice in political life.

This is not the place to run through all the major points that were discussed, but one of great importance that was bound to come up again, as at earlier great meetings, was the question of voting rights: a matter at the heart of every democracy. Once again the smaller States were anxious to ensure that they would not be swamped in the new bicameral legislature by the larger ones. On this occasion they once more succeeded, but only to the extent of obtaining an equal vote in the Senate, though not in the House of Representatives, where population size was to determine the number of seats. Dickinson was one of those who had managed to bring about the Great Compromise, as it was known, which enabled the Congress to settle these major issues. He had been able to call on his experience of office both in the large State that he had represented at Congress, Pennsylvania; and in the State of Delaware, its offshoot, in whose delegation he appeared this time.

John Rutledge had also played a part in the resolution of the voting problem. Shortly before the vote on the Great Compromise, James Wilson hosted a private dinner for the "big states" at his home. Rutledge appeared though not invited. When asked by the host to speak, he asked the big state delegates to subordinate their own interest to the greater good of a union. "I can assure you, gentlemen, that I have been obliged to sacrifice much that I hold dear. However, when I have been tempted to reduce our joint actions to nullity by consulting only my own desire, I have said: 'Is it not better that I should sacrifice one prized opinion than that all of us should sacrifice everything we might otherwise gain?'" Those remarks may have "turned the tide and saved the convention. The big states decided to bow to the inevitable."[42]

Dickinson missed some of the discussions because of illness but contributed significantly whenever present, including the frequently quoted metaphor: "Let our government be like that of the solar system. Let the general government be like the sun and the states the planets, repelled yet attached, and the whole moving regularly and harmoniously in their several orbits."[43]

Once the Great Compromise had been reached, a committee was appointed to draft the new Constitution, with Rutledge as chairman. To Rutledge is given the credit for the inspiring start: "We, the people". Thanks to his legal training and his experience in practice and in politics, the committee was able to produce a draft between 26 July and 4 August. The only major point that can be raised against Rutledge and his colleagues, is that they succeeded, as their forerunners had done in July 1776, in deferring the question of slavery until the next civil war. That was scarcely surprising, given that possibly as many as thirty-five of the fifty-five Framers were slaveholders.44

One reads a great deal about Charles Pinckney's proposals and his claims to have been the Father of the Constitution, which annoyed the hard-working future President, James Madison of Virginia, among others. Bradford stated firmly: "In 1787 he arrived in Philadelphia with a draft version of a new compact. Some of his proposals were embodied in the final version of the Constitution as adopted in 1788, but the draft itself died in committee."[45] The exact extent of his contribution to the final wording of the Constitution does not matter very much now: what remains of importance is the fact that Charles Pinckney was one of those who appreciated the weakness of the Articles produced ten years earlier by Dickinson; that he made sensible proposals for discussion; and that he was one of the lawyers who ensured that all crucial points were fully debated.

As he signed the document he had done so much to bring into existence, Charles Pinckney declared it to be "the best plan in the circumstances." When signing the final draft, C.C. Pinckney stated: "I will sign the Constitution with a view to support it with all my influence, and I wish to pledge my self accordingly." Their fellow Middle Templar, Jared Ingersoll, signed and commented: "I did not consider the signing, either as a mere attestation of the fact, or as pledging the signers to support the Constitution at all events; but as a recommendation of what, all things considered, was the most eligible."[46] Dickinson approved the final draft but, since he had to leave a few days early, asked his Delaware colleague George Read to sign the completed document for him.

There were two further major steps to be taken after the draft of the Constitution had been agreed. Jefferson, who had kept Madison supplied with a "literary cargo", which ensured he was well-informed by many relevant publications, complained to him in a letter from Paris, dated 20 December 1787: "I will now add what I do not like. First, the omission of a bill of rights providing clearly and without sophisms for freedom of religion, freedom of the press, protection against standing armies."[47] The omission of any such bill had troubled some of the delegates at the convention, but Madison and others had persuaded them that the matter should not be included in their draft Constitution. Jefferson's letter helped Madison to change his mind. Two years later, as a member of the new United States Congress, he helped to get the first twelve amendments passed, the first ten being collectively known as the Bill of Rights.

The other outstanding matter was the ratification of the draft Constitution. Middle Templars contributed to the fruition of this stage also, three of them guiding the first three States to ratify. Dickinson, who supported the concept of a strong federal government, became one of the leading and most respected Federalist writers, recommending the ratification of the proposed Constitution in his nine *Letters of Fabius*. They were originally published in the Delaware *Gazette* and later distributed in pamphlet form. One of clarion calls made by Dickinson was: "Trial by jury is our birthright; and tempted to his own ruin, by some seducing spirit, must be the man who in opposition to the genius of United America, shall dare to attempt its subversion." With his leadership, on 7 December 1787 Delaware became the first State to ratify, one of three only that had no votes to the contrary, the other two being New Jersey and Georgia.

When Pennsylvania met to consider the proposed Constitution, Thomas McKean was one of the leading Federalist proponents in favor of ratification He had attended the Stamp Act Congress, signed the Declaration of Independence as a delegate from Delaware and had served as Chief Justice of Pennsylvania for ten years. With his support, five days after Delaware, Pennsylvania ratified.

William Livingston, doubtless feeling much better, used his considerable influence as governor and as a delegate to secure New Jersey's unanimous approval for the new Constitution on 18 December.

In South Carolina the ratification lobby had the advantage being led by Rutledge and both Pinckneys, who were supported by two further members of the Inn: Joseph Manigault and John Julius Pringle. However, it would have been a mistake at the time to regard ratification nation-wide as a foregone conclusion. Not everyone was keen on a strong central government at the expense of the States, and the votes in the three important States of Massachusetts, New York and Virginia, proved to be very close. In the end, of course, every State ratified.

Charles Pinckney, John Rutledge and their five Middle Temple colleagues, had all played their part as Framers of the Constitution and in the subsequent ratification process. The venue for their historic discussions, the State House in Philadelphia, could not have been more appropriate or inspiring. The long road from Jamestown may be said to have led for a second time to Philadelphia—and once more to an equally satisfactory outcome.[48] The long-term commitment of the American legal system to the rule of law and to English common law principles is reflected in the United States Constitution they helped to create. The underlying spirit of that Constitution is the belief expressed to James I by the Jamestown founder, Middle Templar Edwin Sandys, that certain fundamental rights are immutable and must not be subordinated to the changing will of the executive or the legislature.

Commons in the Middle Temple Hall
courtesy of The Honourable Society of the Middle Temple

Chapter 2
AMERICAN STUDENTS AT THE MIDDLE TEMPLE

In the eighteenth century legal education at the four Inns of Court was at an all time low, yet some of their student members became good barristers.[1] That was equally true for students from England and for those making the long journey from the American colonies. The short explanation is that many of the successful ones had come to the law with a good education, and that they were largely able to teach themselves, with the help of books and regular attendance at court. They will also have received some encouragement and guidance from senior members of their Inn, and been able to undertake an element of cooperative learning. John Rutledge arranged with fellow students that they should attend different courts, take detailed notes and then discuss them jointly later. Others cooperated by working on legal exercises with fellow students, when there was always the risk that one might be less enthusiastic than another. For example, in 1749, Edward Shippen wrote home to Pennsylvania about his study partner letting him down in connection with an exercise, a failure that had serious consequences. In 1768, Charles Cotesworth Pinckney and Thomas Heyward worked together in syndicates with four other students.[2]

It is true that the lazy student could avoid such limited obligations as remained, by paying for exemptions, but this book is concerned essentially with students from the colonies who had something about them and wished to learn as much as possible while in London. That they had various qualities becomes crystal clear as one reads of their contribution to the conception, birth and infancy of their new nation.

Many of the students from the colonies additionally attended sittings of the House of Commons and the House of Lords, and some of those definitely benefited from their attendances there. A rudimentary knowledge of the elements of lawmaking and drafting, gleaned while attending debates, was something that the best students, such as John Dickinson and John Rutledge, used to the advantage of their country after leaving London. Although most lawyers would agree that one can learn advocacy better on one's feet than on one's bottom, the intelligent student could certainly learn a great deal merely by sitting to listen to the best speakers in the courts and in Parliament. Dickinson, for one, appreciated that fact.

Many English parents were not concerned to have their sons turned out as professional lawyers: they were content if they returned from the Inns with a better grasp of land law and contract law, so as to be better equipped for running the family estates or business. Parents in the American colonies were often similarly content that their sons should receive a limited legal education, coupled with the experience of living in London, a city that had a great deal to offer—much of it good, some of it bad.

There were undoubtedly hazards that might be encountered in the sinful capital of the Empire, and some fathers were worried about that, having faced temptation there themselves. Chief Justice William Allen of Pennsylvania, for example, was clearly aware of the risks that his two sons ran by coming to the Middle Temple, as he had encountered them himself some thirty years earlier. He wrote to his London agents in July 1761—without making any admission about his own youthful conduct: "I spent six years at one time in England, and am very sensible they are to go through a fiery trial. The many temptations youths are exposed to in your city, and the vice and luxury that is too predominant, make me very anxious on their account."[3]

The hazards were pretty much the same as for students everywhere: women, alcohol, smoking, gambling, idleness and diversions to, and at the theaters and pleasure gardens. William Franklin from Pennsylvania (son of Benjamin) and John Laurens from South Carolina both fathered a child while at the Inn; Laurens married the mother, but not so Franklin, soon to be the Royal governor of New Jersey. It is not inconceivable that Franklin's son was conceived in the Temple, as he chose to name him William Temple Franklin. It would indeed be an extraordinary coincidence if the unknown mother's surname were Temple. Although the Inn records are silent on the subject, there were doubtless other unmarried fathers among the student body, as well as some young men in urgent need of specialist medical attention.

Alcohol was readily available. "London life centered round the tavern, the alehouse, and the club. [Francis] Place says: 'It was the custom at this time, as it had long been, for almost every man who had the means, to spend his evening at some public-house or tavern or other place of public entertainment. Almost every public-house had a parlour for the better class of customer.' In these rooms clubs had their meeting-places. His father when a Marshalsea Court officer and sponging-house keeper, belonged to the 'House of Lords', held at the Three Herrings in Bell Yard, and frequented 'by the more dissolute sort of barristers, attorneys, and tradesmen of what were then called the better sort, but no one who wore a decent coat was excluded'."[4]   Bell Yard was conveniently located opposite the Middle Temple's seventeenth-century gatehouse, and nowadays houses some of the many sets of chambers spilling over from the Temple into Fleet Street,

Chancery Lane and beyond. There was no shortage of establishments selling alcohol in the Fleet Street area, but there were also plenty of coffee houses, such as George's, just outside the Inn at Temple Bar—the arched gateway across the road, which marked the boundary between the City of London and the City of Westminster, to its west.[5]

Smoking was the peculiar habit introduced from Virginia by Middle Temple member, Sir Walter Ralegh. That not every student indulged in the weed is clear from complaints contained in a letter from Peter Manigault (below), who also referred to backgammon as a colleague's vice. Gambling was a pastime of students and card playing was very popular, as Chief Justice Charles Pinckney's wife pointed out when in London. When the Middle Temple Hall floor was replaced in the eighteenth century, hundreds of dice, which had slipped through the cracks, were found under the boards.

For the entertainment of members, including students, the Middle Temple held amusing revels, a custom that continues to the present day, but they were not frequent enough, and possibly not quite bawdy enough, to keep students out of less salubrious places, such as the New Spring (later Vauxhall) Gardens, made more readily accessible for them by the opening of Westminster Bridge in 1750.

Colonial fathers who wanted their sons to become lawyers always had the choice of having them educated wholly in their home colony, so avoiding the long, dangerous voyages entailed, as well as the expense of the traveling and of living in London. They could have their sons apprenticed to a leading local lawyer, who would ensure that they read the papers in their cases, looked up some law, and sat in court regularly. Many leading lawyers qualified without coming to England or joining an Inn, notably, John Adams and Thomas Jefferson. John Quincy Adams could easily have studied at one of the Inns of Court while his father was the resident minister in London. Instead, he attended Harvard and then qualified as a lawyer in Massachusetts only, like his father before him.

One author who studied the South Carolina lawyers of the eighteenth century, came to the conclusion: "Those educated in the province were more successful in their profession than those trained in the mother country."[6] However, it is clear his sample was rather small, as he continued: "Five of the six leading practitioners in the colony (those with more than 500 cases) were products of the apprenticeship method. John Rutledge, Charles Pinckney II, William Burrows and Joshua Ward studied in Charleston, while James Parsons came to Carolina after a term with an Irish attorney. Rutledge and Ward later supplemented their training by enrolling in the Middle Temple, but their practical knowledge of the law undoubtedly came from their apprenticeships."

It seems likely that the American students benefiting most from their time at one of the Inns, were the ones who already had a good grounding in law and were prepared to work on improving their lawyer's skills. The word "polish" is used by some American correspondents to describe the advantage of attending one of the Inns, indicating that they provided a kind of legal finishing school for those colonial lawyers who were newly qualified or almost ready to practice law. It is also clear that when sending their sons or brothers to London, and especially the Middle Temple, a significant number of American lawyers were aware of the shortcomings of English legal education. They knew what was on offer as they had attended the Inn themselves, but reckoned that there were nevertheless benefits to be obtained by their young relatives. John Rutledge attended the Middle Temple and then supported his two younger brothers there. As mentioned earlier, Chief Justice Allen attended and sent two of his sons there, while his successor as Chief Justice, Benjamin Chew, sent a son and a nephew.

There were other factors involved. Some fathers—and others—seem to have thought that there was an advantage in being able to claim membership of an Inn, no matter how much or how little law had been learned. That great friend of America, Edmund Burke, who was admitted to the Middle Temple in 1747, informed a friend: "Even a failure in it stands as a sort of qualification for other things."[7] Similarly, some aspirants, like

William Jones, later a distinguished judge in India and a great authority on oriental languages, thought the Inn would help them into public life. Jones, born in 1746, was admitted to the Middle Temple in September 1770, and called to the Bar in 1774. He was a somewhat unusual student, as is clear from the fact that he was elected as a Fellow of the Royal Society in 1772, while studying law. He was also a keen supporter of the colonists' cause, partly inspired by his American fellow-students.

Jones explained his choice of the law as a subject for study to a fellow linguist, in a letter of 17 March 1771. "My friends, companions, relations, all attacked me with urgent solicitations to banish poetry and Oriental literature for a time, and apply myself to oratory and the study of the law— in other words, to become a barrister and pursue the track of ambition. Their advice, in truth, was conformable to my own inclinations, for the only road to the highest stations in this country is that of the law, and I need not add how ambitious and laborious I am. Behold me, then, become a lawyer, and expect in future that my correspondence will have somewhat more of public business in it."[8]

The most complete picture of student life can be obtained from the entertaining letters of Peter Manigault, an Inner Templar who chose to have chambers in the Middle Temple; and from the more serious ones of John Dickinson, the Middle Templar. Some of the most important products of Dickinson's pen have already been considered, so it is easy to see why he was to be later described as "The Penman of the Revolution." The quotations that follow below suggest that he might with equal justice also be called "The Penman of the Law Students".

Instead of writing one letter to both his parents, Manigault regularly took the trouble to write to each of them separately. The letters to his father were principally about his legal progress and the need for money, while those to his mother were designed to reassure her about his health and well-being. Read together they make an entrancing account of the life of the colonial student. The letters of Dickinson—as one would expect from such a noble writer—were all carefully written and give a detailed corroborating account of life in the Temple. Like Manigault, he also made a point of writing to both parents separately.

PETER MANIGAULT

Peter Manigault, the son of a leading South Carolina merchant, Gabriel Manigault and his wife, Ann, was born in October 1731 and received his schooling in the province. He arrived in England in June 1750, at the age of eighteen, having been admitted to the Inner Temple in the previous August. Once he was considered old enough to have his own accommodation, he chose to live in chambers in the Middle Temple. His parents were content to let him come to London at a young age, because he was escorted all the way by Thomas Corbett, an Inner Templar, who had practiced as an attorney in Charleston. Once in England, Corbett gave private law tuition, with residential accommodation if required. This was a task he undertook for a number of students from South Carolina, and his name appears in many of their letters.

Manigault wrote to his father on 25 June 1750: "Three days after our arrival at Bristol, Mr. Corbett and I set out for London in a post chaise, and got there in three days. I have lost no time since I have been in London; I have been at Westminster Hall every day since the courts have sat, and have kept my commons at the Temple Hall."[9] The reference to commons was to the dinners students were required to eat together, in common with barristers and judges, as part of the collegiate experience. John Laurens, another South Carolinian, was both amused and bemused by the idea, and was to write in 1774: "On Monday I shall be initiated in the mystery of mutton-eating, by which alone I can gain the title of barrister."[10]

The Corbetts were not able to find a house that suited Mrs. Corbett, so they made do with lodgings in Covent Garden on two floors, plus garrets. The accommodation was presumably over or close to a wig shop, as at the end of the letter quoted, Manigault gave the address: "Please to direct for me at Mr. Courteen's, Peruke maker in Bow Street." It was certainly conveniently placed for a law student: in between the Temple and Westminster, hard by the famous magistrates' court (which was to remain on the same spot until 2006) and close to the theaters in Bow Street, Drury Lane and elsewhere in the West End of the city. In August he wrote to tell his mother that his health was good and that he "should like England very well if my friends were here. I found it very lonesome at first for want of acquaintance, but now I am a little used to it, I can make myself very easy." Shortly afterwards he gave the alarming news, "I am become a perfect Englishman," explaining himself by adding, "a mug of porter stands a poor chance when I meet it, and I like red wine better than madeira."[11]

In November 1750 the young man informed his mother: "I like the plays. As I reckon myself very moderate in my other expenses, I think if I may (and I hope you'll think so too) indulge myself in plays."[12] He referred to his fellow passenger Thomas Drayton, also from South Carolina, whose son, William, had just been admitted to the Middle Temple, so it would seem that he had come to see how he was settling into his legal studies. It later turned out that Thomas Drayton would unsettle his son by finding it difficult leave him and return home.

In July 1751 Manigault corrected his mother's confusion over his circuit plans. "You seem to think [Mr. Corbett] and I shall go on a great many circuits together, when in all likelihood we shall go but one. There are only two circuits in a year, one we are going on immediately; the other happens in March, no proper month to travel in! I presume that this time twelve month, which will be the next assizes after March, Mr. Corbett and I shall be quite independent of, and have nothing to do with one another."[13] Sure enough, a year later he wrote to his mother from York, where he was on circuit together with Drayton, Daniel Blake (also from South Carolina), "and two others of the Temple"—but without Corbett. "We are now diverting ourselves with attending the courts, for that is the only diversion we can find. 'Tis well 'tis a good one!"

Manigault turned to his plans for the future: "I hope you will be pleased at my going into the Temple. As I am now of an age to be able to judge a little for myself, I must confess I think it the properest place for me. I mention this because some people think (though 'tis no credit to their understanding) that the Temple is a very wild place, which is by no means true. However, for argument's sake allow that 'tis, yet you can't be against my removing thither from Bow Street, which is situated in the very center of all the bad houses in Covent Garden." Manigault was quite right about Covent Garden: Thomas Pinckney and two fellow American law students got into trouble in that rather seedy area—albeit of their own making.[14]

Though 'twas no credit to his understanding, Manigault's father seems to have believed stories about wild goings on and therefore disapproved of any move to the Temple before his son's twenty-first birthday. The young man demonstrated his maturity when, disregarding any homesickness, he wrote to him on 13 March 1752 about his own plans for the immediate future. "I would not, without your desire, leave England till this time two year, and would employ all the intermediate time in a close application to my improvement. But as I presume you would like to know particularly how I would bestir myself during so long a space, so I ought in duty to inform you that I would choose to stick close to my books all this summer, in London, and in the fall, go the Northern circuit and then have an opportunity of seeing such relatives as I have in that part of England. The next winter I would also choose to spend in London and omit nothing that can possibly be of advantage to me. This you may depend upon, that I don't want to lengthen my stay here, either out of fondness for England, or any dislike of Carolina, but merely for the sake of my improvement."[15]

Manigault wrote to his father again on 2 July 1752. "As soon as I return from the country, it will be time for me to look out for proper apartments in the Temple. I am indeed very sorry to leave Mr. Corbett." He referred to his father's permission to leave the shelter of Corbett's home on October 10, when he was to attain his majority, and expressed his gratitude for Corbett's help. He continued: "When I get into a place which is agreeable to my inclinations, I shall have the greater spirit to go through with my studies, and I must say (though from no motive of vanity) that I have already made some progress in the law, and make not the least doubt, but that by the time I leave England, I shall have made as great a proficiency as can reasonably be expected."

He intended taking furnished chambers in the Temple, but he needed his father's help to ensure that they would be properly equipped for the hospitality to be expected of a southern gentleman - even though he could not have guessed that one of his first guests would be a Chief Justice. "When I am in chambers of my own, I shall from time to time have some of my acquaintances to see me, whom I would treat after my own Country fashion; and for that purpose, I, (who seldom write a letter without asking a favor) would be thankful to you for a little madeira wine and some rum." As though to reassure his fond father that he was not turning into an alcoholic, he added to the foot of his letter: "Please to direct for me, at George's Coffee House, Temple Bar."[16]

On September 25 Manigault was able to report to his mother: "Since I have been in London, Mr. Corbett and I have been often searching for apartments in the Temple, and have at last found a very good set, into which I am soon to remove. If you have occasion to direct any one to me, I am to be found at No. 3, one pair of stairs, Brick Court."[17] The great William Blackstone's chambers were next door, at 2 Brick Court.

Manigault went on: "I fancy you would be pleased to know what sort of a place it is that I am to live in. The Temple is situate remote from noise, and all paved with flat stones, so that no carriage can come into it. The buildings have commonly four floors, and every building has one staircase. At the landing place of each pair of stairs, there are two doors, each of which lead into apartments, where people of the best fashion live." This was an interesting point: the chambers were not all taken up by barristers and students. There were more than enough for them at that time, so outsiders were permitted to take tenancies. He continued: "These apartments, or according to the common phrase 'chambers', consist of different numbers of rooms, from six to two, according to the size of the building. Mine have three rooms, besides a large light passage and a small place for a servant to lie in. Mrs. Motte has promised to come and see them, that she may give you a particular account of them."[18]

James Boswell, Samuel Johnson's biographer, was at one time such an outsider resident in the Temple. His description of it in his journal for 6 April 1763 complements that of Manigault—and remains true to the present day: "We strolled about the Temple, which is a most agreeable place. You quit all the hurry and bustle of the City in Fleet Street and the Strand, and all at once find yourself in a pleasant academical retreat. You see good convenient buildings, handsome walks, you view the silver Thames. You are shaded by venerable trees."[19]

Displaying all the exuberance of a young man with his own place for the first time, Manigault continued his letter: "Here I promise myself vast satisfaction, as I shall have nothing to consult but my own convenience. If I stay out late at court, I have nobody waiting for me to dinner. If I am up early, I can have my fire made without any disturbance to a family. If I have a friend to visit me, I can entertain him without inconvenience to anyone. When I am in an humor to study, I have no noise to interrupt me, and I am near the Temple Library, whither I may at any time resort. I am in the midst of my acquaintance and the profession I am in pursuit of. These are advantages of no slight moment."

In the following year he informed his mother about his catering arrangements, when not eating one of the required number of dinners, or commons, in Hall. "I never know, nor indeed desire to know, what my dinner is before I see it upon the table. There is an eating house within twenty yards of me, kept by the inimitable Miss Sally, a lady much caressed by the Templars; at the shrine of her larder, I constantly pay my adorations when I am hungry."[20]

Gabriel Manigault wrote to Corbett about his son's progress, prompting a letter from the young man on 18 October 1752. "Mr. Corbett tells me that you would be pleased to hear that I spoke readily and fluently. This is an attainment which I have all along had in my eye, and as I thought myself apt to stutter, and be at a loss for words, I have always endeavored by speaking slow and carefully, to break myself of this ill habit. As to the purchase of law books, there are every week sales of them about Temple Bar, which I shall attend in order to pick up bargains of that sort. Mr.Freeman t'other day sold all his uncle's books, as well law as others, for the value of £45. If I had known his intentions, and had given him £5 more than he got for them, I should have had them for less than half the prime cost, though they were very little the worse for use. I am afraid when I tell you that the chambers that I am to live in will cost near £50 a year. I assure you that no tolerable place can be got for less money, and that mine are reckoned among the cheapest apartments in the Temple."[21]

It was as well that the young man's speech impediment was cured, as he was to become Speaker of the South Carolina Commons. The reference to law book bargains is of interest as it marked the beginning of his valuable collection, one that he might never have started to build up, had he stayed in South Carolina for his legal education.

When Manigault was nearing the end of his studies, his father received reports of his frivolity and expressions of concern that he might not be serious about the law. The young man explained to his mother, with characteristic humor, how the misunderstanding had arisen. "My father seems to be under no small uneasiness for fear I should not mind the law. The truth is that I make it a rule whenever I am in company to be as merry and good humored as possible, and many wise folk take it for granted that mirth and the law are incompatible."[22]

By 2 February 1754 the studies were all completed. Manigault informed his mother: "I am now in my state of probation in order to be called to the Bar; and the very next week, the rude hands of a barber must take off my head of hair, which I have been cultivating with great care for these four years; and a tye wig must cover my shoulders. My friend Drayton was to have been called with me; but his good friend Mr. Shubrick advises him to put it off till remittances come from Carolina. Happy I! who by the goodness of an indulgent father, meet with no such stops in the progress of my education."[23] He did not say where he bought his wig, but he may have gone back to Mr. Courteen of Bow Street for it.

On February 26 the barrister reported to his generous father: "The latter end of last Hilary Term, that is, about a fortnight ago, I was called to the Bar. The whole expense including, tye wig and everything else, amounted to very little less than £50." After his call Manigault remained in London for a few more months. On March 29 he gave his father an account of his latest expenditure on law books and his tailor. He added the great news that he had argued, and actually been paid for his first case, which had been heard by the most senior judge in the country, no less. "I will not make any apology for putting you to so large an expense, as I know you are content, provided 'tis made good use of. I have already got two guineas and a half by my profession, which lucky beginning seems to be a presage of greater acquisitions. But I did not get this money for nothing. With all the effrontery I could muster, I hardly knew where I was when I first opened my lips before the Lord Chancellor. I am afraid I am troublesome to my good friend Mr. Corbett, I so often go to him for his advice."[24]

"Where do you think I am?" the young man asked his mother in April. "At the Carolina Coffee House, smoked to death with tobacco, between two very greasy old gentlemen, who perhaps are at this moment looking at what I am writing. People ask me how I can leave dear London. My answer is that I am no proud man, and Carolina is good enough for me. Don't be surprised at this incoherent letter, for 'tis not very easy to write in the midst of tobacco smoke and an eternal buzz of busy gentry."[25]

On 12 July 1754, Manigault informed his mother: "All your acquaintances who have abandoned Carolina for the happier climate are safe arrived and I have had much pleasure in paying visits to them all round. Mr. Drayton has fixed his headquarters at his son's chambers, and eats, drinks and what's more than all, sleeps with him. If he continues this manner of living, the young squire will be able to study very little law. You must know I am generally at home from five o'clock in the afternoon till nine at night, and when his son happens to, he comes and plagues me to play at backgammon with him, which is at least as disagreeable as reading Lord Coke. After he had served me thus five or six times, I shut my door and bade my man William to say that I was gone out."[26]

The pained reference to Coke reminds one of the doggerel by John Trumbull, one of John Adams' law students (not to be confused with the famous painter of that name):

> In solemn coif before my eyes,
>
> I see the awful Coke arise;
>
> There Bracton, Fleta, Blackstone, Wood,
>
> And fifty more, not understood.'[27]

Poor William Drayton should have been called with Manigault, but was in fact not called to the Bar by the Middle Temple until another year had passed. Whether it was his father or his backgammon or a shortage of funds to blame for the delay—or possibly all three—is not clear. However, one need not feel too sorry for him: even before the Revolutionary War he was already Chief Justice of East Florida. He fell out with the governor, Patrick Tonyn, and was dismissed by him, but later obtained judicial office in South Carolina.

At about the time Manigault was finishing his studies, Eliza Pinckney, who was then living in London with her husband Charles, the former Chief Justice of South Carolina, wrote to the young man's mother to congratulate her "on the near prospect of having the child of her heart return to her".[28] She added: "While I am pleasing myself with the happiness of one worthy family, my heart aches for another. How sincerely do I pity the good father who has neglected nothing for the advantage of an inconsiderate and thoughtless son." The letter went on to tell the tale of the law student, known also to Ann Manigault, who had fallen from grace.

John Garden was the son of the Revd. Alexander Garden, a South Carolina cleric and botanist, whose name was immortalized when his Swedish friend, the great Carolus Linnaeus, named the gardenia in his honor. John was also in England as a law student but, as Eliza Pinckney related, "now at a spunging house in London." The spunging (or sponging) house was the halfway house on the road to the debtors' prison. "He some time since left his Master, had got a wild scheme in his head of taking a house in the country and giving up all thoughts of the law, of which he seemed to have a contemptible opinion. Mr. Pinckney heard of this by accident, informed Mr. Corbett of it and begged the favor of him to assist him in finding him, which they did; and after some time brought him to a better way of thinking and to consent to go back to his Master, an eminent attorney, provided he would receive him. His Master and some of his friends were for having him carried to prison. A fine school for the reformation of youth!"

There was more to the story of young Garden, but it need not be recounted here. The point of the above extract is to give an example of the occasional student failing to pursue his studies sensibly, and to demonstrate how responsible adults from the home colony could help out. Garden, who was not a member of any Inn, was lucky enough to have the help not only of the ever present Thomas Corbett, but also of the former Chief Justice. In the published papers of Henry Laurens there are several similar examples of his, or another colonist in London, exercising an avuncular role and looking after the sons of friends or acquaintances, whether at school or in higher education. Incidentally, Henry Laurens warned his own son, John, about the temptations facing him as a law student in London, particularly from the opposite sex, but that advice, as so often, was ignored.

When Laurens was in South Carolina, his London agent kept an eye on his sons for him. David Hancock has pointed out that on top of their commercial work, "London agents attended to more human concerns, as well, and this rise in an 'intimate social relationship' seems to have been new to the eighteenth century. [Alexander] Grant cared for his clients' relatives in London; often he lodged them in his house or found them a job with his firm. Other associates stood similar watch over their clients' relatives when they attended Oxford, Cambridge, or the Inns of Court. [Richard] Oswald and his wife Mary, for instance, cared for Henry Laurens's children when they were living in London in the early 1770s, and he introduced John Laurens to London's leading legal lights several years later."[29] Corbett was also available to give John Laurens advice about the law.

After returning to South Carolina, Peter Manigault successfully applied his legal training to practicing, business and local politics, serving as Speaker of the Commons House of Assembly from 1765 to 1772, when his health failed him. The new Speaker was Rawlins Lowndes, who was later to take over the wartime Presidency of South Carolina from John Rutledge for a short period. During the time he was Speaker, Manigault gave up practicing law and sold the extensive law library he had started to build up while in London, which by then was worth about £3000.[30] He returned to London in 1773, hoping that his health would improve with treatment, but it declined further, and he had a few miserable final weeks staying with friends, separated from his family on the other side of the Atlantic.

Henry Laurens, a good friend of the Manigault family, wrote to his son John that on 26 September he had "set our friend Manigault down at Mr. [Benjamin] Stead's in Berners Street, where he continues under the sentence of death passed by the eminent surgeons." He later referred to "my daily and nightly attendance on my friend Peter Manigault", and was one of the last to see him alive, shortly after his forty-second birthday. On the evening of 12 November 1773 Laurens wrote to Peter's father, Gabriel, about the poor state of his son when he had left him a short while earlier. He described how Peter had asked him to draft a codicil, leading him, a mere layman, to protest that he did not have the necessary legal skills. Peter Manigault commented, typically, "It would vex me to have it delayed," and wrote it himself.

Laurens reported: "The codicil consists only of two clauses, ordering that the negro woman Moll and her children shall be freed from slavery immediately after his death; and his man July, at the end of three years from that period." In fact, Peter Manigault had died before midnight, shortly after Laurens' departure. A week later a respectful small contingent of London's South Carolinian population escorted Manigault's body to a ship at Tower Stairs, so that he might be buried at home. The party included Henry Laurens, Ralph Izard and Thomas Pinckney, destined to become the President of Congress, one of the first United States Senators and the first Federal ambassador to Britain, respectively[31]

Peter Manigault's wife had died nine months before him, so their children were cared for by their grandparents, Gabriel and Ann, the recipients of Peter's letters. The elder boy, also Gabriel, went to school in Geneva and then proposed coming to London to study. His grandfather, who addressed him as Gay, advised him in March 1777: "When you come to England I would not have you confine yourself to studying the law alone, but to improve yourself in other useful improvement." His late son, despite his distinction in South Carolina, had obviously not succeeded in persuading him that the Temple was "the properest place", or anything approaching that, for he continued: "I don't find the Temple will be a proper place for you, being a very disorderly place. Therefore you must advise with Mr. Savage and Mr. Manning of the most proper place for you."

Whatever criticisms of the Temple may have been justified at the time, Gabriel Manigault had somehow got the wrong impression as to the extent of its failings and could not be shaken in his opinion. Distance did not help. Thomas Jefferson displayed a similar entrenched misconception when he wrote to a friend in 1785, the year *before* his only visit to England: "Let us view the disadvantages of sending a youth to Europe. If he goes to England he learns drinking, horse-racing and boxing."[32] Manigault continued his letter to his grandson: "Your attendance at the several courts of justice must be a great advantage, also on the debates in parliament. Enclosed is Colonel Laurens' opinion of the best route you can take from Geneva to England."[33] Henry Laurens was able to give that advice as his son, John—soon to be a colonel also—had been to school in Geneva before joining the Middle Temple. (William Manning was Henry Laurens' London agent and had just become John Laurens' father-in-law.)

Young Gay took note of his grandfather's views and joined Lincoln's Inn, studying until 1780. In that year he returned to Charleston, just in time to join the militia only days before the fall of the city to the British, and only months before his grandfather died. After the surrender Gay took the oath of allegiance to the Crown and was soon appointed a magistrate. His younger brother, Joseph, was one of the few Americans to join an Inn of Court while the war was still being fought. Gay's diary entry for 3 July 1781 reads: "My brother Joseph went on board the *Prince William Henry* packet in the morning, to sail for England."[34] Doubtless on the recommendation of Gay, on 6 September he joined the Middle Temple, where their father had been very happy in his chambers. After his return home, Joseph married a daughter of Arthur Middleton, one the Middle Temple signers of the Declaration of Independence. He was later a delegate to the State convention, which ratified the Constitution of the United States in May 1788.

The fact that the three Manigaults joined three different Inns, and that the first of them was a member of one Inn and occupied chambers in another, is of no great significance. Various members of the Lee family of Virginia also joined different Inns. Arthur Lee, two of whose brothers had joined the Inner Temple, joined Lincoln's Inn first and then switched to the Middle Temple. He gave at least three different addresses in the Middle Temple—two of them while still a member of Lincoln's Inn only. Then, as now, barristers took chambers in whichever Inn was most convenient, although a prospective head, or legal tenant of a larger set of chambers, might well be required to be a member of the Inn concerned—presumably to safeguard the payment of the rent without resort to litigation. If he was a member of another Inn of Court, then as long as he was of good standing and prepared to pay a small fee, he could be admitted to the landlord Inn as a barrister *ad eundum* (*gradum* omitted), that is, to the same degree.

The Inns resembled—and still resemble—university colleges, in having a head, a governing body of senior members, professors of law or teachers (loosely defined), ordinary members (the barristers) and students, together with support staff. Similarly, like a college, each Inn had its own hall, chapel, library and accommodation for work and lodging. The only exception to this rule is that the Middle Temple and Inner Temple have always shared the Temple Church as their chapel. The *ad eundum* provision copied the practice used by the universities when admitting a member of another university, with status equivalent to that enjoyed in his original institution.

The choice of Inn was influenced greatly by the experience and advice of members of the student's family and friends. In the eighteenth century there was clearly an additional factor at work, favoring the Middle Temple. Once a certain number of students had joined from South Carolina, clearly the word got around Charleston that the Middle Temple was not only the Inn with the most American members, but also the one where one could meet a number of fellow students from one's own 'country', thus reducing the problem of homesickness. The issue of homesickness was, of course, far more serious in the days when students could not go back to their parents during vacations, and when a sad letter home would not receive a tender reply for three months or so, if at all.

JOHN DICKINSON

John Dickinson, whose political career has already been discussed, had several advantages as a young would-be lawyer. His father Samuel was a lawyer and his mother Mary was a member of one of the leading families of Philadelphia, the Cadwaladers. They had ensured that he received a good school education, and then were able to place him with an excellent lawyer as an apprentice, namely, John Moland. Another of Moland's apprentices at the time was George Read, who, like Dickinson, was to be a member of the Continental Congress. Like Dickinson, he decided he could not vote for Independence in July 1776; his decision to vote against Independence, rather than abstain, nearly prevented the assembled colonies' delegates from voting unanimously on the great issue.[35]

Although Dickinson was only a year younger than Peter Manigault, their time at the Middle Temple hardly overlapped. Because of the period Dickinson had spent learning law at home with Moland, by the time he arrived in England to further his studies, Manigault was only two months away from his call to the Bar. When the twenty-one-year-old Dickinson arrived in London 10 December 1753, he went straight to the home of John Hanbury, a leading Quaker merchant dealing with North America, who had helped a number of students from the colonies. "A gentleman in his compting house" took the new arrival at once to the Middle Temple, where he met his relative, Robert Goldsborough from Maryland, who had joined the Inn in the previous December. After Goldsborough's mother had died when he was only five, his father Charles, another lawyer, had married Dickinson's half-sister, so that Dickinson held the exalted rank of step-half-uncle (if such exists). More important was the fact that the two young men, who were to be called to the Bar together three years later, were firm friends in the meantime. After call, Goldsborough was to practice in England for a while before returning home in July 1759 to continue his legal career. He was appointed Attorney General of Maryland in 1766 and later served, with Dickinson, as a delegate to the Continental Congress.

Dickinson wrote home on 18 January 1754 that on his first day in London, Goldsborough "very generously made me an offer of part of his bed till I could procure chambers of my own, which was too acceptable for me

John Dickinson
courtesy of the Delaware Division of Historical & Cultural Affairs, State Portrait Collection

to refuse."[36] Dickinson at once contacted the Middle Temple Treasury and found Charles Hopkins, the Under-Treasurer and chief officer of the Inn, to be extremely helpful. A few weeks later he described Hopkins in a glowing manner: "His humanity and integrity procure him the love and esteem of every one."[37] Dickinson was formally admitted to the Inn as a member on 21 December 1753 and was able to put his name down for a set of chambers at once. Although the rent was normally £15 a year, Hopkins asked for £12 only. However, the premises needed some considerable refurbishment, which he arranged, so Dickinson had to wait for some weeks before he could occupy them. In the same letter the young man demonstrated that he had already grasped one of the basic points: "Every person lives without control in his chambers, and according to his disposition may either prosecute his studies with the greatest quiet in them, or employ them to the worst purposes." He failed to give particulars of the purposes he had in mind.

Dickinson continued with some domestic details, to set his mother's mind at rest. "A laundress attends by seven in the morning, lights our fire, brings the bread, milk and butter and puts on our tea kettle. We wait on ourselves at breakfast, which is no manner of trouble, and after, she returns, makes our beds and sweeps the rooms. We then follow our studies till three or four o'clock, which in winter is just dark; then we go to a chop house and dine, after which we step into the coffee house, and in a little time return to our chambers for the evening. This account of one day will serve for all the rest, except the occasional breaks of visits, business &c." He made it clear that he preferred to live in chambers, rather than being a boarder with a family outside the Temple, for much the same outlay. As Dickinson had omitted to bring his books with him, he asked his father to send them on, "for as I am now to polish myself for the last time to make my public appearance, I am resolved to omit nothing."

On the next day Dickinson wrote a long letter to his mother, making it plain that he was already being extremely well looked after—unlike Manigault, whose early days in London had clearly been lonely. "At Mr.

Hanbury's I am entirely at home, for so he commands me to be, and he would not like it if I were to stand on ceremony. I drop in at dinner, tea or supper, and pass away two or three hours with the greatest happiness." Rebecca Anderson, originally from Maryland, whose husband was another London merchant, had heard he was in town and had invited him to dinner on Christmas Day. "I frequently go to see them." He was also invited by Moland's sister, who lived in London. Dickinson reported that he had been to the theater several times already and had managed to skate during the very hard weather. Goldsborough "behaves with all the affection of a brother towards me; I shall stay with him till I get into my own chambers."[38]

His lawyer father must have been delighted when he read his son's letter of 8 March. "I tread the walks frequented by the ancient sages of the law; perhaps I study in the chambers where a Coke or Plowden has meditated. I am struck with veneration, and when I read their works, I almost seem to converse with them. When I view the Hall where the most important questions have been debated, where a Hampden and a Holt have opposed encroaching power and supported declining justice, in short, upon whose judgments the happiness of a nation has depended, I am filled with awe and reverence. When I see men advanced by their own application to the highest honors of their country, my breast beats for fame! Such are the rewards of diligence; the same means are in my power. Why do I loiter? I quicken at their glory, I turn from their sight, and fly to my books, to retirement, to labor, and every moment is an age until I am immersed in study. I now have an opportunity of seeing and hearing the most learned lawyers and the finest speakers. Since my last, I have heard some of the greatest men in England, perhaps in the world."[39]

In the same letter Dickinson made shrewd comments about some of the judges and lawyers he had seen in action. Serjeant Poole seemed to be lost if he was not able to use the exact words of the law book in front of him. "Many of his brethren are like him, so that their heads are a kind of index to all books in general, and are instances of the necessity of a lawyer's not confining himself barely to acquiring knowledge, but of qualifying himself to communicate it to others."

On the same day the dutiful son also wrote to his mother about his improving health. He had been terribly seasick for thirty-five days of his fifty-nine day voyage and then suffered from a bad cold after his arrival in London. By 8 March he was able to report: "I grow heartier every day and am in great hopes not only of enjoying my health while here, but that my stay in England will strengthen my constitution and confirm it for the future part of my life." He added a surprising statement: "There are numberless instances of it in my own countrymen even within the Temple, who have come here in a much worse state than I did, and in two or three years have become different persons. Indeed, I begin already to hear some jests on the difference between roast beef and hominy."

With the approach of spring, he was beginning to enjoy London more and going for walks. "The fields beyond St. James's towards Kensington are inconceivably delightful; the Serpentine river glides through them, whose banks are covered with grass and regular as the nicest pastures." On 29 March, having recovered his health, he felt he could reveal to his mother how ill he had been after his arrival. "London did not agree with me very well at first, when I was prodigiously weak with the fatigue of the voyage, but I soon recovered by retiring for a month to a country village called Clapham, about four miles from London. It is remarkable for its pure air, which quickly recruited me."[40] (A few years later Benjamin Franklin, as a scientist, tried pouring oil on the troubled waters of a pond at Clapham, successfully calming them.)

When he read his son's letter of 22 April, if not earlier, Samuel Dickinson must have felt that the expense involved in sending his son to London was amply justified. "Besides there is great variety and entertainment in the study of our profession, especially in England. Here we are not always plodding over books: Westminster Hall is a school of law where we not only hear what we have read repeated, but disputed and sifted in the most curious and learned manner, nay, frequently hear things quite new, have our doubts cleared up and our errors corrected. The bar is a perfect comment upon the written law, and *every great man at it is in some measure a master and instructor to these young students* who have the wisdom to attend."[41] His last comment was perhaps prompted by his critical view of the students, who could not be bothered to take advantage of what was available and then complained that they were receiving no legal education.

In his letter of 25 May, young Dickinson continued his enthusiastic reporting, widening it to include a reference to the broader advantages available to him. "It would be impossible to enumerate all the benefits to be acquired in London, but it cannot be disputed that more is learned of mankind here in a month than can be in a year in any other part of the world. Here a person sees and converses with people of all ranks, of all tempers. He acquires an ease and freedom of behavior with his superiors, complaisance and civility to his inferiors. The wise are his patterns to imitate. The weak show him, as in a glass, the faults and follies he ought to avoid. Here a man learns from the example of others what in another place nothing but his own sufferings and expense could teach him. London takes off the rawness, the prejudices of youth and ignorance. If the adding practice to study will be more likely to fix the law strongly and clearly in the memory, if the seeing and hearing the finest speakers at the Bar can contribute anything to improving and polishing one's addresses, and if frequent conversations on your studies with numbers engaged in the same will instruct one in controversy, then those advantages are to be acquired here."[42] Dickinson would doubtless have agreed with the observation of Dr. Samuel Johnson, his near neighbor in Gough Square, on the other side of Fleet Street, and a regular visitor to the Temple: "When a man is tired of London, he is tired of life; for there is in London all that life can afford."

Dickinson went on to give his father two reasons why he thought that another two years in London were desirable. The first was the point he had already made to his mother: his general health was improving all the time.

The second made it clear that his father had not insisted on his being called to the Bar while in England: he was clearly content that his son should merely further the legal studies he had begun at home. Dickinson wrote: "But another very weighty reason is that in two years I can procure the degree of a barrister, which I cannot do by next spring. Since my last, I have entered into commons, that is, dining in term time with the barristers and students of the Society in the public hall. We always have with us some of the governors, who are called benchers, and frequently some of the judges and greatest lawyers. Now to obtain the degree of a barrister, a person should be entered five years and keep his commons for two, but Mr. Hopkins assures me that on keeping my commons for the term prescribed, he will by his interest procure me to be called to the Bar. This is a thing, in my opinion, not to be despised, as it will certainly be more to my credit to return with a degree and a recommendation from the Society than in the same character I came away with." He was correct in referring to "a degree": the Inns of Court were deemed to be the third university in England and capable of granting the degree of barrister.

Dickinson not only had the advantage of invitations to both American and English households, but also of having companions from both side of the Atlantic. "My other acquaintances are Mr. Jennings's son, two or three Americans and as many Englishmen, all young fellows of good parts and remarkable industry, and as we are all engaged in the same studies, we find great benefit from our acquaintance." When he visited Vauxhall Gardens for the first time, he was in a party that included the Hanburys' daughter and Peyton Randolph from Virginia, the colony's most distinguished lawyer. Randolph, a cousin of Thomas Jefferson, had been called to the Bar by the Middle Temple in 1744, and was to serve as the first President of Continental Congress, with Dickinson as a member. He was in London as the agent for the House of Burgesses, of which he was a member.[43]

By 15 August Dickinson was working extremely hard on his studies, reporting to his mother: "I am now busily engaged in reading, which I can bear better than ever. I rise constantly at five, and read eight hours every day, which is as much as I can or ought to do, for greater application would not only hurt me, but would be of no service, as it would fatigue me too much. I dine at four and am in bed by ten. In short, I live in a manner the most proper to answer the purposes for which I came, and nothing gives me more delight than to think I do every thing which I believe you would have me."[44]

The father approved the suggested extension of the stay in England. In his letter, dated 21 January 1755, thanking him, Dickinson stated he had been busy reading, "but Hilary Term coming on the 23rd of this month, I shall run down to Westminster Hall every morning by 9 o'clock and shiver in that great open place till two or three."[45] The ancient Hall was large and cold, and as the courts had been created in it by the erection of very basic partitions, one can readily believe the report about shivering when listening to cases. Dickinson, who seems to have been an early jogger, did not mention the fact, but his chambers were not much more than a hundred yards away from the River Thames and the landing stage belonging to the Temple Inns as riparian owners. The short journey upstream to Westminster could have been undertaken by boat.

Before leaving America, Dickinson had sometimes suffered from chest pains. In March 1755 he had a recurrence of the problem and sought medical help. He was ordered to stop studying and to go to the country, so he and Goldsborough, and the newly wed Mrs. Goldsborough, took lodgings together at Kingston in Surrey, near Hampton Court Palace. Goldsborough had met an English heiress, Sarah Yerbury, at the turn of the year, and had married her in March. The fact that he, like several other Americans law students in London, had acquired an English wife, may explain why he decided to practice law in England for a while, before returning to Maryland.

By the end of September Dickinson felt "extremely strong and hearty", so much so that he had begun his reading again. He decided to return to the Temple on 1 November, for his last three months of study in London. The doctors had advised him to stand up and read from a lectern or high book support, rather than sitting down, hunched up, so it looks as though they had diagnosed back problems caused by bad posture.[46]

On 8 February 1757 Dickinson and Goldsborough were called to the English Bar by the Middle Temple and Dickinson arranged to go home. In his letters he had often discussed current political problems: he was clearly interested in more than merely cramming law. He had learned enough about both law and politics to be well equipped for the next stages of his life. After his return to Pennsylvania he practiced law but also became a successful property owner. Eleven years later, he became a political writer. His wider reputation was made by his very first letters to the *Pennsylvania Chronicle*, which claimed to be written by a Farmer in Pennsylvania and were soon published in book form and widely read on both sides of the Atlantic.

In his first letter Dickinson kept quiet about being a lawyer, but gave some indication of the breadth of his reading. Many of the books he referred to will have been bought or read by Dickinson in London, where he studied not only law but also history. One of his biographers made a point that applies to other students also, whether American or English: "In addition to studying law, Dickinson read history, for he was eager to understand how Englishmen in the past had acquired the freedoms guaranteed by the British Constitution. His study at the Middle Temple laid the foundation for a life-long love of history."[47] The author might have added, "and for his ability to apply the lessons of history."

Dickinson began the first published letter, dated 5 November 1768: "Being generally master of my time, I spend a good deal of it in a library, which I think the most valuable part of my small estate; and being acquainted with two or three gentlemen of abilities and learning, who honor me with their friendship, I have acquired, I believe, a greater knowledge in history and the laws and constitution of my country, than is generally attained by men of my class, many of them not being so fortunate as I have been in the opportunities of getting information."

It would be difficult to overestimate the importance of Dickinson's letters, which clearly owed a great deal to the broad education he had received in London. His first biographer commented: "In these letters Mr. Dickinson appears as a statesman, discussing the questions in controversy, not on speculative grounds, as was the habit of many writers of that day— men who had very little knowledge of and still less reverence for positive law—but as one who firmly believed in the traditions of English liberty, and who thought that English law rightly interpreted by English history was the basis of the freest political condition of which the human race up to that time had shown itself capable." The literary expert on the period went so far as to call Dickinson's *Letters* "the most brilliant event in the literary history of the Revolution."[48]

When it became known that Dickinson was the author of the Farmer's Letters, the fame and respect he achieved made him one of the most influential advocates for America's rights. Prior to 1776, with the exception of Benjamin Franklin, probably no American was better known or quoted more often for his sound opinions.

Pamphlets, generally, played an important part from the time of the Stamp Act dispute to the end of the war. We shall later briefly consider the contribution made by the pamphlets of Middle Templars, such as Arthur Lee of Virginia and Daniel Dulany, Jr., of Maryland. When considering their importance, and that of Dickinson's letters, it worth bearing in mind what Benjamin Franklin observed in a letter of 13 June 1782 to Richard Price, a London dissenting minister and great friend of the colonies. "The ancient Roman and Greek orators could only speak to the number of citizens capable of being assembled within reach of their voice. Their writings had little effect, because the bulk of the people could not read. Now by the press we can speak to nations; and good books and well-written pamphlets have great and general influence."[49]

Joseph Kelley, when writing about Pennsylvania before the Revolution, made a valid comment both about the value of a legal education in London generally, and specifically about its effect on Dickinson. "The availability of the courts at Westminster, reports of case, text books on special phases of law, moot courts, and learned conversations and discussions with judges and lawyers were of immense psychological value to a young attorney when he returned to the colonies." Kelley continued: "The boldness with which Dickinson asserted a position on the heady issue of taxation attests the confidence of statutory construction and familiarity with English constitutional law well beyond the reach of an equally meticulous John Adams at a comparable stage of his career."[50]

Dickinson has a strong claim to be considered the foremost American member of the Middle Temple, as his reasoned arguments and carefully drafted documents were extremely influential during the years of the Revolution. However, John Rutledge, the first President of South Carolina, who attended the Constitutional Convention with him, may be considered to have contributed as much as Dickinson overall, so that perhaps it would be fair to regard them as coming equal first. Edward Rutledge, John's younger brother and the youngest signer of the Declaration of Independence, is perhaps entitled to be placed third, after Dickinson and his own brother, John. Joseph Reed, Washington's first military secretary, who declined the post of Chief Justice of Pennsylvania but then accepted that of President of the State, may fairly be considered to rank joint third with Edward Rutledge. The two Rutledges inevitably come first on the list of most successful brothers, but with Charles Cotesworth Pinckney and Thomas Pinckney close behind them. The saddest distinguished brothers were Peyton and John Randolph, both of whom had served as Royal Attorney General of Virginia. Peyton, a leading patriot in Virginia, after serving as the first President of Congress, died in October 1775, not knowing whether the Revolution would succeed. John fled to Britain as a loyalist, leaving his patriot son Edmund behind to become the first Federal Attorney General.

A number of Americans formally joined the Middle Temple as student members but, for one reason or another, never arrived there. The signs of a coming war were enough to deter some families. Others must have been affected by a change in the health, physical or financial, of the student or his father, after the date of the formal admission. William Livingston had the following explanation for his non-attendance in London.

After he had obtained a degree from Yale, his father insisted on Livingston embarking on a legal career, despite his lack of interest in the law. He became a legal apprentice in New York and decided that if he was going to be a lawyer, he would be the best kind, and so at his request was admitted to the Inn in October 1742. Unfortunately, his father was investing money in the building of an ironworks and thought that "an expenditure of several hundred pounds seemed like an unnecessary extravagance, particularly when weighed against the meager education received in return." Rather surprisingly, even with his university education, Livingston felt ill-prepared for his studies as an apprentice in New York, which he completed successfully, and later suggested to a son that he should take a year to read law books before setting foot in a law office. "Despite his inability to come to London to study law, Livingston was inordinately proud of his membership of the Inn and used a bookplate that described him as 'of the Middle Temple'."[51]

Livingston practiced law successfully in New York and for a time served on the Royal Council, together with two other Middle Templars, John Chambers and Joseph Murray. One of his colleagues at the Bar was John Jay, the future first Chief Justice of the United States, who objected to the incompetence of some of the judges, who were laymen, "taken from among the farmers." In 1772 Livingston and Jay suggested to the governor and Council that lawyers should be appointed as legal advisers to such judges.[52] In that year also, Livingston saw his daughter Sarah married to Jay; while he himself retired to New Jersey at the early age of forty-nine. In that State he succeeded Middle Templar William Franklin as governor, a post he held from 1776 until his death in 1790. He attended both the Continental

Congress and the 1787 Constitutional Convention as a delegate for New Jersey. However, he did not sign the Declaration of Independence, as he felt obliged to give priority to his military duties rather than continue at Congress in Philadelphia, but he was there eleven years later to sign the Constitution he had helped to draft. He was a very effective governor during the war, "and to the military warfare against the enemy added a most vivacious literary warfare—bombarding them through the newspapers with intermittent showers of shot and shell, in the form of arguments, anathemas, jokes and jeers."[53] Benjamin Franklin would surely have approved.

WILLIAM ALLEN
Chief Justice of Pennsylvania.
Nat. 1704.— Ob. 1780.

From the original painting in the possession of Baron Hammond of Kirk Ella.

William Allen
courtesy The Historical Society of Pennsylvania (HSP), Society Portrait, by Albert
Rosenthal from the original painting held by Baron Hammond of Kirk Ella

Chapter 3
THE CHIEF JUSTICES OF PENNSYLVANIA
I: WILLIAM ALLEN AND HIS SONS

A separate look at the Chief Justices of Pennsylvania before, during and after the Revolution may be profitable for a number of reasons. Between 1750 and 1805, four of them in succession were members of the Middle Temple—although one of them did not attend the Inn. From their histories and their correspondence one can not only obtain clues about the life of the American student at the Inn, but see how established colonial judges and lawyers might well lean towards the Crown once the crucial choice could no longer be avoided. Even if they disapproved of the actions of the London government in relation to taxation and were prepared to voice their support for the colonists' case on that issue, once the question of independence— yea or nay—was put, many judges and others felt driven to remain loyal to the King.

That was partly because they had taken the oath of allegiance: the judges on appointment to the Bench, others on assuming certain posts, such as that of Attorney General or trustee of the new College in Philadelphia. Neutrality was considered by some to be a possible way out, but it proved difficult for any single person to remain neutral when his neighbors were asking, in no uncertain terms, and sometimes with bricks through the window: "Are you with us or against us?" The third option of remaining neutral was hardly ever open.

The Pennsylvania experience shows that one commentator was doubtless correct when he wrote of colonial lawyers generally: "Although professional lawyers led the movement for American independence, most of those who became revolutionaries did so with unease. Successful practitioners in some colonies, particularly those associated with the imperial establishment, tended to hold back or to side openly with the mother country."[1] It is also interesting to see something of Pennsylvania during the troubled years, because it was one State that experienced the extremes of the revolutionary movement. Furthermore, Philadelphia was not only the leading city and port but, as already discussed, the site of the Independence and Constitutional talks in 1776 and 1787.

The cases of the Chief Justices illustrate how well or ill a loyalist might be treated. If a judge was highly respected and did nothing positive against the independence movement, then—just like some Tory merchants - he might be able to return to his career after the war was over, once a sufficient interval had elapsed to allow strong feelings to simmer down.

Looking at the lives of the Chief Justices one can see that the doctrine of Separation of Powers was not strictly adhered to before the Constitutional Convention met in Philadelphia in 1787 and, following the lead of the new State constitutions, laid it down as a fundamental rule. Judges in Pennsylvania, as in other colonies, sometimes played leading roles in two, or even all three branches of government.

Chief Justice Allen's story is of interest because he was involved in Pennsylvania's history during many of its turbulent years. Allen, having attended the Middle Temple himself, chose it for two of his sons, as did

Benjamin Franklin for his only son, William. Allen's and Franklin's paths crossed regularly over the years, and William Franklin was involved in some of their conflicts. One of the Allen boys became Attorney General of Pennsylvania; the other, while not being a serious lawyer, kept a revealing diary.

William Allen was born in August 1704. His father, also named William, was a successful Philadelphia merchant; his mother was Mary Budd, whose sister married into the influential Shippen family, which included Edward Shippen, the Chief Justice of Pennsylvania at the end of the century. Young Allen came to England to attend Clare Hall at the University of Cambridge and was admitted to the Middle Temple in 1720, as one of its earliest students from America. While there he may have wasted most of the opportunities available for a good grounding in the law. "William received little legal training, however, preferring to spend his time touring on the very generous bills of credit given to him by his father."[2]

Having enjoyed some of the traditional education of an English gentleman, Allen rounded it off by going on the Grand Tour of Europe. After his return home on the death of his father in 1725, he took over his business, comprised of mercantile, property, mining and ironworks interests, and became a very rich man. His connections with the Penns, the Proprietors of the province, often proved helpful. For example, when the Delaware Indians were dispossessed of some of their lands, "Traders and settlers made significant inroads into the Upper Delaware Valley in the late 1720s and early 1730s. Among the first was William Allen, who received a grant from the Penn family of some ten thousand acres." He made a part of that land available for settlers of the Moravian religion, including the site of their little town of Bethlehem, where they were able nurse the soldiers injured in the fighting around Philadelphia in 1777, including the Marquis de Lafayette.[3]

Allen used some of the money he made, including all his judicial salary, for various benefactions related to education and health. He supported the search for the Northwest Passage, but that was on a strictly commercial basis. He also founded the town of Northampton, later renamed Allentown and, together with his future father-in-law, Andrew Hamilton, was largely responsible for the erection of the State House in Philadelphia, the birthplace of both the Declaration of Independence and the United States Constitution.

By February 1734, when Allen married Margaret Hamilton, his success was already assured. In the following year he was elected Mayor of Philadelphia and in 1736 was able to give a memorable banquet to mark both his retirement from that office and the completion of the banqueting hall of what was then known as the new Provincial House and only later as the State House. He and his wife had six children who survived infancy: two girls and four boys, the middle two of whom were to study at the Middle Temple. John was born in 1739 and died in February 1778. Andrew, the most successful, was born in 1740 and lived until 1825. James was born in about 1742 and also died in 1778, seven months after John. William was born in 1751 and survived until 1838, despite a military career on both sides.

Allen cooperated a great deal with Franklin over a number of years: they were both good citizens and helped each other with various projects for the benefit of the public, such as setting up educational and cultural facilities. In addition, in times of danger they were involved together in matters of defense. Franklin was responsible for the idea of raising a local militia. When at the end of 1747 he had the idea of having a lottery to raise funds for defense, Allen became the treasurer. In March 1748 the two of them, with two colleagues, traveled to New York to ask the governor for the loan of some urgently needed guns. They were successful in obtaining twelve twelve-pounders and two eighteens. A "strong battery" was then erected in gun emplacements on some of Allen's land to the south of Philadelphia, and named Fort Allen.[4]

In 1739, after serving for nine years in the Provincial Assembly in the Penn Proprietary interest, Allen declined to serve any further, "as most of our disputes seem to be at an end and the Province affairs upon a very good footing." Some of his colleagues also dropped out, so the Quaker party, led by Franklin despite the fact that he was not a Friend, was able to take over control. However, in 1742 Allen and his colleagues wanted to get their seats back. During the election he found, to his great annoyance, that the Quakers were obtaining a great deal of support from German immigrants, some of whom were not qualified to vote, but may nevertheless have accepted the well-known advice of the corrupt, "Vote early, vote often."[5] A large party of sailors also resented the participation of the unqualified Germans and made it clear that they were prepared to use violence.

When an appeal was made to Allen, as a leading citizen and as the Recorder of the City, to keep order, he was unable to prevent a disturbance. Instead of being elected, he was accused of encouraging the rioting, but as Norman Cohen concluded, "Sufficient proof to support this view has never existed, and certainly Allen had nothing to gain by the riot. William Allen was a clever politician, who never in his long career had to use such crass methods."

In 1750, after nine years as the Recorder of Philadelphia, a part-time judicial appointment, Allen was appointed Chief Justice of Pennsylvania and retained the post until he was almost seventy in 1774. Finding a well-qualified lawyer to replace Chief Justice John Kinsey, who had died, proved impossible for Governor James Hamilton, Allen's brother-in-law. It was only after a "good deal of difficulty" that he persuaded Allen to accept the post.[6] Allen had never practiced law in England or America, so his appointment to the highest judicial post is, at first sight, a little startling. However, there were several factors in his favor: he had studied some law and certainly had a great deal of involvement with private law as a property owner, merchant and employer. He also had considerable experience in public life and therefore of public law. Furthermore, he had been a satisfactory part-time judge, both as a Recorder and in other minor judicial posts.

It should also be borne in mind that the concept of the layman as a judge—rather than as a juror—was not at all a strange one in the British Empire. The justices of the peace were mainly non-lawyers, and laymen serving as civil or colonial service administrators regularly presided over colonial courts until comparatively recently, as did military men at courts-martial. In the American colonies, if there was no suitable lawyer available, a layman was quite often appointed or elected to fill a judicial vacancy. Alfred Jones gave an interesting confirmation of this point when describing the career of William Dudley, who had followed his brother Paul to the Middle Temple. Paul was admitted to the Inn in 1697 and called to the Bar in 1700; he later served as Attorney General and then as Chief Justice of Massachusetts. William was admitted in 1706 and also became a Massachusetts judge. Jones commented: "William Dudley is believed to have been the first trained lawyer to sit on the Common Pleas of Massachusetts."[7]

Nathaniel Jones of the Middle Temple, when appointed Chief Justice of New Jersey in 1759 on the strength of judicial recommendations, gave up his English practice and sailed for America. On arrival he found that Robert Hunter Morris, who had been serving as Chief Justice for some years, would not surrender his place on the Bench, claiming that his earlier resignation had not been accepted. Although the King was consulted about his refusal to leave, nothing was done about it, so Nathaniel Jones had to concede defeat. In an attempt to salvage something from the wreck, he applied for the post of Chief Justice of South Carolina, but failed to get it. Possibly the most infuriating element for him was that Morris was not even qualified as a lawyer.[8]

Benjamin Franklin was one Pennsylvanian layman who sat in a judicial capacity for a while. In his autobiography he wrote: "The office of justice of the peace I tried a little, by attending a few courts and sitting on the bench, to hear causes. But finding that more knowledge of the common law than I possessed, was necessary to act in that station with credit, I gradually withdrew from it, excusing myself by my being obliged to attend the higher duties of a legislator in the Assembly."[9]

In 1753 Allen "in a great measure" retired from the family business and thereafter concentrated more on the law, his family and the cultivation of his garden, but he never relinquished his interest in politics. Although he may have withdrawn from running the family business, he continued to be involved. In April 1754 he wrote to Edmund Butler, presumably a joint venturer, in the Temple in London: "The three houses in Chestnut Street sold for the following sums: £117.16.6, £250, £650; and the 500 acres of land in this county for £750 (all Philadelphia currency). All which, I think well sold."[10]

In 1755 Allen succeeded in securing supplies of flour for General Edward Braddock's expedition (in which George Washington participated) and then, from his Chief Justice's bench, appealed to the public to provide an adequate numbers of horses and wagons for the troops.[11] In July, shortly after Braddock's force had been defeated by the French and their Indian allies, and the general had been mortally wounded, the Chief Justice sent an unusual request to the Barclays, his London agents—one not often emanating from a judge. "As there is some appearance of our being roused from our lethargy, we are about putting the Province in some small position of defense. But as we are much in want of arms, we are desired to send for a thousand muskets, which we are told may be bought at the Tower from 11 to 13 shillings a piece with bayonets and cartouche boxes, being such as the Army formerly used. We are informed that the East India Company purchase such for their settlements. We beg therefore that you would purchase the above quantity on the best terms you can and ship them by the first opportunity with a tun of musket balls."[12]

This was not an isolated instance of a judge being involved in some of the functions of the executive and/or legislative arm. Allen did not feel in the least inhibited by his office from participating in politics in the interests of the pro-Penn Proprietary Party. His political allegiance to the Penns repeatedly brought him into conflict with Franklin, who had obtained the post of Deputy Postmaster for all the colonies in 1753 with his significant help, including financial—a point Franklin has been accused of forgetting.[13] In fairness to Franklin it should be added that his indebtedness to Allen for his help, did not require him to agree with him on all points from then on.

In October 1755 Allen wrote to the Penns' solicitor in London, John Ferdinando Paris, at his address in Surrey Street, very close to the Middle Temple, about pending legislation and the dangers facing the province, which included the unwillingness of the Quaker population to take up arms, even in self-defense. He suggested that two or three of the best lawyers should be retained to put their case in London, "among which we would have the [English] Attorney General for one." He continued: "The remedy we would request is that we may be included in the Bill for uniting the colonies, and our case properly provided for in the same, should that measure take effect. If no such Bill passes this session coming on, we would fain hope his Majesty and his ministers will not suffer this Colony, situate in the center of his Majesty's American Dominions, to remain any longer defenseless, but will recommend it to the Parliament to restrain our Quakers and Germans from sitting in the House of Assembly and the latter from even voting, till they know our language and are better acquainted with our Constitution."[14]

Although Franklin did not agree with the Quakers about their unwillingness to defend themselves or their colony, he continued to lead their party, opposing not only Allen and his allies, such as John Dickinson, but the whole concept of the Proprietary interest. He was in favor of a change from rule by the Penns to Royal government—but his timing for such a suggestion proved unfortunate for Franklin. Existing British demands for tax did not assist his idea of *more* rule by the government in London. "The fears of the Penns and of the oligarchy men—like his one-time friend William Allen—were now confirmed. Franklin the manipulator was revealed as a 'popular' man, an enemy of the Gentlemen's party, a 'grand incendiary'."[15] Many others were similarly dismayed by Franklin's proposal.

In 1764 Franklin mocked Allen and his colleagues, listing some of their actions. "They, who by numberless falsehoods, propagated with infinite industry, in the mother country, attempted to procure an Act of Parliament for the actual depriving a very great part of the people of their privileges. They too who have already deprived the whole people of some of their most important rights, and are daily endeavoring to deprive them of the rest! Are these become patriots, and advocates for our constitution? Wonderful change! Astonishing conversion!"[16]

Franklin was defeated in the Assembly election that year, but was appointed once again as Pennsylvania's agent in London by a majority, with Allen and Dickinson voting against the appointment. Allen was by then so disenchanted with Franklin that he described him as a "turbulent plotter" who was "fully freighted with rancor and malice." Franklin referred bitterly to Allen's "long success in maiming or murdering all the reputations that stand in his way, which has been the dear delight and constant employment of his life."[17] He had clearly ignored one of the four rules he had made for himself as a young printer, on leaving England back in 1726: "I resolve to speak ill of no man whatever."[18]

In 1748 Francis Rawle, a prosperous young man, who was to send his own son, William, to the Middle Temple in due course, "initiated the Philadelphia custom of making the Grand Tour." In the same year, Edward Shippen, then a Middle Temple student, followed suit. "But the great impetus to Italian travel occurred in 1760, when Chief Justice Allen arranged letters of credit for his twenty-one-year old son, John, who 'had an inclination to see a little of the world'."[19] It is worth looking at the background of that trip briefly, as it indicates both what a good father Allen was, and how he helped Benjamin West to become one of London's leading painters.

Benjamin West was born in Pennsylvania in October 1738 and as a young artist attracted the attention of Dr. William Smith, the Provost of the College of Philadelphia, who introduced him to a number of potential patrons. An early commission came from Benjamin Franklin, for a portrait of his daughter Sarah. As West's biographer put it, "West's career took an upward turn when he met William Allen, called 'the Great Giant' and known to be the richest man in Philadelphia."[20] The idea of the trip to Europe came from Allen's cousin, the twenty-seven-year old Colonel Joseph Shippen, who had put up some money to take a ship with a cargo of sugar to London. He asked Allen to invest in the scheme, and the Chief Justice readily agreed to contribute £1000, subject to two conditions. The first was that Shippen should change the destination to Leghorn (Livorno) in Italy. The other was that he should let his eldest, John, accompany him. John Allen was not interested in the law but was thinking of a life in commerce. Then, prompted by Provost Smith, Allen suggested that Shippen might care to make room for the promising young artist, who was bursting to see a cross-section of classical art in Europe.

In April 1760, Allen wrote to his commercial agents in Leghorn about the plan, asking for their help. He also put in a similar plea to the British diplomatic resident in Florence, Horatio Man, who had been a fellow student of his at Clare Hall, Cambridge. To the agents he added: "In this vessel comes a passenger, Mr. West, a young ingenious painter of this city, who is desirous to improve himself in that service, by visits to Florence and Rome, but being unacquainted how to have his money remitted, has lodged with me £100 sterling, which I shall remit to David Barclay and Sons upon his account."[21] He called Benjamin West "a very deserving young man."

In fact, Allen was far more generous than that letter indicates. In the autumn of that year, when he was entertaining members of the government of Pennsylvania at dinner, he read out a letter from the Leghorn agents, reporting on West's continued success. He thought that West's own money must be running out, and announced: "I shall regard this young man as an honor to the country, and as he is the first that America has sent to cultivate the fine arts, he shall not be frustrated in his studies, for I have resolved to write to my correspondents in Leghorn to give him, from myself, whatever money he may require."[22] Governor James Hamilton, Allen's brother-in-law, then insisted on being allowed to help the young artist financially as well, as did other members of the company, including Samuel Powel, a future mayor of Philadelphia.

In August 1759 both Andrew and James Allen were formally admitted to the Middle Temple, but they only arrived there two years later. In July 1761, while the Seven Years' War was still raging, the Chief Justice wrote a long letter of introduction for the young men to give to the Barclays, which included the extract quoted earlier. "This comes by my two sons Andrew and James, whom I send to England in order to study the law in the Temple. I had, as I wrote to you, thoughts of accompanying them, had peace taken place, but I must delay my voyage till that event happens, which I presume and hope will be within the compass of this year. In the meantime I request you would be so good as to afford them your countenance, friendship and advice. I spent six years at one time in England, and am very sensible they are to go through a fiery trial. The many temptations youths are exposed to in your city, and the vice and luxury that is too predominant, make me very anxious on their account. I have taken the greatest care in my power of their education hitherto, and in forming their minds to virtue. And as yet their conduct has been such as rather to give me pleasure than pain; but they are now embarking in a new scene. They will be, in great measure, left to themselves, remote from me, their parent, and from their very affectionate uncle, Governor [Andrew] Hamilton, who seems greatly interested in their welfare, and to whose kind lessons and example they are much indebted."[23]

Their uncle Andrew had been admitted to the Middle Temple in 1729 and called to the Bar by the Inn three years later. That he had kept in touch with some of his contemporaries at the Inn is implicit in what followed in Allen's letter. "I must further beg you would be so good as to supply them with money for the expenses; which I would not choose should exceed £200 a year for each of them, exclusive of books, and the first fitting them with clothes and a few other necessities. I would have them take chambers in the Temple, in the procuring of which their uncle's friends may be able to advise them, he having wrote to some of them for their friendly countenance and advice." Unlike his father, the distinguished Andrew Hamilton, this Andrew never practiced law after his call, but he entered his son William at the Middle Temple in January 1764.

Shortly before Christmas 1761, Allen wrote again to the Barclays. "I am apt to think a peace will, as you formerly mentioned to me, make them produce good interest for money in the end. Should that event happen, as I am still inclined to see England once more, I shall take a trip over and see my old friends and examine how my young Templars are going on." Peace did not come to England then; nor did the Chief Justice. In February 1762 he wrote to the Barclays: "Andrew and James are soliciting me very hard for an increase of their allowance, and their uncle is of opinion that I should do it. I must therefore instruct you to increase the same £50 a year to each of them, though I fear it will enable them to have more avocations from their real business, the study of the law. If it should have that effect, it would be very vexatious to me. I should be very much obliged to you, if you would be so as to give me any information you may receive how they spend their time, and whether the large expense I am at will be counterweighted by their good behavior and diligence."[24] One suspects that the Barclays did not go out of their way to find out how these two students spent all their waking hours. Neither of the brothers seems to have worked very hard, but Andrew may have been more inspired by his studies than James.

Allen concluded that last letter with a scathing reference to Franklin's return home from London. "One would fain hope his almost insatiable ambition is pretty near satisfied by his parading about England &c. at the province's expense for these five years past, which now appears in a different light to our patriots than formerly, especially as he has already stayed near two years longer than they expected."

The fact that Allen had a happy time in England as a young man was confirmed in a letter he wrote to the Barclays in October 1762. "I spent a good part of my youth in England, which makes me have an earnest desire, once more, to revisit it, and I firmly believe I shall, though the Governor and some other of my friends laugh when I talk of it." He referred again to his days as a student when attempting to cap his sons' expenses, writing to the agents in March 1763: "My sons' expenses I think to be more than I am willing they should continue to spend. I am sure they are more, by near one half, than I was allowed, and *I lived handsomely*, and kept as good company as they do, and never left any tradesmen's bills unpaid."[25] He added that he had at last arranged his trip to England, and hoped to arrive in June, bringing his daughters Anne and Margaret with him. As he was going to be away for a considerable time, and his wife had died, he offered to lend his country home, at Mount Airy near Germantown, to his friend Benjamin Chew, who was delighted to accept the offer.

As soon as he arrived in London, Allen rented a house in Golden Square, near Piccadilly, but shortly afterwards took his daughters on an extended tour of England. On 5 July 1763, Chew wrote to Allen about Pontiac's Amerindians' attack on Detroit and the resultant alarm in Pennsylvania. "We are in all probability on the eve of a general Indian war, which may prove more bloody than any that has been experienced since the settlement of the continent."[26]

Allen replied from Bath on 7 October: "Your very kind letter reached me at York at the time of the Races. The dismal account you gave me plunged me into a great deal of grief and concern. I then much regretted that I had left my country and friends, and could not with any satisfaction mingle with the men of pleasure when joy was far from my heart." It is to be noted that he did not add that he would be catching the next ship home. He did, however, go on to give an account of his efforts on his country's behalf to stave off new taxes, and of his meetings with possible allies, such as Lord Shelburne.[27] He also reported that he had met the new governor, John Penn (who was to marry his daughter, Anne) and that he was much esteemed by everybody. "My sons speak of him and his brother [Richard] in the highest terms. They had a very close and intimate acquaintance with them, and they assure me they are both men of the strictest honor and worth."

85

The letter also gave a charming picture of Allen as an indulgent father, for he continued: "I am now at Bath. I have already been to Harrogate, Scarborough, York, Matlock and Bristol. I am almost surfeited with the amusements of these public places, and want to snug it in a family way at my house in London. I have in order to satisfy my girls' curiosity taken this tour, and have given them an opportunity of seeing the best company in the kingdom. I shall return to London by way of Blenheim and Oxford, my whole excursion will be between 7 and 800 miles. After all it vexes me that they, I mean Nancy and Peggy, are not satisfied nor willing to return at the time I have set. England is a bewitching place to young folk, but it is not at all suitable to such as are to spend their life in America, as it teaches them things that are fit only for those who have a great deal of money to spend."

Allen met many friends and acquaintances in London, including Benjamin West, who had arrived there shortly after him, on 20 August. West was extremely lucky with the timing of his arrival: not only was his principal benefactor in town, but by coincidence, so were Hamilton, Smith and Powel—all on separate missions. Between them they were able to introduce West to a number of potential clients. Allen was delighted to see West making speedy progress, but soon accurately foresaw a possible consequence of his runaway success, writing to Chew in January 1764: "He is really a wonder of a man and so far outstripped all the painters of his time as to get into high esteem at once. If he keeps his health he will make money very fast. He is not likely to return among us, so that you will not be able to have Mrs. Chew and your little flock painted." West found it difficult to decide and consulted Allen and Smith about returning home, but they both advised him to stay in London. He accepted their advice and became one of the King's favorite painters.[28]

Once back in London, Allen made a point of poring over his sons' accounts and expressed his dismay in a note to the Barclays on 25 September 1763. "Upon examining the same, I find my sons' expenses exceed much any thing I could have imagined; it was full time to put an end to it; I hope they will turn their thoughts to business, and I think, of getting money for their future subsistence, and become useful to themselves and their country."[29] Despite the hard words, the soft-hearted father let the young men continue their studies.

On 9 December 1763, Allen wrote to Chew from his London house, giving an account of his further endeavors to delay the introduction of new taxes. He added a note indicating that he was not prepared to give in to his daughters any more: "I every day grow more and more anxious to return; my children are not yet quite satisfied to go back and beg hard that I will stay till September, but I tell them the first good opportunity about mid-summer we must be turning our faces homeward."[30] Allen clearly worked hard at his lobbying. A letter from London, dated 24 March 1764, was published in the *Pennsylvania Gazette*, and referred to the success of his attempt to avert or delay the evil day when fresh taxes would be imposed by the British government. The correspondent stated: "The 15th Resolution relating to the Stamp Act will certainly pass next session, unless the Americans offer a more certain duty. Had not William Allen Esq., been here and indefatigable in opposing it, and happily having made acquaintance with the first personages in the Kingdom and the greatest part of the House of Commons, it would inevitably have passed this session."[31]

Some years before his trip to England, Allen had acquired a considerable girth, inviting comparison with Shakespeare's justice, "In fair round belly with good capon lined", but he referred to it with good humor in a letter to Chew towards the end of his stay in England. Unlike some American visitors, he did not complain about English cooking, but wrote instead: "I cannot tell what is the occasion of it: I do not relish my victuals well and have no joy when I sit down to a well spread table. But I am daily falling off in flesh. I can sit cross leg, which I have not done for some years, tie my garters above knee, and weigh some forty pounds less than when I left Philadelphia. Instead of being a terror to the chairmen, I am every day saluted with, 'A chair, your Honor?' and as my girls frequently use the coach, I am wafted about in chairs like a shrimp."[32] Before he came to England he was often called "The Great Giant", presumably mainly by his opponents; they may have been dismayed to see him return in a new slim-line version.

From letters Allen wrote after his return home in August 1764, it appears that he had not only talked about important political topics of the day with Members of Parliament and others, but that he had also bothered some of them, rather like the traditional American snake oil, or elixir of life salesman. Once back in Philadelphia, on 25 September he wrote to William Pitt: "I am one who has for fourteen years past been afflicted with the gout; and as I perceive by the public papers you are visited with that malady, I have taken the freedom to send you some of the pine buds which, being made into tea, have been of infinite service to me and many others in this part of the world. I am lately returned to my native country from England, where I spent a twelve month, and carried over with me about fifty weight, which I distributed to sundry physicians and other gentlemen. The physicians had a high opinion of it, particularly Dr. Fothergill. I gave some of it to the present Lord Chancellor and to my Lord Ellebank and to sundry gentlemen at the Club at Saunders, of which place I was a member." In his letter ordering more books from Robert Davis, his bookseller in Piccadilly, he boasted: "I have an account that my Lord Chancellor and my Lord Chief Justice Pratt have both received considerable benefit since I left England by the use of them, which has emboldened me to send about three gallons of them to that worthy patriot Mr. Pitt, out of my own stock."[33]

When Allen arrived back in Philadelphia, he received a visit from Franklin, who was making "an overture." In the presence of other visitors, Allen rounded on him about his scheme to replace the proprietors with the British government, so they never made up their quarrels.[34]

Allen had returned in time to encounter the introduction of the Stamp Act provisions, which required that all legal documents be stamped. There were public protests, including one in which his son James played a leading part, "spiriting up the mob and enraging of them to persist in the affair they had met about," according to Franklin's wife.[35] In November 1765, John Hughes, the collector appointed under the Act on Franklin's recommendation, was hanged in effigy. Joseph Galloway reported to Franklin: "Several came out to view the agreeable spectacle, even the Chief Justice's curiosity so prevailed over his discretion and his oath, that he could not help sneaking to see."[36]

Allen and Benjamin Chew, the Attorney General, were in a dilemma. They could speak against the Act, and even enjoy seeing protests against it, but they could not very well run the courts with illegal documents. They were spared any significant problems by keeping the courts almost entirely shut until the arrival of the news of the repeal of the Act. Thomas McKean, another future Chief Justice, decided to keep his lower court in Delaware open, using unstamped documents in defiance of the law.

Allen unfairly accused Franklin of having opposed that repeal and Franklin's supporters were indignant about this false accusation. Galloway wrote to Franklin on 7 June 1766: "The Chief Justice's malevolence against you never will end but with his breath. He publicly asserted in the House that you were the greatest enemy to the repeal of the Stamp Act, of all the men in England." Conduct of that kind on the part of the most senior judge in the province was most regrettable, but if William Franklin was correct in his assertions in a letter to his father later that year, Allen followed it up with a further indiscretion. An essay had accused Benjamin Franklin of being one of the principal promoters of the original Bill. "I really think it not at all unlikely that Mr. Allen is in some degree out of his senses," William Franklin wrote. "Upon finding the essay did not take with the people, he cried out against it in the House as much as any body. And yet at the last session, when the Assembly were about appointing their agents, he made that very piece the foundation of a great deal of abuse he threw out against you, and spoke from it as if it had been his brief."[37]

In 1767 the legislature decided to improve the quality of Allen's court by means of the Judiciary Act, which provided for him and his unqualified colleague, William Coleman, to be joined by two judges who had received some legal training: John Lawrence, and Thomas Willing, who had briefly attended the Inner Temple.[38]

James Allen did not take his legal studies very seriously while in London, despite the fact that he had earlier been a student of one of Pennsylvania's best lawyers, Edward Shippen. James's attitude towards studying may be gauged from a comment made by Esther Reed, the English wife of Joseph Reed, the future second President of Pennsylvania. Her father, Denys De Berdt, had kept open house for American students in London, including Reed and the Allen boys. In October 1772 Esther wrote bitterly to her brother, Dennis De Berdt, about a problem being created by Chief Justice Allen. Her husband, Joseph Reed, was by then making great progress in the legal profession, mainly because of his own talents, but partly because of the limited opposition. "There is but one person (Mr. Chew) who can make much figure against him, as they are almost all youngsters. Mr. Reed is very much out of favor with Mr. Allen, who is the judge of the court here, for no other reason than that he thinks he will stand in the way of his two sons, who have just taken it into their heads to be great lawyers. You may remember how differently they studied when they were in the Temple; but it is no great matter, as their fortune will excuse their want of application."[39]

Some ten years after leaving the Middle Temple, when he had matured somewhat, James Allen mused in his diary entry for 30 October 1773: "I often reflect how happy it was for me that I took to the practice of the law. Added to the uneasiness that it gave my father and all my friends to find that after having served a regular clerkship and been three years at the Temple, I should continue an idle man, I say added to this consideration I have now made myself easy in my circumstances. I compute my business this year 1773 will be between £300 and £400, which added to my estate will fall but little short of £1000 per annum. For these last two or three years, which is the time that I resumed the practice of the law, I have read pretty diligently and have overcome the difficulty of speaking in public. In short, both the study and practice are become agreeable to me."[40]

Alexander Graydon, who later wrote some useful memoirs, spent a few months studying with James Allen shortly before the Revolution and called him "very assiduous and attentive." He added: "As this gentleman was without a clerk, my being there was considered as a matter of mutual convenience. In return for the use of his books, I did the business of his office, which was not very burdensome, and left me sufficient time for reading. As he was very gentlemanly in his manners, good-humored and affable, I passed my time with him altogether to my mind. He also took a friendly interest in my improvement, submitting the cases in which he was consulted to my previous examination and opinion, and treating the timidity which many feel on first speaking in public, as a weakness very easily overcome."[41]

Andrew Allen was the most successful of the Chief Justice's sons. Before going to England to further his legal studies, he had studied law with Benjamin Chew, his father's friend and successor. He seems to have taken more advantage than his brother of the opportunities afforded for learning during their lengthy stay at the Middle Temple. He was admitted to the Pennsylvania Bar in 1765 and appointed Attorney General of the province in 1769, aged twenty-nine. Doubtless he was then too young and inexperienced in the law for such an important post, but probably grew into it. In 1774 he became Recorder in succession to Chew. In 1775, Andrew Allen was one of the moderates trying to put a brake on the more revolutionary contributors to the discussions at the Continental Congress, much to the annoyance of those who wanted to speed up the revolution, notably members of the Virginia-Massachusetts junto, led by the Lee brothers and the Adams cousins, John and Samuel.

His brother James wrote to Ralph Izard in England from Philadelphia on 29 October 1774: "I received your letter dated Paris, 8 July, and plainly discover that you are sick of the iniquity of the present times. I heartily agree with you that profligacy of manners has swallowed up all ideas of liberty amongst the people of England. The situation of this country is critical, and a few months will determine whether we are to enjoy the rights of Englishmen, or be involved in all the horrors of a civil war. For no proposition can be clearer, than that nothing but a military force—and a powerful one—can produce an acquiescence to the oppressive measures now carrying on against us."[42] "All the horrors of a civil war"—how apt.

The First Continental Congress had concluded its session on the previous day and Allen enclosed a copy of the printed report of the proceedings for William Lee, one of the Virginian Lee brothers based in London with Izard. He added the comment: "If the people of England are not dead to every feeling of humanity and virtue, it must rouse them. It is not only their cause but the cause of human nature; and to attribute the opposition of America to a desire of independence, or to any other motive than a wish to enjoy English constitutional liberty, is diabolically wicked and false." It looks as though Allen was siding with the patriots, but many of his compatriots, including his father and brothers, were expressing similar indignation, while having no intention of breaking with the Crown.

James's dairy entry for 26 July 1775, three months after the initial shots at Lexington and Concord, also reads as though he was going to end up on the patriot side: "The eyes of Europe are upon us; if we fall, Liberty no longer continues an inhabitant of this globe: for England is running fast to slavery. The King is as despotic as any prince in Europe; the only difference is the mode; and a venal parliament are as bad as a standing army." However, once independence was declared in July 1776, William Allen and all four sons felt obliged to side with that "despotic" King.

On 15 May 1776 James Allen, together with his brother Andrew and other moderates, was elected a representative of the Assembly—much to the dismay of the radicals, who had expected a resounding victory following on their call for Independence. As early as 16 June, shortly before the decision in favor of Independence was reached by Congress, James recorded: "This day I set off with my family for Northampton, with the chariot, phaeton and sulky. I have met the Assembly and sat from 20 May to this time and have been very active in opposing Independence and change of government, but the tide is too strong."

William, the youngest of the four Allen brothers, was the only one with real military experience. James wrote of him: "My brother Billy, returning from Ticonderoga, soon after the Declaration of Independence, immediately resigned his [Pennsylvania] commission of Lieutenant-Colonel, as he had always determined to do in case of such declaration." He later commanded a loyalist unit.

Despite the strength of feeling on both sides of the argument, James Allen decided in September 1776 to go as a tourist to visit the armies of the two sides. He unashamedly wrote in his diary: "I set out from Philadelphia with Dr. Smith, through mere curiosity, to see the state of both armies." Although a loyalist, Allen had the nerve to call on the American army when it was fully occupied with the British attack on New York. Instead of being told in no uncertain terms to depart, he was able to record, "General Washington received me with the utmost politeness; I lodged with him and found there Messrs. Joseph Reed, [Tench] Tilghman, Graydon, and many others of my acquaintance, and was very happy with them." As they all had a war to fight, which their guest opposed, it is unlikely that the feeling was mutual. Reed wrote to his wife: "Jemmy Allen was here the other day with a view to discover, I suppose, what prospects *we* had, so that the party might take their measures accordingly." Alexander Graydon, Allen's unpaid clerk and student, later wrote: "I remember once seeing him on New York Island, towards the close of the summer of 1776, where he probably came to see how the land lay."[43]

Towards the end of 1777, James Allen's three brothers all went over to the British lines. They were responding in part to panic. A young lawyer, Christian Huck, found out that the radical faction in Philadelphia had a list of the names of about two hundred suspected loyalists, including his own. He told others about it, and many, including the Allens, were stampeded into the arms of the British army. There were wider consequences: "Still others, frightened by the extremists, hid in the countryside for a time and returned to Philadelphia only when a degree of stability had been restored. The significant result of this flare-up, brought on by an irresponsible minority, was that some of the ablest men in the State were alienated, driven to the British permanently."[44] Andrew Allen went to live in England, where he was awarded a lump sum and a small pension under the scheme set up to compensate loyalists. His son, also Andrew, joined Lincoln's Inn in May 1796 and later served as the British consul in Boston from 1805 to 1812. Andrew Allen was succeeded as Attorney General by a sound patriot, John Morris, who had been admitted to the Middle Temple in 1754.

James Allen, alone of the four brothers, though a loyalist, did not go over to the British lines. His diary, and other evidence, suggests that James was the fool of the family, so he may have thought that his influential friends would save him, if he were to stay and flatter them. The irritating thing is that he proved to be right: he got away with outrageous behavior. He joined the local militia, explaining in his entry for 14 October 1775: "My inducement principally to join them is that a man is suspected who does not; and I choose to have a musket on my shoulders to be on a par with them; and I believe discreet people mixing with them, may keep them in order." Discreet he was not. His actions and statements made it clear to his militia colleagues that he was not really hostile to the British. When he was eventually arrested as a Tory and then released on giving his parole, his militia colleagues let out a howl of protest: they had clearly seen through him and felt he should remain in custody.

Their breathless long petition to the Council of Safety, dated 26 December 1776, began: "We, the officers of the fifth company in the second battalion of militia, for ourselves and our company, take this method to inform you that it gives us no general satisfaction on hearing that James Allen Esq., was apprehended and conducted as a prisoner in order to be examined by your Honorable Board and to be dealt with according to his deserts, the behavior of his nearest relations in flying from their fellow citizens and seeking refuge amongst our common unprovoked cruel enemies, we thought was sufficient cause for securing such a person as the aforementioned James Allen Esq., but to our great astonishment we are informed that he is set at liberty."[45] The petitioners then gave an account of various minor follies committed by Allen, which had offended them. Allen probably never learned of this screed, for in the following year he went crashing on with further ill advised conduct, instead of using a little discretion.

Alexander Graydon, after commenting on James' foolish behavior, added that his brother Andrew Allen had also joined the militia, but "not long after, recognizing his error, he withdrew, giving out that he would hang up his cap and regimentals as monuments of his folly, and, upon the Declaration of Independence, he sought asylum with General Howe."[46]

In December 1777, James Allen called at the Valley Forge headquarters of the Commander-in-Chief, although in fairness to him, it should be added that this time he was not coming merely as a sightseer, but on account of his wife's pregnancy. He had written to Washington to ask for leave for his wife to be allowed back into Philadelphia for her lying-in, "and to my utter astonishment met with a refusal, though I knew people were permitted to pass into and out of Philadelphia at liberty without any license. Wherefore I rode to headquarters and dined with the General, who was very civil to me—no doubt my visit was unexpected. Immediately on my coming, Mr. Tilghman, who had settled the matter with General Washington, told me the General would be willing to permit us all to go in, but not return. I accepted the terms."

Tench Tilghman, Washington's aide, later tried to explain this bizarre visit to Timothy Matlack, the secretary of the Executive Council: "Although I had ever differed with him in political sentiments, yet from my family connection with him I thought it my duty to give him my advice as a friend." That advice had been that he should apply to the appropriate authorities: he had certainly not suggested an approach to his general, who—as he knew better than anybody else—was fully occupied with somewhat more important matters. It is possible that the considerate Washington tolerated the intolerable Allen, merely because he did not want to cause further embarrassment to his young aide, who was already embarrassed enough by having several loyalist relatives, closer than Allen. The Allen and Tilghman families were to be further linked in 1794, when James's daughter Margaret married Tench Tilghman's brother William, who was to be appointed Chief Justice in 1805.

Despite his concern about his wife's imminent confinement, Allen still went on his travels in February 1778, visiting his sister Anne and her husband, the ex-Governor John Penn, as well as ex-Chief Justice Chew, at their place of exile, the Union Ironworks in New Jersey. He also managed to dine with the British general, Sir William Howe, presumably to demonstrate his lofty neutrality. Allen was delighted when on 27 February 1778 his wife gave birth to their first son, after five daughters, but he suffered a blow when he learned that his eldest brother, John, had died on 2 February "of a putrid fever" (typhus), while still in his thirties. James himself died in the September of the same year, 1778. William Allen in one year lost two of his four sons, on top of losing his country.

William Allen's retirement in 1774 had proved fortunate, as he was a loyalist and would have been dismissed soon after that—as was to happen to his successor, Chew. He would seem to have been an adequate, rather than an outstanding Chief Justice during his twenty-four years in office. His sole biographer, Norman Cohen, paid him the compliment of asserting, "Despite Allen's closeness to the Penns, and the fact that he held his position as Chief Justice by Proprietary appointment, he still handled his court with strict independence."[47] He lived on his own at his country house, which though damaged during the battle of Germantown, had not been fought over in the same way as Chew's House.[48] He died in September 1780, two years after his two sons. The conflict must have caused him much sadness, as he clearly had strong attachments to both America and England. At least he had the limited consolation, not granted to all parents in his position, of knowing that all four of his sons had decided in the same way as he had done. He was on the losing side, but at least he was spared the kind of pain that his old opponent, Franklin, suffered from his son's unequivocal choice of the loyalist side.

That Franklin never got over that pain is evident from the letter he wrote to William, in response to his approach for a reconciliation after the war. "Nothing has ever hurt me so much and affected me with such keen sensations as to find myself deserted in my old age by my only son; and not only deserted, but to find him taking up arms against me in a cause wherein my good fame, fortune, and life were all at stake. You conceived, you say, that your duty to your king and regard for your country required this. I ought not to blame you for differing in sentiment with me in public affairs. Your situation was such that few would have censured your remaining neuter, though there are natural duties which precede political ones and cannot be extinguished by them. This is a disagreeable subject. I drop it."[49]

A large number of loyalists chose to live in Canada or the West Indies, while some returned to the United States. Like many others, William Franklin decided to live in England, until his death in 1814. In 1783 his portrait, together with that of other loyalists, was painted by Benjamin West, but it no longer exists. In the following year he had a brief visit from the son born while he was a student at the Middle Temple, William Temple Franklin, who had been living and working with his grandfather in Paris. As soon as Jefferson had arrived in Paris, he had contacted the bookshop in London recommended by John Adams, who had stayed there for two months with his son, John Quincy. His letter to the bookseller, John Stockdale, dated 1 September, is relevant to the present account for two reasons: the first, for its reference to Blackstone, the second, for William Temple's address.[50]

Jefferson wrote: "I asked the favor of Mr. [William Temple] Franklin, who lately went from hence to London, to send me a book or two which you had published. As he will not have left London when you receive this, I will beg the favor of you to procure for me a copy of the small 12mo. edition of Blackstone's *Commentaries*, published I believe in Ireland. I would choose it unbound, because I can then have it bound into one or two more volumes whichever may best suit me as a traveler." He added that young Franklin, who would pay for it, was to be found "at Govr. Franklin's, Norton street, London."

William Franklin, like his father, lived to a good age, eighty-two, and was buried in St. Pancras Churchyard, not far from the Middle Temple. A biographer has commented that his pride in his military expertise, gained as a teenager before coming to England, "was rivaled only by the importance he attached to his education at London's Middle Temple."[51]

One further loyalist who fled from Philadelphia should be mentioned, if only because of the joy that one of his sons gave to Britain as a poet, writer and editor. Isaac Hunt was admitted to the Middle Temple in 1765 and practiced very successfully in Philadelphia until he left for England in 1775, after he had been roughly handled by a mob for daring to represent a loyalist medical practitioner in court. In London he took Holy Orders and helped Benjamin West, his wife's uncle, to secure the release of fellow painter John Trumbull, one of Washington's first aides. Trumbull had retired from the war and had come to England to study with West; he later acted as secretary to Chief Justice John Jay, when he was negotiating the treaty that bears his name, which will be considered later.[52]

Americans who wanted to see Divine retribution for George III's conduct towards them, were not aware of the trials and tribulations that were to be heaped on his head by his sons—more than adequate punishment for most offences. It is a moot point as to which of his sons was the most obnoxious, but the Prince of Wales, who became Regent and then King George IV, has a weighty claim to the title. In 1812 the London *Morning Post* praised the Prince Regent in ridiculously extravagant terms, including, "You are an Adonis in loveliness," which proved too much for Leigh Hunt, Isaac's son.

He published a reply in *The Examiner*, which he and his brother John edited. His outburst predictably landed him in prison—but he probably thought it was worth it. He felt obliged to point out, "That this Adonis in loveliness was a corpulent gentleman of fifty! In short, that this delightful, blissful, wise, pleasurable, honourable, virtuous, true and immortal Prince was a violater of his word, a libertine over head and ears in debt and disgrace, a despiser of domestic ties, the companion of gamblers and demireps, a man who has just closed half a century without one single claim on the gratitude of his country or the respect of posterity."[53]

Benjamin Chew
courtesy of The Historical Society of Pennsylvania (HSP), Society Portrait, photo of
painting by unidentified artist in unidentifed collection

Chapter 4
THE CHIEF JUSTICES OF PENNSYLVANIA II: BENJAMIN CHEW AND HIS SUCCESSORS

Benjamin Chew, who was born in November 1722, when William Allen was in London as a student, certainly had a proper legal education and in due course was considered to be one of the finest lawyers in Pennsylvania. He was fortunate enough to study with the great Andrew Hamilton from the age of about sixteen until Hamilton died in 1741. Chew's father, Dr. Samuel Chew, who was not a lawyer but a physician, was appointed Chief Justice of the Lower Counties, which became Delaware, at about the same time, so young Chew spent some time assisting him as an unqualified clerk, before going to England to join the Middle Temple in 1743.

The father's connections proved useful. On 26 June 1743 Samuel Chew wrote to Thomas Penn in London. "My son Benjamin, who you may remember, lived some time with Mr. Hamilton, having since his death pursued his studies in the law, comes to London with a view of residing for a year or two about the Temple or some of the Inns of Court in order to complete them. He has a letter from the Governor to Colonel Martin and another from Mr. Allen to Mr. Paris that I hope will be useful to him. Mr. Paris may certainly be of very great advantage to him." Paris, as has been mentioned, was the Penn's legal representative in England. The judgment of Paris was clearly regarded as sound, even though he was known for his bad temper.[1]

Chew made the most of his father's introductions. While in London, "he gained both the sophisticated professional skills and the personal connections with the Penns on which his career was to be based."[2] Unfortunately, like Allen, he had to cut his time at the Middle Temple short when his father died, and he returned home in late 1744. He brought with him a package from William Strahan, Franklin's printer/bookseller friend, whose shop was close to the Temple in Wine Office Court, on the other side of Fleet Street. Franklin's acknowledgment shows that he was catering for customers of different political colors, for he wrote, with typical humor: "I received your favor per Mr. Chew, dated 10 September. I would not have you be too nice in the choice of pamphlets you send me. Let me have everything, good or bad, that makes a noise and has a run: for I have friends here of different tastes to oblige with the sight of them."[3]

Chew built up a very successful practice in Pennsylvania and the three Lower Counties. He was a member of the commission appointed to fix the boundary between Pennsylvania and Maryland and eventually drafted the final report, basing himself on the findings of the surveyors Mason and Dixon, whose line continues to this day. He moved to Philadelphia in 1754 and after his first wife died, leaving him with four young daughters to bring up, married again. His second wife was the niece of Allen's business partner, James Turner, and soon provided Chew with a son, also Benjamin. When the boy was christened, Chew had all four daughters baptized at the same time, so cutting his links with the Quakerism of his forebears.[4] Young Benjamin Chew in due course followed his father to the Middle Temple, being admitted in January 1784, immediately after the formal ending of the war.

From 1755 to 1769 Chew served as Attorney General of Pennsylvania and as the Recorder of Philadelphia, earning a reputation that was second to none. In 1758 he accompanied Governor William Denny to one of the conferences with the Amerindian population at Easton. At one stage several of its members had too much alcohol and could not be persuaded to behave in an orderly manner. The governor threatened to send them to Philadelphia to be "swinged" but Chew advised him that such a course would be not only dangerous and dishonorable but also illegal. The governor responded churlishly to this advice from his official legal adviser, leaving Chew to muse, "What a strange peevish petulant creature it is."[5]

One of the students lucky enough to learn from Chew, before setting off for London to complete his legal education, was Andrew Allen. Two other of his students were the cousins, William and Edward Tilghman; Edward was not only Chew's nephew, but also became his son-in-law. These Tilghmans were to be so successful in the law that they were both offered the post of State Chief Justice in 1805.

As a young man, Edward Tilghman was at one stage, in the winter of 1772, thinking about cutting short his time in London, but Chew persuaded him to continue with his studies at the Middle Temple. He advised him: "The requiring a polish, as you call it, or a view of your making a proficiency in the study of the law, were not the sole ends proposed by your friends by the tour to England. But besides the reputation arising from a gentleman having attended Westminster Hall, you must allow no small advantages may be gained by it. The address and manner of speaking gracefully, and with proper elocution, is in some degree to be acquired by anyone disposed to improvement in these matters; and although there are not a great number of cases debated at bar in a term, yet as the ablest counsel are employed in these that are argued, you are sure to have the whole law on the point cited and exhausted, of which your note will be a treasure for your whole life to come."[6]

Chew seems to have realized that his advice was rather solemn, for he continued in a lighter vein. "Let me caution you, however, not to risk your health by too sedentary a life and intense application, a rock I myself had like to have split on when I was at the Temple. Mingle the *dulce* with the *utile* [the sweet with the useful], and let your time be divided between the law, history, belle lettres, society and exercise, and learn to profit by the views and foibles of others, and by copying the virtues and manners of those worthy of imitation."

When Chew gave up the post of Recorder of Philadelphia, he cut down his practice to some degree. He had been the leading lawyer of the city for some time, and his place as such was taken by Nicholas Waln, another Middle Templar. However, Chew continued to take some cases, as is shown by a revealing comment by the Deputy Collector of Customs at Philadelphia, dated 5 September 1771: "The claimants have much the advantage in respect to lawyers—they have got Mr. Chew, the late Attorney General (who resigned) at the head of them, and the Deputy Collector can get nobody to appear for him except Mr. [Andrew] Allen, the present Attorney General, who is a young man and has not much experience."[7]

In March 1773, Chew was ill and wrote to James Tilghman, William's father: "I must lessen, if not altogether give up the business of my profession, or shorten the thread of my life. Old age is creeping on and my mind can't bear up under the burden it has hitherto supported." These remarks came from a man still only fifty years of age. It was just as well for Chew that William Allen was continuing for a while as Chief Justice. Had the post become vacant at that time, it is doubtful whether Chew would have wanted it, or whether he would have got it in any event, if his ill-health was really as bad as he indicated.

Six weeks later he wrote to Edward Tilghman at the Middle Temple that he was "absolutely worn down by hard service," but nevertheless gave his former student an account of the trial in which he had just been engaged. He thought that Joseph Reed had distinguished himself, adding, somewhat surprisingly, that John Dickinson had signally failed to do so. In a speech lasting three-and-a-half hours, Dickinson, Chew's colleague in the case, had "butchered the cause most horribly," so that Chew had to repair the damage done. "I was never more in distress than when I got up to speak and conclude on the part of the Proprietary at four in the morning."[8] It is highly likely that everyone else who had to stay until the whole case was concluded *after* four o'clock was also in distress.

Fortunately for Chew, his health improved during the course of the next twelve months, so that he was ready, able and willing to become Chief Justice when Allen resigned in April 1774. Allen, whose seventieth birthday fell on 5 August 1774, had been thinking of retiring earlier, as is clear from the diary kept by his son. On 30 October 1773 James Allen recorded: "I am laboring to persuade my father to resign his office of Chief Justice as he has now entered his seventieth year, which he is inclined to do, but he is anxious to know who is like to be his successor." Allen was keen to have Chew take over as he was the most able lawyer available. Chew was offered the appointment and accepted it; he may well have decided that it was a case of "now or never." He must have realized that in the event of a breach with the Crown, his chances of attaining high judicial office would be nil; and must also have had a lingering concern that his health would rule him out in the near future, despite his comparative youth.

Chew's political views were at all times close to those of his friend William Allen. He supported the Proprietary interests, opposed the Stamp Act and other English abuses, but opposed Independence. Like Allen, he was disturbed by the Quaker attitude towards defense and other matters and abandoned Quakerism for the Anglican Church. He shared Allen's views of Franklin. After Franklin had lost his seat in the Assembly in 1764, he continued to run it, though the lawyer Joseph Galloway was by then the formal Quaker party leader. In November of that year, Chew commented that Franklin and Galloway met regularly before each session of the Assembly to plan the party's next move there.[9]

In all the circumstances, it is scarcely surprising that the scholar who made a study of the Pennsylvania Supreme Court, should have commented: "The Chew court essentially was the Allen court under new leadership." However, he added one important distinction: "As such, it was without question the most professional and formally trained high court to date."[10]

In April 1776 Chief Justice Chew was charging the members of a grand jury about the principal offences they might be called upon to consider, when he was asked by the foreman for further guidance on the crime of treason. Somewhat surprisingly, in view of his loyalist leanings, and perhaps influenced by the fact that the Continental Congress was at that moment meeting in the same building, Chew replied: "I have stated that an opposition by force of arms to the lawful authority of the King or his ministers is high treason; but in the moment when the King or his ministers shall exceed the constitutional authority vested in them by the constitution, submission to their mandates become treason."[11]

Chew's pro-American views and actions were not enough to save him, after the Declaration of Independence and the rise of the Whig radicals, coupled with the threat to Philadelphia from the British forces. The Provincial Convention of Pennsylvania took over the government, and Crown appointees, such as the Chief Justice, lost their jobs. However, Chew was not persecuted in the way that some out-and-out loyalists were, as his record of speaking out against British abuses was well known. It was not until the following year that his liberty was restricted.

Together with Governor Penn and some thirty others, including Edward Shippen, a future Chief Justice, Chew was arrested in August 1777 and paroled to the Union Iron Works in New Jersey, owned by Allen and his associates. The only member of the Allen family who had not already fled, James, was among those arrested. The Chief Justice did not "come quietly", to use the classic police expression. "Chew refused to take the action of the Council seriously at first, and thoroughly intimidated the young soldiers from the City Troop who were sent to pick him up. Eventually realizing his predicament he signed a parole that he would go to, and remain at, the

Union Iron Works, although he insisted that there was no charge against him except that he had held office under the Proprietor."[12]

The conflict around Philadelphia included the battle of Germantown on 4 October, during which the lives of four Middle Templars intersected in an extraordinary way: those of the two Chief Justices, Allen and Chew; and those of Washington's two aides, Joseph Reed and John Laurens, who were also members of the Inn. Chew's country house became the focus of fierce fighting at a crucial stage of the battle. The house itself had an interesting background. As related earlier, when Allen had gone to England, he had lent his house at Germantown to Chew. In a letter of 27 January 1764, Allen referred to Chew staying there, and added a point that gives rise to the first of two "What if?" questions. "It gives me pleasure to hear that your abode there contributed to your health, and that you are like to build and be my neighbor."[13]

Chew did indeed build his new house near Allen's, naming it Cliveden, in honor of the English mansion of that name, which had been occupied until his death by the respected Frederick, Prince of Wales, the father of George III, and by the young future King himself. The Pennsylvania Cliveden became better known as the Chew House (although it is still there with its first name) after it was used as a strong-point by the British army during the fighting at Germantown, immediately after Chief Justice Allen's nearby house had been taken without difficulty by the Continental army. Despite repeated attacks by American troops, and notably by John Laurens, who had recently joined the general's staff, the British succeeded in keeping possession of the house and in holding up Washington's advance. The delay led to confusion and confusion to Washington's defeat. Had Chew not stayed at Allen's house for a year, he might well never have built his own substantial stone house there. Had that house not been built, or been built of timber, the battle of Germantown could well have gone Washington's way on 4 October. Given the surrender of the British army under General John Burgoyne at Saratoga to General Horatio Gates a mere thirteen days later, the war might then have ended speedily with an American victory.

There is another twist to the story, giving rise to a second "What if?" As will be discussed shortly in some detail, Middle Templar Joseph Reed, who had been Washington's first military secretary and then his army's Adjutant General, had a few weeks before the battle turned down the offer of the post of Chief Justice, in succession to Chew. He was with Washington at the height of the battle, considering with him the problem caused by Chew's stone house, when General Henry Knox said that "the fort" must be reduced. The principles of war, he asserted, did not permit an advance that left an enemy in the rear of the advancing army. Knox had been a Boston bookseller until 1775, and then became a brilliant artillery commander. Reed, the lawyer, who had even less experience of those principles, was all for bypassing Chew's house, with its small garrison, and pressing on to a possible victory. He protested: "What! Call this a fort, and lose the happy moment!" Had the lawyer's views prevailed over those of the bookseller, Washington might still have had his victory and an early end to the war, with the saving of thousands of lives on both sides.[14]

At least one other Middle Templar participated in that battle: Charles Cotesworth Pinckney, whose brother Thomas was to take part in the final battle at Yorktown together with Laurens. The significant contribution of those three men from South Carolina will be considered further later. Four days after Germantown, Thomas McKean, a Middle Temple signer of the Declaration of Independence and Chew's newly-appointed successor as Chief Justice, wrote a note of consolation to Washington about the casualties sustained. His letter contained a shrewd comment that proved to be amply justified. "If your Excellency attacks and disables a thousand of the enemy a week, and are constantly reinforced equal to the numbers you lose, as I trust you will, you must soon prove triumphantly victorious."[15] The British commanders' inability to replace all the men lost in action, by sickness and by desertion, placed them at a great disadvantage.

After Washington's failure at Germantown, there was one important consequence of the success at Saratoga, which involved John Laurens. Following on the defeat of Burgoyne by General Gates, a number of critics queried whether he or General Thomas Conway might not be more effective as Commander-in-Chief. The movement to oust Washington became known as the Conway Cabal. On 3 January 1778 young Laurens, who was with Washington at Valley Forge, wrote to his father, since November the President of Congress, to inform him about the plot. Henry Laurens wrote back five days later that Washington's ruin would involve the ruin of the cause. He added, "On the other hand his magnanimity, his patience, will save his country and confound his enemies."[16] John Laurens doubtless felt able to show that letter to his general, who was able to see off all the opposition. "By keeping the President well informed of certain manoeuvres of the Cabal, the young Carolinian was able during this unpleasant episode to be of particular service to his adored Chief."[17]

On 10 May 1778 Chew and John Penn wrote to Henry Laurens, as President of Congress, from the Union Iron Works in New Jersey, where they were required to live under the terms of their parole. They asked for leave to return to Philadelphia, so that they could comply with a new law, "requiring all persons who had enjoyed office under the Crown to take the Test prescribed by a former Act by 1 June next, under pain of confiscation of their estates."[18] Laurens sent the necessary authorization, so on 30 June 1778 Benjamin Chew was escorted from New Jersey to the western shore of the Delaware River, and released from his parole. He wrote, "I would retire to Cliveden for a time if it was habitable. At present it is an absolute wreck, and materials are not to be had to keep out the weather." He accordingly sold the house. After some repair work it was occupied by Washington in the winter of 1781-82. That particular story had a happy ending, as Chew was able to buy it back eight years after selling it.

Chew's own career had a happy ending also, thanks to his solid reputation. During 1778 the Pennsylvania Assembly discussed how best to deal with the various land holdings of the Penn family; in the following year there were hearings to determine a solution that would be fair to the public as well as to the Penns. Chew, together with his nephew and son-in-law, Edward Tilghman, was able to represent the Penn family, without any hindrance. One of the reasons that it was possible to come to a satisfactory conclusion, was that the President of the State, Joseph Reed, and Governor John Penn both behaved in an exemplary manner.[19]

Pennsylvania at first made no provision for any appeal from its Supreme Court, but in February 1780 legislation established the High Court of Errors and Appeals. It was empowered to hear appeals from the Supreme Court and also from the Court of Admiralty and the Register Court. The judges named for this highest court included the President, Joseph Reed and the Chief Justice, Thomas McKean, who presided over it until 1791. In that year Chew received the highest compliment Pennsylvania could pay him: he was appointed by Governor Thomas Mifflin as President of the High Court, despite the fact that he was by then close to seventy. He presided over the court until 1804 and died in January 1810. Brilliant lawyer though he was, Chew's fears in 1773 of an early demise would seem to have been prompted by his incorrect assessment of the medical evidence.[20]

JOSEPH REED

To coin a cliché, Joseph Reed may be called the best Chief Justice Pennsylvania never had; he was selected for the post in March 1777 but declined it. He would obviously not have been chosen at the early age of thirty-five, but for his distinguished record, which included a comparatively short but brilliant legal career, followed by service with General Washington. Reed was undoubtedly one of the most interesting men to participate in the Revolution and we make no apology for discussing him at some length, nor for including him in this chapter, where we feel he belongs.

Reed was born in Trenton, New Jersey, in August 1741 and graduated from the New Jersey College at Princeton as a Bachelor of Arts at the age of sixteen. He then studied law with Richard Stockton, a leading New Jersey lawyer. Reed was admitted to practice in May 1763, but decided to complete his legal education at the Middle Temple. His biographer, John Roche, concluded that it was undoubtedly the governor of New Jersey, William Franklin, who had recommended him to do so, having studied at the Middle Temple himself.[21] On 20 October he sailed for England, and was admitted to the Inn on 16 December 1763, together with Nicholas Waln, who had probably traveled with him. Like Arthur Lee of Virginia later, he obtained chambers in Garden Court, adjoining the Hall of the Inn, and was provided with his own key for the Middle Temple garden.[22]

Like other American students before him, Reed was befriended by an English merchant of Flemish descent, Denys De Berdt, whose Protestant family had emigrated from the Spanish Netherlands in the seventeenth century on religious grounds. De Berdt had commercial connections with America, including the business run by Reed's father and his son-in-law, Charles Pettit. He also had contacts with several members of the government in London, notably the Earls of Shelburne and of Dartmouth, who were well disposed towards the American colonies. De Berdt had many visitors at his two homes: one off Chiswell Street in the City of London, in Artillery Court, which led to the entrance of the historic Artillery Ground; the other just north of the capital, near Enfield (one correspondent referred to it as being at nearby Broxbourne). In those two welcoming homes the students were able to discuss the politics of the day, including the problems being created for the colonies by the government.

Arthur Lee, then still a medical student, who had not yet turned to the study of law, was one of the regular American visitors, as was Stephen Sayre, who was later described by Reed's grandson as "a volatile, untrustworthy adventurer, of extremely plausible address and attractive manners."[23] The latter two characteristics were probably largely responsible for his success in worming himself into a partnership with De Berdt, and into the City of London establishment, where he and Arthur Lee's brother, William, were both elected Sheriff.

Joseph Reed
courtesy of The Historical Society of Pennsylvania (HSP), Society Portrait, engraved by
John Sartain after a painting by Charles Wilson Peale

Richard Stockton, the eminent New Jersey lawyer with whom Reed had studied in America, also turned up at the De Berdts'; he was essentially in the British Isles as a prosperous tourist, spending fifteen months there in all. Although they later had opposing political views, William Franklin regarded him as "a particular friend of mine." Stockton nearly became Franklin's successor as governor, but was narrowly defeated by William Livingston. He did, however, serve on the New Jersey Supreme Court and as a member of the Continental Congress. Stockton signed the Declaration of Independence, but five months later he had the misfortunate to be kidnapped by a party of loyalists and flung into prison. The experience gravely harmed his health, but it was probably cancer that was the cause of his death in 1781 at the age of fifty.

De Berdt's daughter, Esther, had her sixteenth birthday in October 1763 and within a few weeks met Reed, who was some six years older than her. They got on extremely well, as Arthur Lee noticed, concluding a note that he wrote on one occasion to Esther, "Lay me in the next chamber of your heart to that which Mr. Reed inhabits." The couple discussed marriage, but ran into the opposition of Esther's father and the difficult problem of deciding where they could live together. On 1 November 1764, when Reed was still in London, Esther wrote: "As to my going to America, *it cannot be*. You by several hints seem to mean that you could not live in England; you told my father that the trade in the law never was so dull as it is now; these things all tend to sink my hopes."[24] The word "dull" was obviously used to indicate that work prospects were not bright. It was certainly true that many London barristers were then, as at other times, unable to earn a living or to support a family.

Reed made a point of attending debates in Parliament on America, and was most impressed by William Pitt's eloquence. He also took note of the views of some alarmed friends back home, such as those of Daniel Coxe of Trenton, who wrote to him on 12 April 1764: "What in the name of sense has possessed the English nation, or rather its Parliament? For I find a paragraph in the last paper that a scheme is on foot for obliging us to furnish £500,000 sterling among the colonies. My God, what madness this is: think they that we are any ways able to raise that sum, or half of it?"[25]

In June 1764 Reed wrote to Charles Pettit, his brother-in-law and closest friend, expressing the view that taxation of the colonies was being considered partly because "the exaggerated accounts the officers from America have given of its opulence, and our manner of living, have had no small share in it, as there has, in this way, been raised a very high and false notion of our capacity to bear a part of the national expenses." When Pennsylvania suffered from Indian raids, there was some brutal retaliation by frontiersmen known as the Paxton Boys, and their calls in Germantown for better protection. Reed was appalled; he could see an additional danger and wrote home with an astute warning. "As the weakness of the civil authority was a pretext made before to send over troops, which we are to maintain, you may be sure the ministry will consider every such disorder as an additional argument to prove the necessity of such a measure and, however injured the inhabitants of the frontiers may have been, their Germantown expedition may be the means of saddling their fellow subjects with an increased expense."[26]

As discussed earlier, Chief Justice Allen of Pennsylvania visited England for about a year, from mid-1763 to mid-1764, when his two sons were at the Middle Temple. Reed was concerned about the worsening political situation and was therefore very pleased with the efforts made during his stay by the Chief Justice and by Richard Jackson, a Member of Parliament, who was the agent for the province. He wrote to Pettit on 11 June 1764: "Mr. Allen and Mr. Jackson exerted themselves, with great spirit and industry, to moderate and soften the designs of the ministry, and not without success. Both of them are entitled to a great share of American gratitude."[27]

Reed sailed from England in February 1765, without being called to the English Bar, as he was urgently needed by his family back home in Trenton, where he started at once to practice law. Fortunately, Esther's parents had consented to an engagement and to an exchange of letters, and Reed looked forward to returning before long to claim his bride. The year 1765 saw the passing of the notorious Stamp Act and also the appointment of De Berdt as agent for Massachusetts Bay and the Pennsylvanian Lower Counties of New Castle, Kent and Sussex, the future Delaware.

After a year apart, the prospects for a reunion seemed distinctly gloomy for the couple. Reed's friend Pettit, who had married his half-sister and had three children by her, was not doing well in the business that he shared with Reed's ailing and absent father. Reed nobly took on the support of the extended family, explaining to Esther from Trenton on 13 January 1766: "I have been, much against my inclination, obliged to keep house ever since my return, and you will perhaps be surprised when I tell you that my family consists of nine persons besides servants—but so it is, and I have been under the unavoidable necessity of supporting all these, besides my father, who chose retiring to the country, where he still continues."

Reed clearly had a big heart. He had also taken his brother Bowes into his law office, though with "no expectation of his making a great figure." One could not have a better illustration of the harm done by Britain's foolish legislation, than Reed's sad reflection on his difficulties, "However, my income I believe would have been equal to them all if the Stamp Act had not interfered. This has hurt me prodigiously, and exhausted all the little store my first success had given me."[28]

He was sufficiently indignant about the Act to write some articles about its effects, copies of which he sent to De Berdt, doubtless with the dual object of informing him and of impressing him as a potential son-in-law. Before that letter arrived, Esther wrote: "Mr. Sayre is thinking many ways of opening a way for your coming to settle in England; and we have some few pleasant hours in talking of them." As Stephen Sayre, a classmate of Reed's from Princeton, managed to contribute to the ruin of her father's firm, it was just as well that Reed was never induced to follow up any of his schemes.

De Berdt's importance may be gauged from his response to the repeal of the Stamp Act in 1766, when together with other colonial agents, he chartered a ship specially to carry the good news to America. Furthermore, later in the year, Esther wrote about the change of government, adding, "If Lord Dartmouth had been made Secretary of State, my papa intended to have spoke for you to have been his Law Secretary." Dartmouth had been impressed by Reed's reasoned attacks on the Stamp Act, which her father had passed on to him. Roche made the point that the ground for Dartmouth's later important exchange of letters with Reed, was laid on this occasion.[29]

On 4 October 1766, Reed made his excuses for not writing more often, revealing how successful he had become: "The practice of the law is extremely fatiguing in this country. There are sixteen courts, which I am obliged to attend from home, oftentimes near a whole week at each, besides attending the assizes once a year through the whole province, which contains thirteen counties." The practice continued to flourish and on 24 April 1767 Reed informed Esther, with a rare glimpse of humor: "My business now produces me at the rate of £1000 per annum, and is increasing beyond my ability to go through it, though my two brothers, and a young gentleman who is serving a clerkship with me, assist me. My family is decreasing, contrary to the usual custom of families, and I hope in a little time to get my brothers into business, when I shall only have my father and sister to take care of."[30] Esther must have thought that Joseph was a wonderful family man, but wished that he were creating one with her.

As De Berdt at one point suggested that Reed might like to help him with the Massachusetts agency, the lawyer thought he had better learn more about that province before returning to England. In the summer of 1769, together with his fellow Middle Templar, John Dickinson, he spent about two months in Boston, meeting "the most active men of the day on the side of the colonial rights."[31] One of them was Josiah Quincy Jr., who later called on him at his home and then sailed for England on a lengthy visit to Franklin and other Americans, as well as their English supporters. On 25 October

1774, Reed wrote to Quincy from Philadelphia: "I hope this will find you safely arrived in Great Britain, a country wherein I have spent many happy hours, before she began to play the tyrant over America."[32] The exact nature of Quincy's mission, and whether it was successful or not, remains unclear, partly because he died of tuberculosis at sea while on the return journey.

On 14 March 1770 Reed was at last able to set off for England, after an absence of five years. His own father had died in the previous December; when he landed in Europe, Reed saw a copy of the *London Gazette* announcing the death of Denys De Berdt, Esther's father. That second death was a blow, as he had been hoping that his future father-in-law's many contacts would lead to a good job in England. However, all turned out for the best, as Esther agreed to live in America, where Reed was able to lead a far more rewarding life than would have been possible in England as a rebellious colonist. Their marriage was celebrated on 22 May 1770 at the parish church close to Artillery Court: St. Luke's in Old Street (designed by Nicholas Hawksmoor and now the home of the London Symphony Orchestra). Mr. and Mrs. Reed sailed for Philadelphia on 3 September, and her mother came, too.

Arthur Lee, who had decided to practice law rather than medicine, wrote from Essex Court in the Middle Temple on 18 January 1771, to thank Reed for having recommended him for the post of colonial agent when he was in England. They had by then both made contact with the Boston radical element. Lee had succeeded in being appointed as deputy agent, in case of the illness or death of the elected agent, Benjamin Franklin. "Unknown and unworthy as I was, the idea of being agent for Massachusetts Bay never possessed me; I therefore never solicited that honor, and considered your recommendation of me as flowing more from your great partiality for me than from an expectation of success. I am now tempted to believe that had I moved the rest of my friends here, especially Col.[Isaac] Barré and Mrs.[Catharine] Macaulay, to exert themselves in my favor, Dr. Franklin would not have gained so easy a victory." The new law student managed a weak legal joke for the experienced lawyer when he added: "There is no probability of his departing from hence, but at the irresistible summons of fate; therefore my contingent remainder is of no great value." Had Reed decided to stay in England, he might well have been chosen as the Massachusetts agent in preference to both Franklin and Lee.[33]

Reed's proficiency soon made him one of the leading lawyers in Philadelphia, the city he had decided to make his home. Esther wrote to her brother Dennis on 29 February 1772: "Providence has remarkably favored our settling in this place. Out of the four greatest lawyers in the city, three have resigned practice. Mr. Galloway, being a good deal advanced in life, and having a very large fortune, cares very little about it. Mr. Dickinson also, married to a wife worth £30,000, is improving and building on his estate; and Mr. Waln, who you may remember in the Temple with Mr. Reed, is, on a sudden [impulse] turned Quaker preacher. He had very great business— they say near £2000 a year, but he has resigned on principle, as he says no good man can practice law. Mr. Chew has recovered his health and practices as usual, but he cannot be on both sides of a question." It is perhaps not without significance that of the "four greatest lawyers", only Galloway was not a member of Reed's Inn, the Middle Temple. In April Esther sent her brother a request indicating how reliant some American lawyers still were on London for their books, apart of course, from pirated copies of Blackstone's *Commentaries*, which were available locally. "Mr. Reed will be glad if you will send him all the new law books, which are received by those that understand the matter. Dr. Lee will be a good person to inquire of."[34]

Reed exchanged a number of letters with Lord Dartmouth, and it is clear from those that he was constantly trying to persuade the British government to adopt a more reasonable attitude towards the colonies. He argued their case rationally and objectively, as is demonstrated by an extract from his letter of 4 April 1774. "The other project now forming is to distress and harass the admiralty courts, so as to make all the officers in them odious and disgraceful. It is to be wished that the mode of trying revenue causes was more agreeable to the English Constitution, but at the same time I must acknowledge that at present there seems little probability of justice being done to the Crown by an American jury. It is therefore an object well worthy of your lordship's attention to make the mode of trial in these courts as honorable and acceptable as may be."[35]

After the Boston Tea Party had led to more repressive legislation in London and the closure of the port of Boston, Reed was approached for help by his Massachusetts contacts, who had dispatched Paul Revere to bring their message. Together with three colleagues Reed arranged for public support in Philadelphia. They were Dickinson, who also knew the Bostonians; Thomas Mifflin, who was to be a general and then governor of Pennsylvania; and Charles Thomson, who later acted as secretary to every Continental and Confederation Congress meeting. On 26 May 1774 Edward Tilghman wrote a letter to his father about the political efforts of two of his Middle Temple colleagues that he had witnessed in Philadelphia. "In regard to the meeting at the City Tavern, Mr. Reed, a rising lawyer among us from New Jersey, made a motion to address the governor to call the Assembly, that we might show our inclination to take every legal step in order to obtain redress of our grievances. He was seconded by Mr. Dickinson. It is agreed on all hands that he spoke with great coolness, calmness, moderation, and good sense. Charles Thomson, as well as Reed, was more violent. He spoke till he fainted, and then went at it again. They were opposed by Alexander Wilcocks and Dr. Smith, but upon a division the motion was carried by a vast majority."[36]

On 25 September Reed informed Dartmouth about the meeting of the First Continental Congress that month, warning him, "Unless some healing measures are speedily adopted, the colonies will be wholly lost to England, or be preserved by her in such a manner as to be worse than useless for years to come. I am fully satisfied, my lord, and so I think must every man whose views are not limited to the narrow bounds of a single province, that America never can be governed by force; so daring a spirit as animates her, will require a greater power than Great Britain can spare, and it will be one continued conflict, till depopulation and destruction follow your victories, or the colonies establish themselves in some sort of independence."[37] On the following day he wrote to Dennis De Berdt: "If Parliament will repeal the tea duty, and put Boston in its former station, all will be well, and the tea will be paid for. Nothing else will save this country and Britain too. My head and heart are both full."

The first significant acknowledgment that Reed's abilities were not confined to the courtroom, but extended to the political scene, came on 23 January 1775, when the Pennsylvania Provincial Convention elected him as chairman. From then until 1781 he was a leading contributor to the revolution, both locally and nationally.

On 9 May 1775 Samuel Curwen, who kept a journal, "passed the evening at Mr. Joseph Reed's in company with Colonel Washington, a fine figure and of a most easy and agreeable address."[38] Apart from Washington the company included two other Virginian delegates to the Continental Congress: Richard Henry Lee and Benjamin Harrison. Also present were Dr. William Shippen; Mrs. De Berdt and Mrs. Reed. Mrs. De Berdt was not only Esther Reed's mother, but had been William Shippen's landlady when he was studying medicine in London. On one occasion he had been called upon to bleed his landlady's young daughter—who was now his hostess. As mentioned earlier, another American who had been a regular caller at the home of the De Berdts was Arthur Lee, Richard Henry Lee's younger brother. The Lees' sister Alice, while living in London, had met and married William Shippen, and they had put Washington up at their home on 4 September 1774, when he arrived to attend the First Continental Congress. Other meetings and events were to take place before decisions and appointments were made, but this dinner party at the Reeds' may well have played a part in the future roles of some of those present, including the host. Apart from anything else, Washington later made William Shippen the army's chief medical officer.

The Virginian delegate, Benjamin Harrison, who was a guest of the Reeds and later signed the Declaration of Independence, is worth an interjection. His grandfather, also Benjamin, had been a kind of pathfinder, having been admitted to the Middle Temple as early as 1697. He had then served as Attorney General and later as Treasurer and Speaker of the House of Burgesses in Virginia, before his early death in 1710. Alfred Jones pointed out that the ninth and twenty-third Presidents of the United States were his direct descendants. They were William Henry Harrison, a soldier, who served for a few days only in 1841, before having the dubious distinction of being the first President to die in office; and yet another Benjamin Harrison, who had been a practicing lawyer. He served from 1889 to 1793 and also achieved a first—a rather more pleasant one—in that he was the first grandson of a President to follow in his grandfather's footsteps. Furthermore, although the Reed's guest was not a member of his grandfather's Inn, his brother Carter Henry Harrison joined it in 1754, and his brother-in-law was one of the most distinguished members of the Middle Temple: Peyton Randolph, the first President of the Continental Congress.[39]

Dennis De Berdt kept in touch from England not only with his sister but also his brother-in-law. On 4 October 1775 he gave him some military information which proved to be essentially sound. "As to the first dependence, on English soldiers, though all the world would admit their bravery, still in this bad cause many doubt their fighting with zeal and usual intrepidity. Recruits are with difficulty raised, the men disliking the service. Every garrison is bare of men, and this day's paper says, out of forty officers drafted for Ireland, thirty-eight have resigned their commissions."[40]

The war started after the first shots had been exchanged at Lexington and Concord in April 1775. The British withdrew to Boston, where they were hemmed in by the local militia. After the Second Continental Congress had promoted Colonel George Washington to the rank of general and appointed him Commander-in-Chief of the American forces, he set off at once to conduct the siege of Boston. He was escorted from Philadelphia by a small mounted honor guard that included Joseph Reed, by then, like Dickinson, a Pennsylvania militia lieutenant-colonel. Unlike most of the general's escort, Reed stayed with him all the way to the new headquarters at Cambridge, outside Boston. By the time they arrived there Washington had decided that he wanted Reed on his personal staff: he had clearly been able to form a good impression of the lawyer over the past few weeks. On 4 July 1775 Lieutenant-Colonel Reed was appointed as Washington's military secretary, with Major Thomas Mifflin as an additional aide.

Those two appointments marked the start of a remarkable body of men: Washington's aides, some of whom were promoted out of the job, others of whom stayed on. They had one thing in common: an amazingly close-knit family relationship, thanks mainly to the attitude of the considerate, childless General, who regarded them more like sons than military subordinates. Reed very quickly developed a close relationship with him and felt able to advise him frankly, as for example when Washington gave offence to New Englanders with some unfortunate remarks. Washington took his minor rebuke well and wrote: "I will endeavor at a reformation, as I can assure you my dear Reed that I wish to walk in such a line as will give most general satisfaction."[41]

After four months with Washington, Reed felt obliged to return home, for an unspecified time, to the family and clients he had abandoned without notice, and he was soon elected to the Pennsylvania Assembly to take Mifflin's place. Washington wanted Reed to return and wrote him several warm letters, such as that dated 28 November 1775, a month after his departure: "I can truly assure you that I miss you exceedingly, and if an express declaration of this be wanting to hasten your return, I make it most heartily, and with some pleasure."

On 23 January 1776 Washington gave John Adams, his future Vice-President, a letter to bring to his absent secretary. "Real necessity compels me to ask you whether I may entertain any hopes of your returning to my family? My business increases very fast, and my distress for want of you, along with it."[42] The Washington "business" was presumably that of defeating the British and setting up a new nation. Incidentally, Adams had also been impressed by Reed when he met him at the time of the First Continental Congress, noting in his diary for 11 September 1774: "This Mr. Reed is a very sensible and accomplished lawyer of an amiable disposition—soft, tender, friendly &c. He is a friend to his country and to liberty."[43]

When the post of Adjutant General of the army became vacant on the promotion of General Horatio Gates, Washington attended Congress and on 5 June 1776 obtained approval for the appointment of Reed, with the rank of colonel. Reed accepted the post but soon found that his military experience was too limited for him to do a good job. An Adjutant General needed a great deal of such experience, for the post carried with it major responsibilities, including that of discipline for the whole army. Discipline obviously included trying to stop troops from returning home for personal reasons—as Reed himself had done.

In October Reed wrote to his wife that he had informed Congress of his wish to be replaced, adding: "As I am of opinion that some person may be found more skilled in military matters, and of more temper to bear the rubs and obstacles which ignorance and impudence are constantly throwing in my way, I think I may, with a safe conscience, resign it into other hands. To attempt to introduce discipline and subordination into a new army, must always be a work of much difficulty; but where the principles of democracy so unequivocally prevail, where so great an equality, and so thorough a leveling spirit predominates, either no discipline can be established, or he who attempts it must become odious and detestable."[44]

The British troops were eventually forced to withdraw from Boston, but returned in force to Long Island, New York, in August 1776. Reed played a useful part in the retreat from New York and through New Jersey, but was unhappy about Washington's failure to withdraw in time from Fort Washington, which was eventually lost with all its 2,800 defenders.

Unfortunately, he indicated his sentiments in a letter to General Charles Lee, which included the passage: "Oh, General! An indecisive mind is one of the greatest misfortunes that can befall an army; how often have I lamented it in this campaign." Lee gleefully replied: "I received your most obliging flattering letter—lament with you that fatal indecision of mind which in war is a much greater disqualification than stupidity or even want of personal courage."[45]

As ill luck would have it, Reed being away from headquarters, Washington opened the letter and felt bitterly disappointed that his closest adviser seemed to have written in critical terms to Lee, his second-in-command. Washington never saw the letter Reed had written, so its author was able to lie about its contents, assuring his chief that his remarks had been perfectly innocent and had contained "nothing inconsistent with that respect and affection which I have and shall ever bear to your person and character." If lies can be placed into categories, then this one possibly qualifies as a white one. Although Reed was saving his own skin, if he had not reassured Washington in this manner, the general's morale might well have sunk to a dangerous level and prompted his retirement. He had a thankless task, and had earlier in the year written to Reed: "I have often thought how much happier I should have been, if instead of accepting a command, I had taken my musket upon my shoulder and entered the ranks."[46]

Washington's letter of 14 June 1777 reveals a great deal about the two men and their close relationship. "True it is, I felt myself hurt by a certain letter, which appeared, at that time, to be the echo of one from you. I was hurt, not because I thought my judgment wronged by the expressions contained in it, but because the same sentiments were not communicated to myself. *The favorable manner in which your opinions, upon all occasions, had been received*, the impression they made, and the unreserved manner in which I wished and required them to be given, entitled me, I thought, to your advice upon any point in which I appeared to be wanting."[47]

Shortly before Christmas 1776, Reed was sent on a mission, during which he spoke to some senior officers, including General Hugh Mercer, who was to fall at Princeton. Reed's hometown was Trenton and his college had been at Princeton, so he knew the area Washington was approaching extremely well. On 22 December he wrote a letter which—bearing in mind the passage written six months later and emphasized above—may have stiffened the Commander-in-Chief's resolve to go over to the attack. After making it clear that he was speaking for his colleagues as well, Reed wrote: "Some enterprise must be undertaken in our present circumstances, or we must give up the cause. In a little time the Continental army will be dissolved. The initiative must be taken before their spirits and patience are exhausted, and the scattered, divided state of the enemy affords us a fair opportunity of trying what our men will do, when called to an offensive attack. Will it not be possible, my dear General, for your troops, or such part of them as can act with advantage, to make a diversion, or something more, at or about Trenton?"

Reed made plain his personal feelings, when he added: "I will not disguise my own sentiments, that our cause is desperate and hopeless, if we do not take the opportunity of the collection of troops at present, to strike some stroke. Our affairs are hasting to ruin, if we do not retrieve them by some happy event. Delay with us, is now equal to a total defeat."[48]

Washington replied on the same day: "Christmas day, at night, one hour before day, is the time fixed upon for our attempt on Trenton. For Heaven's sake, keep this to yourself, as the discovery of it may prove fatal to us, our numbers, sorry as I am to say, being less than I had any conception of; but necessity, dire necessity, will, nay, must justify any attempt. Prepare, and, in concert with Griffen, attack as many of their posts as you possibly can with a prospect of success."

Reed was not present at Trenton when Washington attacked it after crossing the Delaware, but participated in the later action at Princeton, where his local knowledge of the terrain proved useful. The success of those limited attacks on Trenton and Princeton had far-reaching effects. Thousands of Americans realized that they were not obliged always to retreat; that they could attack, despite appalling conditions; and that they could defeat professional soldiers, whether from Britain or Germany. Even more important was the fact that the French then appreciated that the colonists had a reasonable chance of eventual success and merited further support. There was one other after-effect of those victories, which is little known. Congress had earlier decided that the names of the signers of the Declaration of Independence should be kept secret, lest any of them fall into British hands. After Trenton and Princeton Congress felt sufficiently confident to lift the embargo and to order that the names of all the signers be sent to the thirteen States.[49]

Washington did not hold the unseen Lee letter against Reed. He was so impressed by him that in January 1777 he recommended him to Congress for promotion to brigadier-general and for the command of the cavalry, stating: "He is extremely active and enterprising, many signal proofs of which he has given this campaign." A lesser man than Washington might well have allowed his initial irritation with Reed, for writing the "certain letter", to prevent him from recommending his competent subordinate for promotion. However, Washington was the reasonable man personified— and he was not aware of the full extent of Reed's critical remarks, either to General Lee or to Dr. Benjamin Rush.

Many years later, Rush, another signer of the Declaration of Independence, recalled a conversation with Reed, which confirmed that he had indeed been a severe critic of Washington. Rush wrote to John Adams on 12 February 1812: "After the defeats and retreats of our army in 1776, I went as a volunteer physician to General [John] Cadwalader's corps of Philadelphia militia. During this excursion I rode with Colonel J. Reed from Bristol to the camp on the Delaware opposite Trenton. On our way he mentioned many instances of General Washington's want of military skill, and ascribed most of the calamities of the campaign to it. He concluded by saying he 'was only fit to command a regiment'."[50] As Rush became a leading member of the Conway Cabal, one is driven to the conclusion that had the plot succeeded, Reed's comments could have contributed to Washington's downfall.

There can be few lawyers who, in the space of a few weeks, turn down the offer of three prestigious appointments: that of general, cavalry commander and Chief Justice—but Joseph Reed did just that, though his full reasons are not clear. He may have declined the two military posts because he was offended that Congress had taken so long to recognize him, or because he was once more justifiably diffident about his military experience being adequate, but whatever the reason, he made the decision to continue to fight the war as a volunteer. The post of Chief Justice of Pennsylvania was vacant because Benjamin Chew had lost it, as described earlier, and it was offered to Reed by the new radical Supreme Executive Council. After considering the offer for some four months (from March to July 1777), he turned it down, probably because he was troubled by the new State constitution and by the oath he would be required to take to uphold it. As a result he was free to continue with the army and, after the fall of Philadelphia to the British, to participate in the battle of Germantown and the discussion about the wisdom of by-passing the Chew House.

Had Reed at that stage of his career been accused by a latter-day Brutus of being ambitious, Washington might well have countered with Mark Anthony's defense of Julius Caesar:

> You all did see that on the Lupercal
>
> I thrice presented him a kingly crown,
>
> Which he did thrice refuse: was this ambition?[51]

The next public appointment was one for which Reed was well qualified: one that enabled him to use his combined political and military experience. Late in 1777 he was elected as one of the delegates to the Continental Congress and then as a member of its Army committee. In view of his overall experience and his useful contributions to the work of the committee, he was soon made chairman, paying regular visits to the Army to inquire about its needs. On 2 December Washington sent a request to Reed: "If you can with any convenience let me see you today, I shall be thankful for it. I am about fixing the winter cantonments of this army and should be very glad of your sentiments on the subject, without loss of time."[52]

The cantonments were those at Valley Forge, where the remnants of the Continental army endured a long, cold and hungry winter, and where Reed visited them more than once. From then on he doubtless from time to time gave his wife graphic descriptions of the privations of the soldiers. The shortage of food was so serious that Washington dispatched another member of the Middle Temple, "Light Horse Harry" Lee, and his own aide, Tench Tilghman, to forage further afield. Fortunately, in the nick of time, "Lee found large droves of cattle that had been fattening in the marsh meadows of the Delaware River for the British army, and Tilghman was able to collect abundantly in New Jersey."[53]

Four years earlier, Arthur Lee, who knew both Esther and her mother well from his visits to their London home, had written to his friend Reed: "I dare say the ladies hardly think of poor old England any longer. It is more natural to worship the rising sun than the setting sun, and certainly America is the former." Lee was correct in his surmise. As well as raising a number of children, Esther Reed became an American patriot wife. "The pinnacle of women's wartime involvement in Philadelphia came in the summer of 1779, when Esther and Sarah Franklin Bache, daughter of Benjamin Franklin, organized a campaign to raise money for Washington's tattered army."[54] They put up posters appealing for help, headed "The Sentiments of an American Woman". They also knocked on doors, raising some 300,000 paper dollars, with which they bought sufficient linen to make 2,200 shirts for the boys.

The restless Reed resigned from Congress in April 1778 and rejoined the army. In June, after the British had abandoned Philadelphia, he was present

JARED INGERSOLL.
Nat-1750 — Ob-1822.

From the original painting in the possession of Edward Ingersoll, Esq.

Jared Ingersoll, Jr.
courtesy of The Historical Society of Pennsylvania (HSP), Society Portrait, by Albert
Rosenthal after a painting by Charles Wilson Peale

at the battle of Monmouth Court House, where General Charles Lee possibly threw away the chance of a victory. At his resultant court-martial, one of the principal witnesses to testify as to Lee's incompetence was John Laurens. When Lee later made disparaging remarks about Washington, Laurens, who did not share Reed's admiration for Lee, challenged him to a duel, in which he wounded him. Laurens' friend and fellow aide, Alexander Hamilton, acted as his second.[55]

Monmouth not only proved to be Washington's final battle fought outside the South, but also Reed's last military engagement, for in August he was appointed as a special prosecutor to assist the Attorney General of Pennsylvania in his pursuit of traitors. One of Reed's successes in his new post was that of unmasking General Benedict Arnold as a British agent. However, that appointment was also short-lived, for on 1 December 1778 Reed was elected to preside over the Executive Council, becoming the second President of Pennsylvania.

Two weeks later he wrote to an old friend, Jared Ingersoll, Sr., a loyalist who had moved from Connecticut from Philadelphia in 1771, bringing with him his son Jared, a Yale graduate. The younger Ingersoll had then studied law with his father, who sent him to the Middle Temple. Ingersoll joined the Inn in July 1773 and was in London until early 1777. He decided he could not share his father's loyalist views and became a firm patriot, doubtless discussing the progress of the revolution with fellow Americans at the Inn, such as Arthur Lee and John Laurens. He also paid close attention to the law propounded by Blackstone and Chief Justice Lord Mansfield. Following the example of Chief Justice Allen and others, he then spent more than a year traveling in Europe, during which time he met Franklin in Paris. Reed wrote to the father: "Our lawyers here, of any considerable abilities, are all, as I may say, in one interest, and that not the popular one. The conduct of your son abroad, and the testimonials which I have no doubt he has brought from our friends in Europe, will, I am persuaded, enable me to introduce him here to advantage, and I am clearly of opinion that it will

Thomas McKean
courtesy of the Delaware Division of Historical & Cultural Affairs, State Portrait Collection

depend upon himself entirely, to carve out his own fortune. The sooner he can come the better."

The young man took the hint and came back to Philadelphia. He then acted as attorney for the President. In 1781 Ingersoll was elected to the Continental Congress and in 1787 he attended the Convention in Philadelphia, signing the Constitution as a Pennsylvania delegate. From 1791 to 1800 and for a further five years in the new century, he served as Attorney General of the State. He ended his days as the chief judge of the District Court for the City and County of Philadelphia.[56]

Reed served out his three-year term as President, but it was marred by the death of his wife Esther in September 1780, at the age of thirty-four. During 1783 Reed suffered from fainting fits and was often ill. In the December he sailed for England for the sake of his health, accompanied by his mother-in-law and eldest daughter. His health did not improve and he returned home in September 1784, surviving only until 5 March 1785. He died at the young age of forty-four. Alexander Hamilton, another of General Washington's aides, later became President Washington's first Secretary of the Treasury. Had Joseph Reed lived longer, given his talents, experience and his chief's admiration, he would almost certainly have been invited by Washington to join his administration in some important capacity.

THOMAS MCKEAN

Thomas McKean was born in New London, Pennsylvania in 1734 and thereafter spent a considerable time in the Lower Counties, eventually representing Delaware at the Continental Congress. He left school at sixteen and went to New Castle to read law with his cousin, David Finney. He was admitted to practice when still only twenty and embarked on a lifetime in the law, coupled with local and national politics. Four years later, in May 1758, he was admitted to the Middle Temple as a student member, but he never went to London to polish his legal skills. He presumably joined the Inn with the intention of going over at some convenient time in the not too distant future, and changed his mind either because he regarded the expense as not justified, or because he was doing so well in his early years as a lawyer, that he felt there was no point in going. Having regard to what has been stated earlier about McKean's public life, his fascinating career will be related only briefly.[57]

It is not difficult to guess the identity of the lawyer who recommended the Middle Temple to McKean: John Dickinson, who had been admitted in 1753 and called to Bar by the Inn in February 1757. During his time in England he had befriended McKean's elder brother, Robert, who was in London to study medicine and theology. Dickinson met his friend's brother Thomas on his return home and clearly liked him also and started a correspondence with him in October. In the following century, McKean recalled: "From the year 1757 until his death, I was his constant and confidential correspondent; few months passed by for fifty years without a letter from each other."[58]

McKean's public career may be said to have started in 1762, when he was elected to the Assembly of the Lower Counties, but it was in the year 1765 that it took off, when he received his first judicial appointments and then shortly afterwards attended the Stamp Act Congress in New York as a delegate. The Congress provided a useful trial run for the later Continental Congress meetings—and particularly for McKean, who was to attend that Congress for nearly all its sessions and to serve as its President in 1781. After the New York Congress, McKean was never out of the public eye, so that even in "the early stages of the contest", according to one witness, "on the Whig side of the question, Mr. John Dickinson, was most prominent and distinguished. Next in conspicuousness to Mr. Dickinson, among the members of the city bar, were Mr. Reed and Mr. McKean."[59]

On 10 May 1776 John Adams and Richard Henry Lee put a resolution before Congress that the thirteen colonies should each assume the powers of government, in place of the existing authorities. That fundamental proposition was accepted on 15 May. John Coleman has cleverly shown how busy McKean was by creating his notional diary for the momentous days of the summer of 1776, and by pointing out that on 20 May he attended a crucial public meeting at the Philadelphia State House Yard in three capacities. He was there as one of the militia colonels, as chairman of the city committee and as a delegate from Delaware at the Congress, and he successfully guided the meeting to a number of decisions.[60] The principal one was a unanimous resolution: "That a Provincial Convention ought to be chosen, by the People, for the express purpose of carrying the said Resolution of Congress into execution."

On 2 July Congress voted on the issue of Independence, against a background of long discussions on whether the time had yet come for such a step and on the desirability of unanimity. McKean played his part in securing that historic vote. As mentioned earlier, when he realized that as his only colleague present, George Read, was going to vote against the motion, he took immediate steps to ensure that their colleague, Caesar Rodney, joined him. Rodney rode nearly eighty miles through a stormy night and arrived in the nick of time to join McKean in making Delaware's vote count in favor of Independence.

Edward Tilghman, Chew's son-in-law, who had been a delegate to the Stamp Act Congress, had foreseen the particular problem that had arisen. On 4 February he had written to his father about the division of opinion between the different colonies on the issue of Independence. He listed those in favor as New Hampshire, Massachusetts, Connecticut and Virginia, adding: "All the others breathe reconciliation, except that the Lower Counties are sometimes divided by the absence of Rodney or Read. Colonel McKean is a true Presbyterian and joining the violents."[61] After voting against Independence on 2 July, George Read faced up to the realities of the situation and signed the Declaration. He was the only delegate to blow cold and hot in that way.[62] He then threw himself whole-heartedly into the Revolution, later serving as one of the first United States Senators until appointed Chief Justice of Delaware.

Dickinson's reputation suffered significantly as a result of his decision not to support the vote for Independence, and he lost his place in Congress for a time. He also had a serious falling out with Joseph Reed, his former ally, "which apparently remained a source of bitterness for both men."[63] He returned to public life as a member of Congress in 1779, when he pressed for the ratification of the Articles of Confederation, which had been largely drafted by him. In 1781 he was elected President of Delaware for three years, but resigned after being elected to the same post in Pennsylvania in the following year. For three months he served as President of both States.[64] McKean had his reservations about the radical nature of the new constitution of his own State, which followed the Provincial Convention, but when Joseph Reed declined the post of Chief Justice in 1777, McKean felt able to accept it. The two men were obviously required to work together, especially once Reed became President in the next year.

Although he eventually served for twenty-two years, at an early stage of his career as Chief Justice, McKean had considered retiring. In May 1784, when he was visiting London for the sake of his health, Reed wrote to Attorney General William Bradford, indicating his opinion of the judge: "Though the Chief Justice not always pleases me in law or politics, I should be sorry he should leave the Bench, and be succeeded by Mr. Wilson. The Chief Justice, I think, will repent his descent if he should actually make it." The possible successor referred to was James Wilson, who had studied law with Dickinson and had been a delegate at the Continental Congress. He was later to play a significant part at the Constitutional Convention, speaking no less than 168 times before signing the draft Constitution, so he might have made a good judge—provided he could curb the number of his interventions. In the event, McKean soldiered on for many years.[65]

He was a very successful Chief Justice: his "dominating personality and legal skills" helped to reshape the court and to ensure its proper separation from the legislature and executive. "McKean proved to be the dominant voice on the court. For all his personal failings—his uncontrollable temper and exasperation with those unable to grasp things as quickly as he did and lacking knowledge of the law—McKean proved to be superior to any of his predecessors."[66]

EDWARD SHIPPEN

In 1799, when McKean gave up his post of Chief Justice and became Governor of Pennsylvania, he appointed Edward Shippen to succeed him, despite the fact that he had turned seventy in that year, and had been a loyalist during the war. However, by 1799 Shippen had given many years of good service as a judge and McKean appreciated his skills, preferring him to Chew, who was recommended for the post by a number of influential people.[67] If some people recalled that one of Shippen's daughters had been married to the traitor Benedict Arnold, they were prepared to accept that the sins of the daughter and her husband should not be visited on the father.

Shippen was born into a wealthy and well-known merchant family in 1729 and after school was placed with Philadelphia's leading lawyer and Attorney General of Pennsylvania, Tench Francis, for his initial legal training. He was admitted to the Middle Temple in November 1744, and seems to have treated his studies there seriously. Following the example of William Allen, in 1748 he went on the Grand Tour of Europe, starting out from London. He was eventually called to the Bar by the Inn in February 1750. His call would have been a few months earlier, but for his being let down by a study companion, as he reported to his father. "I am sorry that I have to inform you that I am disappointed in my expectations of being called to the Bar at this term; the occasion of it, I could not possibly prevent. Every student, before he comes to the Bar, is obliged to perform six vacation exercises, three candlelight exercises and two New Inn exercises; which he is not allowed to do alone; but must be joined with another student. I had calculated matters so as to have performed them all before the end of this term; but, unluckily for me, the gentleman who was my companion in the exercises, having some engagements in the country, could not attend at the time appointed for the performance of one of the vacation exercises, which obliged me to defer that duty until next vacation."[68]

With his sound legal training, helpful family background, and support for the Proprietary party, Shippen got off to a good start with his practice in Philadelphia, for in 1753 he married Margaret, a daughter of Tench Francis, and two years later was appointed the judge of the Admiralty Court—by no means a sinecure, as Philadelphia was the largest port in the colonies. Like William Allen, he managed to combine his judicial work with a role in the legislative and executive arms of government: in 1758 he became a member of the Philadelphia Common Council and in 1770 of the Provincial Council (the Governor's council). Like Chief Justices Allen and Chew, he opposed the Stamp Act and other oppressive steps taken by the British administration, but like them, he felt unable to contemplate a complete break with the King and Britain.

Shippen took on as one of his students his nephew Edward Burd, whose letters demonstrate that the training of the would-be lawyer was much the same in Philadelphia as in London. Burd wrote about buying or being given standard law books and about attending court. For example, on 12 May 1769 he wrote: "I am now just released from the load of business which each Supreme Court brings along with it, and may study again without much interruption. I bought at the auction of Mr. Stedman's books in February, Hawkins *Pleas of the Crown* and Pufendorf's *Law of Nations*, with the money Uncle J.S. had of mine, as I thought it could never be laid out for a better purpose. Uncle E.S. bought at the same auction two law books, viz, Fitzgibbon's Reports and Hobart's Reports and very kindly made me a present of them."[69] Transport often presented a problem for students: on one occasion Burd was concerned that he might not be able to borrow one of the family horses in time for a distant court session. He seems to have been a serious student and learned his professional skills well enough, for he ended his career on the Pennsylvania Supreme Court bench with his trainer, Edward Shippen.

Shippen attempted to be neutral once Independence had been declared, but such a status was not recognized by the radical patriots of his city. As a result, in 1776 he lost his judicial post and also the remunerative post of Prothonotary of the Pennsylvania Supreme Court. He may have derived some consolation from the fact that in 1778 the Prothonotary appointment went to his nephew, student and by then, son-in-law, Major Edward Burd, who had been captured at the battle of Long Island and then exchanged. In 1777, like other loyalists and would-be neutrals, Shippen was arrested but quickly paroled.

Any pleasure that Shippen derived from his lawyer son-in-law was in marked contrast to his reaction to his other son-in-law, General Benedict Arnold, who met and then married his daughter, Peggy, when in the Continental army in Philadelphia. It need scarcely be added that Arnold was the man who was prepared to sell West Point, the American stronghold on the Hudson River, to the advancing British army, and whose name is synonymous with treachery. This was not the first hazardous relationship of Peggy Shippen: she had earlier, when the British army was occupying the city, been associating with the British Assistant Adjutant General, Major John André, who was shortly afterwards hanged as a spy on the specific orders of Washington.

Shippen may be considered to have been rehabilitated when he was appointed to preside over the Common Pleas Court in 1784, doubtless on the recommendation of McKean, who had known him for a number of years by then. In 1791 he was promoted to the State Supreme Court. As already related, he succeeded McKean as Chief Justice in 1799, but instead of living out his last few years enjoying his office, was impeached in 1804 on dubious grounds. Although acquitted, he resigned in the following year and died in 1806. Rowe summed up his service as Chief Justice by pointing out that his age and health were against him. "Though Shippen's strengths were many as a lawyer and jurist, he was unable to provide the focus and direction to his court achieved by his predecessor."[70]

The vacant post of Chief Justice was offered to Chief Justice Chew's nephew and son-in-law, Edward Tilghman, but he declined it, suggesting that his cousin, William Tilghman, who had studied with Chew, would be very suitable. William was a grandson of Tench Francis, the Attorney General of Pennsylvania, and the brother of Tench Tilghman, Washington's aide, who had been embarrassed not only by James Allen's visit to the General, but also by a request from his own brother. When William, a loyalist, wanted to go to London to study at the Inner Temple during the war in 1781, he asked Tench for his help in getting permission. Tench, who had a number of other loyalist relatives, declined to help, adding words one can readily accept: "I am placed in as delicate a situation as it is possible for a man to be."[71] As mentioned earlier, William Tilghman later married Margaret, a daughter of James Allen and granddaughter of Chief Justice Allen.

Apart from serving as a State judge, William Tilghman had also briefly been a Federal judge, having been appointed as one of the outgoing President Adams' "midnight judges". He accepted the offer of the office of Chief Justice in 1805 and served as such until 1827. Had both Joseph Reed and Edward Tilghman accepted the post when it was offered to them in 1777 and 1805, the Middle Temple might have been able to claim six Chief Justices in a direct line. As it was, the four who did accept it served Pennsylvania reasonably well for a continuous period of fifty-five years, even if they were, jointly, not as helpful to the revolutionary movement as they might have been.

Arthur Lee
courtesy of the Virginia Historical Society, Richmond, Virginia, by Charles Wilson Peale

Chapter 5
THE LEES AND RANDOLPHS OF VIRGINIA

The Lees and the Randolphs were two of the leading Virginia families with Middle Temple links, whose members contributed to the success of the Revolution. It may be helpful to consider the Lees first, particularly the six sons and two daughters of Thomas and Hannah Ludwell Lee, who were born in the fourteen year period from 1727 to 1740.[1]

THE LEES

The eldest son, Philip Ludwell Lee, was of importance as he became the head of the family when his father died in 1750. Born in 1727, he attended school in England and later returned to that country as an adult because he liked the life there. He was admitted to the Inner Temple only a year before his father's death, which brought him home and made him abandon the idea of a legal career. He later became a member of the House of Burgesses and then a member of the Council of the colony, but he was unable to contribute much to the cause for freedom as he died in 1775. Unfortunately for his siblings, Philip had earlier become an exasperatingly slow executor of their father's will and an unreasonable guardian.

His co-executor was the second son, Thomas Ludwell Lee, born in 1730, who had also joined the Inner Temple. He stayed in England after his father's death to complete his studies and so he had little influence over his brother or the distribution of their father's estate. However, he was able to play an important part in Virginia politics after his eventual return and in due course became a judge.

Richard Henry, born in 1733, went to school in England, but never joined an Inn of Court; instead, he qualified as a lawyer in Virginia. He and the brother born a year after him, Francis Lightfoot, were both important members of the Virginia delegation at the Continental Congress in 1776 and both signed the Declaration of Independence.[2]

The youngest two were also born within a year of each other: William in 1739 and Arthur in 1740. William became a merchant in the City of London at a time when Arthur was in England with him. While Richard Henry was undoubtedly the family member with the highest profile in the Revolution, Arthur was the most interesting, in view of his many talents and diverse experiences—and by virtue of the fact that he was the only one of the six sons to be a Middle Templar. Like many a brilliant man, he managed to exasperate some of those who encountered him.

The elder daughter, Hannah, was born in 1729, and was married at eighteen to Gawin Corbin, who died in 1759. The Middle Temple records show that a Virginian with the same name was admitted to the Inn in 1756 and called to the Bar in 1761. He was presumably a nephew or cousin of Hannah's husband. The younger girl, Alice, born in 1736, decided to live in London and was close to her brothers who lived there. While resident in London, as related earlier, Alice met a doctor from Pennsylvania, William Shippen, and they were married in 1762 at the Church of St. Mary-le-Strand, very close to the Middle Temple.[3] After her marriage she lived in Philadelphia, including at the time when Richard Henry and Francis were attending Congress. As the hostess of a number of her brothers' congressional colleagues, Alice entertained George Washington.

We shall consider the political members of the family further below, and especially the youngest, Arthur, but at this stage it is pertinent to point out that the Lees may be said to have had the American Revolution as a family business, which was based in Virginia, with branches in Philadelphia and London, staffed by at least two members in each of the three locations—and in order of seniority, with the oldest members staying home and the youngest having to serve the furthest away.

Arthur Lee was only ten when his father died and when his eldest brother, Philip, became his guardian. Philip had been educated at Eton and sent Arthur there for his schooling until the age of about sixteen, when he went back to Virginia. At the age of nineteen, in 1760, he returned to England with a view to studying medicine at Cambridge. In London he visited his cousin Lucy Ludwell and her husband John Paradise, meeting at their home Dr. Samuel Johnson, who asserted that Edinburgh would provide a better medical education. Arthur accepted the advice and found a number of fellow Americans there, including Benjamin Rush and William Shippen, both from Philadelphia. Rush was to sign the Declaration of Independence and Shippen, Arthur's brother-in-law, became General Washington's principal army doctor. By a happy coincidence, Arthur also became friendly with a Scottish law student at Edinburgh University, James Boswell, later to be Johnson's biographer.[4]

In 1765, despite his indignation over the Stamp Act, Arthur considered staying in England after qualifying in medicine. One reason was that, like his brother Richard Henry, he strongly disapproved of slavery. Another was that he appreciated the intellectual life of London, where he could rub shoulders with leading members of the various professions. In addition, he became attached to England, as is shown by a letter he wrote much later, when back in London in 1774, to Joseph Warren, the Boston doctor and leading patriot, who was to fall at Bunker Hill: "I not only lament the attempts which have been made and are making to enslave us, as productive of great misery to American, but as fraught with danger to this country. Revering as I do the very name of England and loving most sincerely the people, it adds infinitely to the affliction of these proceedings that they must eventually operate to the ruin of this country."[5]

When Arthur wrote to Richard Henry about the Stamp Act, he received a reply questioning the propriety of his staying abroad once he was qualified. Richard Henry referred to "arts and learning" and continued: "But then, my brother, when these, or either of these are acquired, should not their possessor import them into his native country, which, if forsaken by the best of her sons, must fall into barbarous ignorance, and, of course, become a fit subject for tyrannical natures to impose arbitrary and injurious acts upon."[6] That letter probably managed to prick Arthur's conscience, for in the following year he returned home to practice medicine, albeit for a short time only.

While a student at Edinburgh, he had studied botany and written a paper on the properties of Peruvian bark, or quinine, which impressed a number of scientists, including Benjamin Franklin. Franklin proposed Arthur for the Royal Society, and he was elected shortly after his departure for Virginia. Arthur wrote to Sir Joseph Banks, the President of the Society, suggesting that he should perhaps resign in view of the situation that had arisen between the colonies and the mother country. Banks replied that such a step was unnecessary, the interests of literary and scientific societies being universal.[7]

One of the most important preliminaries to Independence was the exchange of ideas between kindred spirits in different colonies, whether by personal contact or by correspondence. Arthur became increasingly drawn toward the case for the colonies and decided to correspond with, and meet others of a like mind, in Massachusetts and elsewhere. Among the men approached were two Middle Templars, known for their important pamphlets and letters: Daniel Dulany, Jr., from Maryland and John Dickinson. "I found Mr. Dulany so cold and distant that it seemed in vain to attempt anything with him. Mr. Dickinson received me with friendship, and the contemplated correspondence took place." On Arthur's recommendation, his brother Richard Henry and Dickinson also agreed to exchange views.[8]

Arthur's great-nephew was probably correct when he wrote: "He determined to return to England; to fix himself in London, the center of political information, and there to aid, by his utmost exertions, the cause of American liberty. For this end, he purposed to commence in that city the study of the law, a profession, which while it might enable him to support himself, would make him acquainted with international law, and the peculiar structure of the British constitution, as well as the municipal laws of England, and thus fit him to take an intelligent and useful part in the great political questions about to be so warmly discussed in that country and in the colonies."[9]

On the journey back to England Arthur was accompanied by his brother William, who intended seeking his fortune in India, but found it on the way in London, in the shape of a bride with a prospect of money: his cousin Hannah Ludwell. William abandoned all ideas of the Orient and settled down in the capital, with his wife's income, as a merchant and City father. This change of plan proved to be very useful for Arthur: not only did he have his brother as a sympathetic companion, but he could make the most of his connections in the City.[10]

Arthur later described the political scene he had found after returning to London: "The proceedings against Mr. [John] Wilkes at this time agitated the nation. Mr. Wilkes was the idol of the people, and the abhorrence of the King. All the powers of prerogative, all the influence of the Crown, and every practicable perversion of the law, were employed to subdue him. Of courage, calm and intrepid, of flowing wit, accommodating in his temper, of manners convivial and conversible, an elegant scholar, and well read in constitutional law, he stood the Atlas of popular opposition." That was quite a recommendation, as Arthur was normally swift to chide and slow to bless. He continued: "Mr. Wilkes was then confined in the King's Bench [prison] as the printer and publisher of the *Essay on Woman*. The City of London was the stronghold of popular opposition, and the Society of the Bill of Rights the most active in conducting it."

Arthur continued with an account of the strategy he had adopted: "I formed the plan of connecting myself with the opposition; and the grievances of America, with those of England. For these purposes I became a member of the Bill of Rights and purchased the freedom and livery of the City of London. By these means I acquired a voice and influence in all the measures of that society, and in the proceedings and elections of the City. An acquaintance with Mr. Wilkes soon grew into intimacy and confidence. The arbitrary views of the Crown originated in the same spirit on both sides of the Atlantic. To sensible men, therefore, the combining of the complaints of the people of America and England, appeared just and politic. I procured the introduction of the grievances of America into the famous Middlesex Petition; and to keep them alive in the popular mind, I commenced and continued a periodical paper under the signature of Junius Americanus. My brother established himself in London, was elected an alderman and one of the sheriffs. Our footing was now strong, and the American cause was thus firmly united with that of England."[11] That last remark was an overstatement of the true position; some of Arthur's similar exaggerations were to prove counter-productive.

After his first year back in England, Arthur was able to report on his regular meetings with Wilkes, the success of Junius Americanus, and the substantial progress he had made in his political life. He wrote on 15 November 1769: "I dine frequently in the King's Bench where I meet the declared patriots of whom I shall be satisfied if we find one Sidney in twelve elect. The City of London is however in our possession, and will support the character it has always maintained, of standing foremost and firm in opposition to arbitrary power."[12] The reference to Sidney was presumably to the earlier "miracle of our age, Sir Philip Sidney". On one of his visits to Wilkes, Lee took along his friend from Edinburgh medical school, Benjamin Rush. The dinner party consisted of no less than fifteen guests, who were well entertained by the prisoner, as according to Rush, "Wilkes abounded in anecdotes and sallies of wit."[13]

Arthur exchanged a large number of letters with Dickinson, who knew London well and approved of his ideas, writing on 25 November 1769: "Surely nothing can more advance this cause than the well concerted plan you mention, of joining our force to that of the public spirited men who are now asserting the rights of Englishmen against the degenerated Englishmen who would destroy them."[14]

As related earlier, Arthur was a regular visitor to the London home of the agent Denys De Berdt, together with Joseph Reed, the future President of Pennsylvania, who was to marry Esther De Berdt. Thanks to a recommendation from Reed and the fact that he had earlier visited the Massachusetts revolutionaries, Arthur was appointed as deputy to Benjamin Franklin, their London agent. The communications he sent over to Boston were later praised by John Adams in a letter to the Comte de Vergennes, the French Foreign Minister, who had questioned Arthur's patriotism. "He held a constant correspondence with several of those gentlemen who stood foremost in the Massachusetts Bay against the innovations and illegal encroachments of Great Britain. This correspondence I had the opportunity of seeing, and I assure your Excellency, from my own knowledge, that it breathed the most inflexible attachment to, and the most ardent zeal in the cause of his country."[15] Perhaps one of Arthur's most important contributions was that he helped to cement the cooperation of the revolutionary leaders of the two important colonies of Virginia and Massachusetts, who were in the van of the movement for colonial rights. Among those leaders were Richard Henry Lee and John Adams, who were to be foremost advocates of Independence, as opposed to an accommodation with Britain.

Arthur was in London for several months before joining Lincoln's Inn on 1 March 1769. He may have decided against joining the Inner Temple, as it was the Inn not only of his barrister brother Thomas, but also of his eldest brother Philip, who had caused him much unhappiness. At some stage Arthur realized that the Middle Temple had the most American students, as well as a number of supporters of Wilkes and the colonies, and joined that Inn on 15 November 1773. (Alfred Jones referred several times in his book to a student "migrating" from one Inn to another.)

Another factor influencing his decision to switch Inns was doubtless that he had lived in chambers in the Middle Temple for some three years: since January 1771 at the latest, when he had written to Joseph Reed from Essex Court. A recently discovered document in the archive of the Inn shows that when Arthur applied for admission, his brother William, of Tower Hill, was one of his two sureties. The other was John Reynolds, of Salisbury Square, Fleet Street, who was Wilkes' attorney. Arthur gave his own address as Fourth floor, 4 Elm Court, Middle Temple, where he may well have occupied the same room as that taken by Charles Cotesworth Pinckney in 1769.[16]

Arthur soon moved a few yards to Garden Court, adjoining the Middle Temple Hall, where he was very happy with his accommodation, writing later: "I was placed in chambers in the Temple, which looked into a delightful little garden on the Thames, of which I had the key. I could go in and out at almost all hours, and have what company I pleased, without being questioned or overlooked."[17] In January 1773 another member of the Lee family, Arthur's young cousin Henry Lee, had been admitted to the Middle Temple. It was unfortunate that he never came to London as he would have made a good companion for Arthur and William. He was later to marry their brother Philip's daughter, but first he decided to become a cavalryman. Once hostilities started he became known as "Light Horse Harry", as the commander of Lee's Legion, which has been described as "one of the elite units of the war".[18] After the British had surrendered at

Yorktown, Henry Lee resigned from the army, the command of his unit passing to the Middle Templar who had negotiated that surrender, John Laurens.[19]

Henry Lee later served as Governor of Virginia and then in Congress, where he was asked to deliver the funeral oration for Washington. Some of his words about the President are still remembered today: "First in war, first in peace, first in the hearts of his countrymen." It was perhaps as well that his decision in favor of a military career trumped the idea of a legal one, as his own son was in due course to be an even more successful soldier. He was General Robert E. Lee, whose reputation and talents were so impressive that he was offered the command of both sides in the Civil War, choosing the Confederacy.[20]

Only one other member of Arthur's family, his cousin Philip Thomas Lee, was called to the Bar by the Middle Temple. Philip had been admitted to the Inn in 1756, after school at Eton and before studying at Christ's College, Cambridge. He was called in 1764 and returned home to Maryland, where his Virginian father, Richard, had settled. His father had joined in 1719 but had never been called to the Bar by the Middle Temple. Both these Maryland Lees were loyalists, the father having earlier served as President of the Provincial Council.

Arthur not only wrote a large number of articles and letters for publication while in London, but also arranged for the publication of the works of other writers. One of the most astute pamphlets was Arthur's own: *An Appeal to the Justice and Interests of the People of Great Britain in the Present Dispute with America*, which he wrote in the spring of 1774, while visiting Paris with Ralph Izard. The pamphlet was ostensibly written by a former Member of Parliament. Franklin, who often used different names on publications, so as to hide the American origin of the writer, passed the manuscript on with his own recommendation to John Almon, the pro-American bookseller/publisher in Piccadilly, another great supporter of Wilkes. Like Arthur, Almon had been a regular visitor to Wilkes during the time he graced the King's Bench prison with his presence, so they had doubtless met.

What Arthur Lee wrote in this pamphlet proved to contain a basic and most important truth of the coming war—and of later wars also. "In a country furnished with fastnesses and defiles without number, intimately known to the enemy you are to combat, where discipline is unavailing or embarrassing, and valor useless, it requires more than human power to succeed to any permanent purpose. God forbid that the bravery of such troops as the English should be so vainly, so fatally employed. Let us suppose it true, as some vainglorious military men have vaunted, that with four regiments you might march from one end of the continent to the other—what would this exploit avail you? The moment you quit one province for another, the commotions your presence suppressed, will revive. When you have marched through, you will have to march back again." The London *Evening Post* was later to make an acid, if not very poetic comment about the British troops being required to fight their way from New York to Philadelphia and back again:

> Here we go up, up, up
>
> And here we go down, down, downy
>
> There we go *backwards* and *forwards*
>
> And here we go round, round, roundy.[21]

Tyler, the authority on the literature of the Revolution, was rather dismissive of Arthur as an author, but probably hit the nail on the head when he described him in the following terms: "A man of ability, integrity and patriotism, the value of all that he did and said was constantly hurt by an inordinate and a fussy sense of his own importance, by a morbid jealousy of others, and by an invincible habit of suspicion, opposition, and disparagement." As it happened, some of his suspicions proved to be justified—but let that pass. Tyler gave a neat illustration of one fault: "It was difficult for him to agree exactly with any statement on any subject as made by anybody but himself. Thus, being caught in a shower, Lee met under a shed a man who, by way of affability, ventured upon a remark which he probably thought a safe one: 'It rains very hard, sir.' To this, however, Lee replied: 'It rains hard, sir; but I don't think you can say it rains *very* hard'."[22]

Arthur's enthusiasm sometimes led to his making statements in his letters that were far too optimistic, and misled some American recipients as to the extent, for example, of the support they had in England. Significantly, on 26 September 1775, five months after the clashes at Lexington and Concord, his brother Richard Henry was sufficiently encouraged by the reports he had received to write the following inaccurate appreciation for Washington: "We have no late accounts from England, but from what we have had that can be relied on, it seems almost certain that our enemies there must shortly meet with a total overthrow. The entire failure of all their schemes, and the rising spirit of the people strongly expressed by the remonstrance of the Livery of London to the King, clearly denote this. The Ministry had their sole reliance on the impossibility of the Americans finding money to support an army, on the great aid *their* cause would receive from Canada, and consequent triumph of their forces over the liberties and rights of America. The reverse of all this has happened, and recruiting business in England has entirely failed them, the shipbuilders in the royal yards have mutinied, and now they are driven as to their last resort to seek for soldiers in the Highlands of Scotland. But it seems the greatest willingness of the people there cannot supply more than one or two thousand men, a number rather calculated to increase their disgrace, than to give success to their cause."[23]

On 13 December 1774 Arthur wrote to Richard Henry: "My anxiety about the public absorbs every idea of private concerns," but nevertheless went on to express such concerns. "Col. Phil remits me nothing, and the additional expenses of my being called to the Bar in April next, will distress me extremely."[24] He was in fact called to the Bar by the Middle Temple on 5 May

1775 and then went out on circuit as a fully-fledged barrister. On 21 August his friend Ralph Izard wrote to him: "Your three weeks circuit must be finished about this time and I hope you are returned in good health, and loaded with fees—rewards for the defense of innocence, and prosecution of guilt."[25] Izard's role was similar to Lee's from about this time. He collected information that could be of use to their compatriots and placed appropriate items in the press. Izard even went so far as to give firm instructions, much like a spymaster, to John Almon, as to what he should publish and what information he should obtain and forward.[26] He later joined Lee in Paris as one of their country's commissioners to European courts and then served in the first United States Senate.

Although Arthur could not have earned any money from the law, save in his last eighteen months in England, he must have earned something with his pen at different times, and possibly as the agent for Massachusetts, after Franklin's return to Philadelphia. He was certainly paid by Henry Laurens for a long pamphlet he wrote for him in 1774: *Answer to the Considerations on Certain Political Transactions in the Province of South Carolina*, which Almon also published. Arthur had a double interest in the subject as it concerned his friend Wilkes and the oppression of the South Carolina legislature by the British.

The legislature had subscribed to the Wilkes Fund and was punished by an Additional Instruction of the British government, dated 14 April 1770, which prohibited it from dealing with money matters. Laurens, like other South Carolinians, had been trying for a long time to free the legislature from this restraint, and eventually commissioned Arthur to put the argument into a form that would reach the wider public.[27] While awaiting publication, Laurens wrote to his son John, who was shortly to start as a student at the Middle Temple, praising Arthur for his anonymous writings as Junius Americanus and also with the pen name of A Bostonian. He added: "To him we shall be principally indebted for a performance which I long to have from the press for your perusal. He is a pretty writer, and hitherto a firm friend to his country's cause."[28]

In 1775, the year of his call to the English bar, Arthur moved closer and closer to being a secret agent. On 25 October Wilkes, the ex-prisoner, by then metamorphosed into Lord Mayor of London, invited Arthur to a dinner at the Mansion House, his official residence. One of the other guests was Caron de Beaumarchais, the witty French playwright, whose character, the barber Figaro, was to inspire operas by Mozart and Rossini, but who was also to be one of the principal conduits for supplies sent to the American patriots.[29] As Beaumarchais spoke no English and Arthur no French, they cannot have had a very satisfactory first conversation. It would have been dangerous, in a public place, for Arthur to adopt the usual English practice of shouting in English at the foreigner unfortunate enough not to know the language. Wilkes had lived for a long time in France as a fugitive from injustice, and may have made the time for a little discreet interpretation.

It did not take very long for Arthur and Beaumarchais, who came back to London in December, to get round to discussing, somehow or other, the supply of arms and equipment by France to the colonists, but with little success at first. On 29 February 1776 Beaumarchais wrote to the King of France to report that Arthur Lee, "discouraged by the uselessness of the efforts he has made through me to obtain from the French ministry aid of powder and munitions, asked if France is determined to refuse all aid, permitting America to become a victim of England."[30] The last few words presaged a mild blackmailing line that several American representatives in Europe were to use, including John Laurens, when he was sent by Congress to Paris to get further aid in 1781. The argument ran: If you, the French, allow the British to defeat us, not only will that leave them free to attack you, but we, as British subjects, might be obliged to fight against you, too—and, as you may recall from the French and Indian War, we are tough fighters, who make better allies than enemies!

At the end of 1775 Arthur was formally appointed by the Continental Congress as one of its secret agents. His letter of appointment was signed by the formidable trio of Franklin, Dickinson and John Jay, and read: "By this conveyance we have the pleasure of transmitting to you sundry printed papers, that such of them as you think proper may be immediately published in England. It would be agreeable to Congress *to know the disposition of foreign powers towards us*, and we hope this object will engage your attention. We need not hint that *great circumspection and impenetrable secrecy are necessary.*"[31]

The foreign power that Congress was most interested in was obviously France. Arthur at once had several meetings with the French ambassador in London, pointing out the advantages to France of combining French and American efforts against perfidious Albion. Vergennes, the French minister, sent Beaumarchais to London to inform Arthur, "that the French court could not think of entering into a war with England, but that they would assist America by sending from Holland this fall £200,000 worth of arms and ammunition."[32]

At the Continental Congress Francis Lee played an active part, but it was Richard Henry Lee who, prompted by the Virginian Convention, had the great honor of moving, on 7 June 1776, "That these United Colonies are, and of right ought to be, free and independent States." For complicated reasons, and much to his distress, Richard Henry was not appointed to be a member of the committee appointed to draft the appropriate Declaration, but he may have derived some consolation from the fact that, in the end, it was drafted by one of his Virginian colleagues, Thomas Jefferson. Francis Lee so impressed his colleagues that for some weeks in 1777 he was seriously considered as the next President of Congress, as successor to John Hancock. As it happened, Henry Laurens was elected unanimously on 1 November. Richard Henry Lee became President in November 1784, but Francis never occupied that prestigious post.

In the Spring of 1776 Arthur had been to Paris for a meeting with Vergennes and others. In December, back in London, he received his appointment as a joint commissioner in Paris with Silas Deane, who was already there, and Franklin, who would soon arrive. The only reason that Arthur was appointed as one of the three commissioners, was that Jefferson had decided to retire from the war and did not want the post. Richard Henry had written to Jefferson on 27 September 1776: "The plan of foreign treaty is just finished, and yourself, with Dr. Franklin and Mr. Deane, now in France, are the Trustees to execute this all-important business." Jefferson pleaded family reasons for declining the post, especially the grave ill-health of his wife.

Richard Henry, though an admirer of his fellow Virginian, was not impressed, writing to him on 3 November 1776: "As I have received no answer to the letter I wrote you by the express from Congress, I conclude it has miscarried. I heard with much regret that you had declined both the voyage and your seat in Congress. No man feels more deeply than I do, the love of, and the loss of, private enjoyments: but let attention to these be universal, and we are gone, beyond redemption, lost in the deep perdition of slavery."[33] Richard Henry was right: the men who returned to their farms at a time of their own choosing, leaving Washington short of troops, almost lost the war for him on several occasions. Jefferson was not setting a good example.

Although Arthur Lee did not have the stature of either Franklin or Jefferson, one can readily appreciate why he was considered as a suitable alternative when Jefferson declined the Paris post. Arthur was extremely well connected, with two brothers in the Congress and admirers such as Adams and Dickinson, who had seen what he could do. His two professional qualifications, coupled with his membership of the Royal Society, were also impressive. Finally, Arthur had one qualification that neither Jefferson nor Franklin had at the time: he was already "over there".

On 23 December Arthur wrote a farewell letter to the Earl of Shelburne, which gave an indication of his feelings at that important time. "A very few hours after my last letter to your lordship brought me the desire of my country that I should serve her in a public character. Your lordship thinks too well of me, I hope, to suppose I could hesitate for a moment. In fact almost the same minute saw me bid adieu, perhaps forever, to a country where I had fixed my fortunes, and to a people whom I most respected and could have loved. But the first object of my life is my country, the first wish of my heart is public liberty. I must see therefore the liberties of my country established or perish in her last struggle."[34]

Arthur was to have all sorts of problems in Europe and back home in America, but this is not the place to consider them—nor indeed, all of his "nine lives", as A.R.Riggs has called them.[35] The generous comment of John Adams on Arthur, Richard Henry and their brothers, perhaps provides a suitable ending to this short account. He referred to them as "that band of brother, intrepid and unchangeable, who, like the Greeks at Thermopylae, stood in the gap, in the defense of their country, from the first glimmering of the Revolution in the horizon, through all its rising light, to its perfect day."[36]

THE RANDOLPHS

The first member of the Randolph family to qualify as a barrister in London was John Randolph, who was called to the Bar by Gray's Inn in 1717. He was very successful as a lawyer in Virginia and served for a time as both Attorney General and Treasurer of the province. In 1730, having made submissions in London on the subject of taxation, which greatly impressed Robert Walpole, the first minister, he was knighted—the only native born Virginian to be so honored. However, he was only able to enjoy his knighthood for seven years, as he died in 1737 at the early age of forty-four, leaving three young sons, two of whom were to follow closely in his footsteps.

Peyton Randolph was the elder of the two boys who both became barristers and Attorney General; born in 1721, he was educated at The College of William and Mary. By his will his father had left Peyton all his books, "hoping he will betake himself to the study of the law." He was

Peyton Randolph
courtesy of the Virginia Historical Society, Richmond, Virginia, by John Wollaston

admitted to the Middle Temple in October 1739; why he chose that Inn in preference to his father's is not clear. Peyton was called to the Bar in February 1744 and speedily made a name for himself as a lawyer in Virginia.

At the age of twenty-six he was appointed Attorney General, a post he was to hold for nearly twenty years in all, but he soon found a conflict of interest arising, as he was also an elected member of the House of Burgesses. Governor Robert Dinwiddie introduced a system of payment for certain land documents, which the House objected to as improperly raised taxation. The Burgesses asked Randolph to make representations in London on their behalf and he agreed to do so. The governor was outraged and dismissed his Attorney General, appointing a distinguished lawyer and law teacher, George Wythe, in his place. Nobody could complain about the choice of Wythe, who was later to sign the Declaration of Independence as a member of the Congress, and to influence many young lawyers, including his student Thomas Jefferson.

Once in London Randolph soon learned that his stay would be a protracted one, as the Privy Council announced that it would not hear the dispute until the following year, 1754. With some months to wait for the hearing, "he welcomed the opportunity to renew the many valuable friendships that he made during his student days at the Middle Temple."[37] He also made contact with John Hanbury, the leading American merchant in London, who had opened his doors to John Dickinson and other students, and whose considerable influence had helped Randolph to become Attorney-General.

When the case eventually came on, Randolph did not appear as an advocate himself, but retained Robert Henley, an Inner Templar, who was later to serve as Lord Chancellor with the title of Lord Northington, together with a Middle Templar, Alexander Forrester. William Murray, who shortly afterwards became Lord Mansfield as Chief Justice, led for the Governor of Virginia. The outcome of the hearing provided a compromise solution, but it was followed by a more satisfactory decision for Randolph. The Board of Trade recommended that Randolph should be reinstated as Attorney General, a recommendation Dinwiddie felt obliged to accept.

As we have earlier considered the vices that might tempt innocent American students attending an Inn of Court in pursuit of legal knowledge, it is worth interposing that Lord Northington demonstrated that young English students could also be tempted. Lord [John] Campbell, a later Lord Chancellor, wrote of Northington's days as a student: "The truth is that hard-drinking was at that time the ruling vice and bane of society, and Henley was not, at his early period of life, fortunate enough to escape the general contagion." Although he gave up drinking to excess, he later paid for his earlier folly by suffering severely from gout. According to Campbell he was once overheard in the House of Lords muttering to himself, "If I had known that these legs were one day to carry a Chancellor, I'd have taken better care of them when I was a lad."[38]

Shortly after his return home, Randolph was so concerned about the failure of General Braddock to dislodge the French and their Indian allies, that he raised a cavalry unit to assist George Washington to defend the colony. His unit—the Virginian equivalent of the London Inns of Court Regiment (or "The Devil's Own", as it understandably became known)—was made up of 150 men, many of them lawyers, who between them had provided all the necessary equipment. "Fortunately, the anticipated French movement into the area failed to materialize, averting a possible disaster for Randolph's cavalry, which was totally unprepared for frontier warfare."[39]

In May 1766 John Robinson, the Speaker of the House of Burgesses, died; he had also been Treasurer and had misused the colony's funds. Peyton Randolph was elected Speaker and from then on until his death in October 1775 was the undoubted political leader in Virginia, impressing nearly everyone attending sittings of the House and conventions with his calmness and authority as a chairman.

The Massachusetts circular letter proposing firm opposition to the Crown

John Blair
courtesy of the Virginia Historical Society, Richmond, Virginia, Carte de Visite of a
painting of the Honourable John Blair, 1732-1800, by Lee Gallery (Richmond, Va.)

was one of the matters that Speaker Randolph was obliged to consider. The governor of Virginia, Francis Fauquier, had died in March 1768 and John Blair, the President of the Council, was acting temporarily as governor until his successor's arrival. Blair had been called to the Bar by the Middle Temple in 1757 and was so highly regarded in Virginia that he was later a delegate to the Constitutional Convention and Chief Justice of the State. In 1789 he was to be nominated for the original United States Supreme Court by Washington—together with John Rutledge of South Carolina. As Blair was "wholly in sympathy with the concerns of the colony," the Assembly was able to support the circular letter from the New England radicals without fear of dismissal.[40]

In August 1774 Peyton Randolph was selected as one of the band of distinguished Virginians, which included George Washington and Richard Henry Lee, chosen to attend the first meeting of the Continental Congress called to meet in Philadelphia. Virginia had a strong claim to provide the chairman for the assembled delegates, as it was the largest and most populous of the colonies, but Randolph's personality and experience undoubtedly helped them to elect him, with the title of President. The delegates were thereafter not disappointed in their choice, save possibly by his need to return to Virginia for Assembly sessions and by his ill health. When Randolph and his colleagues returned to Williamsburg to attend the Assembly in October, he was replaced as President by Hugh Middleton of South Carolina, whose son Arthur had attended the Middle Temple and was to sign the Declaration of Independence.

When he returned to Philadelphia to attend the Congress in the following spring, Randolph was again elected as President, but left soon afterwards, the governor having once more called a meeting of the Virginia Assembly. Thomas Jefferson took Randolph's place as a Virginia delegate and John Hancock replaced him as President. Hancock did not step aside when he returned from Williamsburg, but Randolph was so ill that he was not concerned. On 22 October 1775 he went out to dinner with his cousin

Jefferson and died at the house of their host.

Philadelphia was in a way a fitting place for him to die. Not only had he been a successful President during the important first days of the Congress, but he had helped to establish Virginia's crucial position there. He had earlier played a vital role in uniting the Virginian opposition to the Crown. It was in no small measure thanks to Randolph that one writer was able to make the comment: "Virginia was more united in support of the Revolution than any other state in the rebellion. Its leaders enjoyed virtual unanimity regarding the constitutional issues in contention with Great Britain."[41]

Furthermore, Randolph had encouraged Jefferson on different occasions as a draftsman and his experience as such was to prove invaluable in the following June and July. "It should be remembered that it was Peyton Randolph who brought forward the young Jefferson, who was half a Randolph himself, and really started him on his wonderful career."[42] Jefferson later confirmed the importance of Randolph, and of two of his more formal teachers. "Looking back on his youth for the instruction of his grandson, Jefferson said that when under temptation and difficulties he would ask himself, 'What would Dr.[William] Small, Mr.[George] Wythe, Peyton Randolph, do in this situation? What course in it will insure me their approbation?' "[43]

Apart from his failing health, the last months of Randolph's life were blighted by his younger brother's decision to support the Crown. John Randolph was called to the Bar by the Middle Temple in 1750 and was an immediate success on his return to Virginia. When Peyton resigned his post of Attorney General to become Speaker, he passed it over to John. "The fact that Peyton could pass on an important office to his brother is testimony to the influence of the Randolph family at this time. Offices simply belonged to them." When John had to decide where his loyalties lay, like many other senior lawyers, he was swayed by the fact that he had taken an oath of allegiance, in his case, on taking office as the King's Attorney General for Virginia.[44]

John Randolph decided to take his family to England, where he died in 1784, but he gave his twenty-two-year-old son, Edmund, the opportunity to choose for himself. Edmund chose to stay in Virginia and very quickly demonstrated his commitment to the patriot cause by serving as one of Washington's first aides, until required to go home to wind up his uncle Peyton's estate. John Randolph's departure was a loss for a number of reasons. "Educated in England and renowned for his brilliance in law, Randolph was a pillar of the colony's intelligentsia. Fellow violinists and bibliophiles, he and Jefferson were particularly close."[45] On 25 August 1775 Jefferson wrote to John Randolph: "Looking with fondness towards a reconciliation with Great Britain, I cannot help hoping you may be able to contribute towards expediting this good work."[46] Although his Declaration of Independence was less than a year away, Jefferson, like most of his countryman, was at that stage still regarding Independence as something that might have to be considered in the future.

Unlike his grandfather, father and uncle, Edmund Randolph had not traveled to London to study at one of the Inns of Court, but had qualified as a lawyer after studying with his father in Williamsburg. Like his grandfather, father and uncle, he became the Attorney General of Virginia—but he had the additional distinction of being the first one for the independent Commonwealth. He was later to be Washington's first Attorney General of the United States and to succeed Jefferson as his second Secretary of State. He resigned from the latter office after reacting in a disloyal manner towards the Jay Treaty in 1795, but in 1775 he was a young man who had lost, in different ways, both his immediate family and his influential uncle. Our discussion will be confined to his concern about the position of loyalists, such as his own father. In Virginia he was appointed to be one of the lawyers who considered the individual cases of admitted or suspected loyalists, and he probably dealt with them sympathetically, if his own published words are anything to go by. They are worth repeating here, as we have already referred to the dilemma of the loyalist and the divided family.

"Mr. Jefferson in his *Notes on Virginia* [Query XVI] remarks that a Tory has been properly defined to be a traitor in thought but not in deed. In some cases it may have been the harsh language of the most violent and intemperate, but it cannot be admitted that thinking men, who valued free will as a gift of heaven, were thus indiscriminate in their severity. What multitudes could now be cited, who, confounded by the new order of things suddenly flashing upon their minds and still entangled by the habits of many years, were branded as Tories, though spotless as to treason even in thought; who could not comprehend what was to be the issue of provoking the fury of the British nation and were yet innocent even as to wishes of harm to their country; who believed in a chance of reconciliation, if excesses were spared; who might feel sufficient irritation at the distant danger of an abstract principle."[47]

When Peyton Randolph was the first President of Congress, that body had a crucial part to play. After the successful conclusion of the war Congress was often poorly attended, as it became increasingly clear to everyone that power resided in the individual new States and that the Confederation had little muscle. That was why, as was mentioned earlier, the members of the great Convention of 1787, including its seven Middle Templars, drafted the new Constitution for the United States, rather than merely revising the Articles of Confederation, which was what they had been appointed to do. The new Constitution provided among other institutions for a new Congress. The man who had the honor of serving in the not very onerous position of the last President of the old Congress was, by what may regarded as a happy coincidence, like the first, also a Virginian member of the Middle Temple, Cyrus Griffin.

Griffin had been admitted to the Inn in May 1771, after studying law at Edinburgh, a university more often chosen by American medical students than would-be lawyers. Its medical school was renowned, but Scots law was not usually studied by American students, as the colonies shared the completely different common law of England. It may have been the twinkle in the eye of a Scottish lassie that led to the unusual choice of law school, for while in Edinburgh, Griffin eloped with the daughter of the Earl of Traquair. The approaches for a reconciliation made by the Earl of Dartmouth and his contact with Joseph Reed have been referred to earlier, but in December 1775 Griffin, who was in London on business at the time, had also suggested such a step to the Dartmouth. He later served as a United States judge.[48]

Drastically pruned family tree showing Rutledge/Pinckney/Laurens links

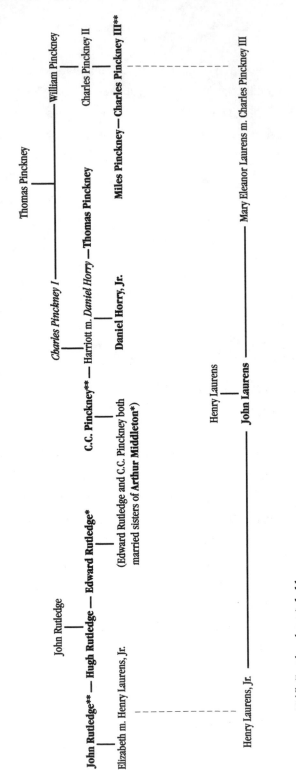

Middle Templars shown in **bold**
Inner Templars shown in *italics*
Signers of the Declaration of Independence marked *
Signers of the Constitution marked **

Chapter 6
THE RUTLEDGES AND PINCKNEYS OF SOUTH CAROLINA

The Rutledge and Pinckney families, who were linked by friendship, marriage, the legal profession and a common interest in politics, played an important part in the development of South Carolina and helped with the birth and early years of the infant United States. Of particular interest to the present story are three men from each family who were members of the Middle Temple: the brothers John, Hugh and Edward Rutledge; and the Pinckney brothers, Charles Cotesworth (or C.C., to distinguish him easily from several relatives named Charles) and Thomas; and their cousin, Charles Pinckney. The latter's younger brother, Miles, was also a member of the Inn, but played only a minor role the in the great events.

THE RUTLEDGES

John Rutledge was born in 1739, son of a physician of the same name,

John Rutledge
From the Collections of the South Carolina Historical Society

Edward Rutledge
From the Collections of the South Carolina Historical Society

who died when he was only eleven years old. His paternal uncle Andrew, a successful lawyer, was elected Speaker of the South Carolina Commons, and played an influential part in his nephew's life for a few years, but then also died before John had attained adulthood. That left his widowed mother to raise him and his brothers on her own and with great financial difficulties. John was formally admitted to the Middle Temple in October 1754, when he was just fifteen, so it may well have been his lawyer uncle who arranged and paid for that admission, shortly before his death.

When he was sixteen John started to learn his law from James Parsons, one of the leading lawyers in Charleston, who had qualified in Ireland and then practiced in London. After two years with him, John set off for London, where he clearly made the most of his opportunities, if his instant success on his return home and his later advice to his brother are anything to go by.[1] John Rutledge was called to the English Bar by the Middle Temple on 9 February 1760, shortly after his twenty-first birthday, but he did not go home immediately. He followed the example of some of his fellow students and attempted to practice for a while and went on a short tour of England.

On his return home, John Rutledge was admitted to the local Bar at once and took over as head of the family from his struggling mother, who owed a great deal of money, some of it to the leading merchant, Henry Laurens. Rutledge was bold enough to ask Laurens both for time to pay and for some legal work so that he might be in a position to make payments. Strictly speaking, that second request may have amounted to the offence of "touting" for work, strongly disapproved of by some members of the legal profession. In his first few months Rutledge had a few small cases only, with little or no income, but his practice very soon took off. Henry Laurens became a good client and the fees he paid helped to improve the family fortunes. John Rutledge was an impressive speaker and had an air of authority: he had not been home for many months before being elected to the Commons House of Assembly to start a distinguished political career. After a mere two years in practice, Rutledge was able to demand a retainer of £100, and could afford to get married to Elizabeth Grimké.

In 1764, at the age of twenty-four, Rutledge was appointed acting Attorney General of the province, but retained the post for less than a year, in view of the conflict that was becoming inevitable. Rutledge obtained his first experience of politics outside South Carolina when he was dispatched as a delegate to the Stamp Act Congress in New York. Neither North Carolina nor Georgia sent a delegation, so the South Carolinians were particularly welcome. Rutledge was appointed chairman of the committee drafting the resolutions of the Congress and honed another skill that was to be useful to him and his country.

Having witnessed John's meteoric rise, two of his brothers wanted to follow in his footsteps, and started by studying in his office before being admitted to the Middle Temple: Hugh in 1765 and Edward two years later. They were supported for their journeys and expenses in London by John's earnings, although it seems likely that the money advanced was in the form of a student loan, to be repaid at some time in the distant future. Although Hugh attended the Inn, unlike his brothers he did not stay long enough to be called to the English bar. He was presumably satisfied that membership of the Charleston bar, coupled with his own talents and his brother's eminence in the profession, would guarantee him a living in the law.

Hugh was right. Like John he obtained a good practice; like him he played his part in local politics, becoming a member of the Provincial Council as well as the Assembly. As soon as South Carolina—thanks largely to John's efforts—became a republic, Hugh obtained a judicial appointment in the Admiralty court. He was Speaker of the lower house in 1777 and 1778 and again from 1782 to 1785; he later succeeded John as Chancellor of the Equity court.

By the time Edward set off for England in 1769, John was the proud possessor of a copy of the *Letters to his Son* by the Earl of Chesterfield, which inspired him to write a long list of guidelines for his brother.[2] The first piece of advice he gave Edward was that he should learn shorthand, "and when you can write it, take notes of every thing at court." He added: "I would take down every public discourse, either at the bar or pulpit, which you hear. And now I mention the latter, by no means fall into the too common practice, of not frequenting a place of worship. This you may do, I think, every Sunday. There is generally a good preacher at the Temple Church, and it will be more to your credit to spend a few hours of that day there, than is generally spent in London, especially by the Templars."

After stressing the obvious need to attend the courts, John gave some practical advice, clearly based on his own experience: "Remember what I hinted to you of attending alternately in the different courts by agreement between you and some of your intimate fellow students, and then of comparing and exchanging notes every evening; by which means, if you select proper acquaintances, in whose judgment you can confide, you will have the same advantage as if you attended all the courts in person. Don't pass too slightly over cases and not note them, because you think they are trifling. Many cases appear so at a cursory overlooking, and indeed may be not very material, and yet you will find use for them."

John turned from the study of law to politics and lawmaking: "But you must exert yourself to the utmost in being able by some means or other to attend the House of Commons constantly, or at least whenever any thing of consequence is to come on." He went on to advise on essential reading, not only law books but also Latin, French and history, but possibly asked too much of his young brother when he counseled him, "Don't neglect to learn surveying." He added the interesting advice, "Consult Corbett upon every matter with regard to your studies in which you are in any doubt."

Exactly how much of big brother's advice was followed cannot be established, but Edward, who was called to the Bar by the Inn in July 1772, certainly gave indications in his later career of having paid attention to the most important parts of it. John Adams, one of Edward's fellow delegates at the First Continental Congress, noted in his diary for 3 September 1774: "Young Rutledge told me he studied three years at the Temple. He thinks this a great distinction. Says he took a volume of notes."[3] Adams apparently did not think that time spent in London studying law could amount to a great distinction, but this may have been an instance of sour grapes, as he never had the opportunity of joining an Inn himself and had studied law in Massachusetts only.

One of Edward Rutledge's contemporaries at the Inn, Thomas Heyward from South Carolina, who was admitted in 1765 and called in 1770, seems to have heeded similar advice. He wrote home in 1767 that he spent his time between "the courts at Westminster Hall, the Parliament, my private tutors, my closet and my friends." For relaxation he attended the theater and tried skating. One of the advantages for students dining in the Middle Temple Hall, was that they were able to eat and drink with senior lawyers and to learn from their shop talk. During the week commencing 6 November 1769, Edward Rutledge and Thomas Heyward dined in Hall with the great William Blackstone, who had just completed his four-volume *Commentaries on the Laws of England*.[4] After returning home both young men practiced law successfully and doubtless used that work, which remained a standard text for many years. As mentioned earlier, together with Edward Rutledge, Heyward was one of their State's delegates in Philadelphia in July 1776, signing the Declaration of Independence. As a judge he took a special interest in legal education.[5]

Edward Rutledge returned to Charleston in January 1773 on board the good ship *Magna Charta*—a propitious name. In the August of that year he successfully argued, during *habeas corpus* proceedings, that the Council had no right to commit Thomas Powell, a local printer, for contempt, as it was not a legislative body with the requisite powers.[6] He soon began to obtain a good practice and to dabble successfully in business. He worked together with C.C. Pinckney, and within a short space of time they both married sisters of Arthur Middleton, another Middle Templar, who was to sign the Declaration of Independence. Pinckney married Sally Middleton and Edward Rutledge married her sister Henrietta. Edward and C.C.'s

Arthur Middleton
From the Collections of the South Carolina Historical Society

younger brother, Thomas Pinckney, had for a while been companions at the Middle Temple.[7]

Many members of the leading South Carolina families married one another, just as many successful families in Pennsylvania and Virginia intermarried. This was scarcely surprising, given the relatively small number of educated and prosperous young men deemed suitable for cherished daughters. Many of the leading South Carolina families lived at nearby plantations, mainly growing rice, but completely dependent on slave labor. It was doubtless those basic facts that led one author to call them "Rice Kings", and to add, somewhat harshly: "The most prominent were the intermarried Draytons, Laurens, Lowndes, Manigault, Middleton, Pinckney and Rutledge families, who may fairly be compared to the robber barons of medieval England."[8] What is most relevant to the present account is that, apart from the Lowndes, each of those families sent one or more sons to the Middle Temple.

In 1774 both John and Edward Rutledge were selected as members of the South Carolina delegation to the First Continental Congress in Philadelphia. Like the majority of the delegates, including John Dickinson, they were against Independence at that stage and felt strongly that an accommodation should be reached with Britain. After the first shots had been exchanged in April 1775, the numbers in favor of Independence rose, but the Rutledges still held back, knowing that their view was shared by many South Carolinians.

In 1775 Henry Laurens became President of the South Carolina Provincial Congress and of the Council of Safety. He was never an extremist at any time during his lengthy public life; one of the ways this was demonstrated was by his refusal, while filling those posts, to sanction the opening of private mail for security reasons. On one occasion a bundle of letters was opened by Arthur Middleton; much to his annoyance, Laurens was accused of having sanctioned that step. John Fauchereau Grimké, who had been admitted to the Middle Temple in 1769, turned the accusation into a major attack on Laurens, who challenged him to a duel. Fortunately neither man was injured. Grimké was elected a South Carolina judge in 1779, at the same time as two fellow Middle Templars: Thomas Heyward, the signer of the Declaration of Independence, and John Mathews (or Matthews), who had served as Speaker of the Assembly and as a delegate to the Congress, and who was to be elected governor in 1782.[9]

In October 1775 New Hampshire sought the advice of Congress on how best to govern itself, the Royal governor having abandoned his post. On 3 November Congress gave what Colin Bonwick called "a carefully evasive answer", recommending that a convention of representatives should, "if they think it necessary, establish a form of government, as in their judgment will produce the happiness of the People." He added: "Since the chairman of the committee which drew up the advice was John Rutledge it was not surprising that it gave his own State of South Carolina identical advice on the following day."[10]

On 8 December 1775 Edward Rutledge, who had only left London three years earlier, wrote a letter to a Carolinian friend in England, Ralph Izard, which gave a clue as to his own state of mind, as well as indicating the amount of hard work he was doing. "Tell me then, I beseech you (before it is too late) what are the sentiments of the English nation—are the people of that country determined to force us into Independence? Or do they really imagine that we are so void of the feelings of humanity and so insensible to the calls of reason, as willingly to submit to every insult, to every injury?" Edward continued: "You must take this as I write it, for we are so closely engaged in business that we have hardly time to eat and drink, what with attendance in the House and committees."[11] In 1776, despite his youth, Edward became one of the most experienced delegates, and was given more and more work and responsibility at the Congress. John Rutledge had stayed in South Carolina, where he was engaged in work of great importance to the province; and Christopher Gadsden, another member of the delegation, had returned home to command the militia forces. That meant that for a time

Edward Rutledge had only one colleague from his own state, namely, Thomas Lynch.[12]

In February 1776 John Rutledge was appointed a member of the South Carolina committee, under the chairmanship of C.C. Pinckney, which was requested to prepare a new interim constitution for the province, even though Independence was not seriously contemplated. The committee also included four other Middle Templars: Charles Pinckney III, Arthur Middleton, Thomas Lynch and Thomas Heyward. Of those six lawyers, the last three named were to sign the Declaration of Independence, while the first three were to be among the most active framers and signers of the United States Constitution in 1787. On 26 March 1776 the Provincial Congress accepted the proposals of the committee and converted itself into a General Assembly. John Rutledge was elected President of South Carolina and Commander-in-Chief of its forces, with Henry Laurens, his lay client, as his Vice-President.

The decision by South Carolina to replace the Royal governor with a native President, and to turn itself into a republic was, of course, open rebellion, and yet in one sense the new republic was still one of the most faithful of the colonies, in that it had little wish for a complete break. In the crucial days of June and July at the Continental Congress, Edward Rutledge was conscious of his brother's conviction that the time was not ripe for Independence, and he himself was not keen on it either. He informed John Jay that Richard Henry Lee's resolution, that the time had arrived for separation, had been opposed by "the sensible part of the House", adding that America would look "ridiculous in the eyes of foreign powers by attempting to bring them into an Union with us before we were united with each other."[13] As a recent biographer of Franklin put it: "To become independent of Britain, they had to become less independent of each other."[14]

The explanation for Edward Rutledge finally delivering the vote of South Carolina in favor of Independence is probably that he did not wish his colony to be the only one voting against it. Unanimity was clearly highly desirable from the point of view of the new nation; and the danger of being labeled forever as the one colony to have voted against Independence, would hardly have been a good neighborly start for South Carolina. When he voted in favor of Independence on 2 July and later signed the Declaration, although he was the leader of the South Carolina delegation, he was the youngest delegate of all, aged only twenty-six.

The British forces, which had been forced to abandon Boston, returned to the mainland from Halifax, Nova Scotia, landing near New York on 2 July 1776, together with strong reinforcements. After being defeated at Long Island, Washington pulled back to the island of Manhattan. On 16 July, Joseph Reed, the Middle Templar who was Washington's first aide, and by then Adjutant General, wrote to his wife from the New York headquarters. "I make no doubt you will be agreeably surprised, as I was yesterday, on receiving a letter from our brother Dennis. It was endorsed 'per favor of Lord Howe' and sent with the seal untouched. He mentions that he had seen Lord Howe, and is well assured that he comes as a mediator rather than as an enemy, and most earnestly pressing me to promote a conference in order to an accommodation." As mentioned earlier, Dennis De Berdt, Reed's London brother-in-law, was a friend of America.[15]

Admiral Lord Howe, the British commander-in-chief, sent a message by an officer under a flag of truce, addressed to Washington as though he were a civilian, without any mention of his military rank. Reed told the British officer that he could not accept such a document. Shortly afterwards Washington was prepared to accept the title of "Gentleman" on the replacement document and met the assistant Adjutant General of the British Army, but as he was able to offer very little in the way of useful terms, the meeting broke up without any progress.

Howe next asked Congress to send representatives to discuss the possibility of reconciliation once more. It is a mark of the respect that he had earned by his hard work in Congress, that Edward Rutledge was selected to accompany Benjamin Franklin and John Adams. "Thus, New England, the middle states, and the South were to be represented, or, as also noted, it could be seen as a trio of the oldest, the youngest, and the most stout-hearted of the members of Congress."[16] Franklin informed Howe, whom he knew personally from London, that he and his companions would meet him on 11 September either at the house in Perth Amboy, occupied until a short time before by Governor William Franklin, or one on Staten Island—which Howe chose.

The Admiral was genuinely a friend of the colonies, and said that he would feel the fall of America like the loss of a brother. Franklin assured him, "My lord, we will use our utmost endeavors to save your Lordship that mortification."[17] The four men talked for hours over dinner but no useful proposal emerged. During the discussion Edward Rutledge made the valid point that Britain might benefit more from an alliance with the independent thirteen States than from the subservient relationship. Unfortunately it took many years for that idea to sink in with the British government. Rutledge added that South Carolina would never return to being a colony, even if Congress wanted it so to do. It turned out that Howe had no power to negotiate a settlement, other than to grant pardons, so nothing came of that meeting either. A few weeks after this mission, Rutledge returned home and undertook military service until taken prisoner in 1780. His departure from Philadelphia was unfortunate: "The state gained a captain of artillery but lost a delegate in Congress whose service in the critical years to come would have been of greatest assistance."[18]

South Carolina may have dragged its feet on the issue of Independence, but it was not slow to fight the British and gave the United States an early inspiring and rare victory, only days before the Declaration of Independence was approved. As Charleston was both the principal city and the main port of the South, it was a tempting target for the most powerful navy in the world, which had great experience of landing complete armies on distant shores. John Rutledge instituted the hasty improvement of the basic fortifications of the city, especially at Sullivan's Island. General Charles Lee, who had been given command of the new American forces in the Southern Department, was convinced—not unreasonably—that the island could not withstand an attack by the British, and wanted Colonel William Moultrie, the South Carolina commander there, to abandon it and deploy his troops in a safer place. Rutledge sent Moultrie a simple message: "General Lee wishes you to evacuate the fort. You will not do so without an order from me. I would sooner cut off my right hand than write one."[19]

The British ships arrived on 28 June 1776 and began a heavy bombardment of the hastily reinforced fort. The South Carolinians held their fire until the ships were close in and anchored. Rutledge instructed Moultrie: "I beg and entreat of you only to fire your heaviest guns very slowly, only now and then, and take good aim; if a brisk fire is kept up on your side your ammunition will soon be expended, and what shall we do then?"[20] Moultrie's men fired four guns at a time and each one was skillfully laid, so nearly every round struck home. The British ships were able to fire a large number of rounds for each one fired at them, but they only managed to do comparatively little damage to the fort. The reason was that the palmetto tree trunks and the earth walls, used to make the emplacements, absorbed most of the broadsides.

The slow, steady gunfire from Moultrie's men took its toll. One British ship was sunk and others were badly damaged. The Royal governor of the colony, Lord William Campbell, who was on board one of the ships, was killed, as were some crew members. The commodore of the fleet, Sir Peter Parker, was injured and eventually withdrew his surviving battered ships. Moultrie was promoted to brigadier-general and the fort was given his name. South Carolina obtained, as a badge of honor, the title of the Palmetto State, in memory of the trees that had taken the punishment of the broadsides, instead of the defenders of the fort. The effects on the morale of the new nation were significant. In South Carolina itself, President John Rutledge had shown himself to be an effective leader. Any lingering doubts that he may have had about the need for Independence, had been blown away by the guns of the British ships. When he formally delivered the copy of the Declaration of Independence to the South Carolina legislature, Rutledge stated: "May the happiest of consequences be derived to the United States from the Independence of America who could not obtain peace, liberty, and safety by any other means."[21]

The March 1776 constitution of the State had been regarded as an interim one, pending a settlement with Britain. Once it became clear in July that there would be no such settlement, a new permanent constitution was drafted, making significant changes to the earlier one, which many considered to be unsatisfactory and undemocratic. Reference was made earlier to the first constitution of Pennsylvania being one of the most radical ones. "At the other end of the spectrum South Carolina and especially Maryland drafted profoundly conservative constitutions."[22] One change made in Charleston by the new draft was that the President's veto was removed; another that the Assembly could no longer choose the members of the upper house, but that the electorate should do so. In March 1778 John Rutledge felt he could not approve the new constitution and resigned. Arthur Middleton turned down the offer of his post, as he had his own misgivings about the changes; it went instead to Rawlins Lowndes, though the title of the head of the state was changed back to governor.

Edward Rutledge was not the only delegate from South Carolina to leave the Congress. Henry Laurens, who had been elected President of Congress on 1 November 1777, was left as its sole representative for a period of eight whole months. Laurens lamented: "O Carolina! O my country! Shame to you that in this great, this momentous cause, so few among your many worthy sons are found zealous advocates—so few will leave their yokes of oxen, their pleasures, their emoluments and apply their talents, their whole abilities, to the one thing needful. This evil seems to pervade all classes in South Carolina; we are lulled by a transient success into a sleep of security which will produce our ruin." He accurately predicted that unless his State kept up its fortifications and troop levels, the British would select it as an easy target. Laurens warned Lowndes in similar terms.[23]

Lowndes was not a success as leader of the State: John Rutledge was sorely missed, and in February 1779 he was elected to head the executive once more. Charleston was threatened by a British force and a strong leader was needed. At Coosawhatchie, during the retreat to Charleston, John Laurens, instead of withdrawing as ordered, impetuously attacked the enemy and endangered a large number of his men. The situation was only saved from disaster by the speedy actions of Captain Thomas Shubrick, a fellow student from the Middle Temple. Moultrie reported the near disaster to General Benjamin Lincoln and added the fair comment: "Colonel Laurens was a young man of great merit and a brave soldier, but an imprudent officer; he was too rash and impetuous."[24]

John Rutledge displayed one of his rare moments of weakness when in May 1779 the British commander, General Augustine Prevost, who had succeeded in surrounding the city, called on Charleston to surrender. Rutledge was prepared to do so, partly because he felt that the other States had failed to come to the aid of South Carolina, and partly because of his concern to save the lives of both his troops and the civilians remaining in the city. He offered to surrender on condition that the State should be allowed to remain neutral after giving in to Prevost. John Laurens declined to deliver such a treacherous message, so Moultrie sent two other officers instead.

Prevost replied that he would not deal with the civilian authorities, but only with the American military commander. Moultrie later wrote: "I then said, 'I am determined not to deliver you up prisoners of war. We will fight it out!' Upon my saying this, Colonel Laurens, who was in the tent, jumped up and said, 'Thank God! We are upon our legs again'."[25] Fortunately for South Carolina, the situation was saved by Prevost's decision to withdraw from Charleston because of the imminent arrival of forces under General Lincoln, which he believed to be stronger than his own.

Charleston, under the leadership of John Rutledge, had beaten the British off in 1776, and in 1779 had been lucky enough to be relieved in the nick of time by the impending arrival of the cavalry—thus starting a good American tradition. The luck did not hold when the British, despite being outnumbered two to one, made their third attempt to take the city. The concerns of Henry Laurens proved justified, and his son John was one of the five thousand prisoners taken by the British when Charleston fell on 12 May 1780. If the repelling of the British in 1776 was one of the high points of the war, the loss of the city and its garrison was undoubtedly one of the lowest. The only consolation that some patriots, including John Adams, could find was that shortly afterwards London suffered from the notorious Gordon Riots, which led to a great deal of destruction in the city and some loss of life.[26]

Charleston was to remain occupied for the rest of the war. Many of the leading local citizens went over to the British, including Henry Middleton (father of Arthur), Colonel Charles Pinckney II (father of cousin Charles, discussed below) and Rawlins Lowndes, who had replaced John Rutledge as governor for a short time. The British must have been delighted about Henry Middleton's defection: he had briefly taken over as President of Congress in 1774 from the very first President, Middle Templar Peyton Randolph. John Rutledge was not captured, as he had been persuaded to leave the city before its fall, so that he could continue to lead the State and rally its remaining forces.

The American fatal casualties at Charleston were relatively light and would appear to have included one Middle Temple patriot only, the twenty-eight-year old Philip Neyle, who had signed a number of the protest petitions while at the Middle Temple, before being called to the Bar in November 1773. C.C.Pinckney was one of the many taken prisoner, but was eventually lucky enough, like young Laurens, to be exchanged after a period on parole. Some of the prisoners, soldiers and civilians alike, including Edward Rutledge and Arthur Middleton, were less fortunate: they were interned by the British in St. Augustine's in Florida for the best part of a year. John Rutledge continued as the governor and active head of government until the end of the war: although he had his critics, there was really no alternative leader.

After the war was over, the Rutledges, like many other Carolinians, set about rebuilding their lives. With continued bitter feelings about the British, they were opposed to conciliatory measures, such as Jay's Treaty, which will be considered briefly later. Fond memories of happy times spent in London could not eradicate more recent unpleasant recollections.

There were probably four principal reasons for the bitterness of the Carolinians. First, their country and their capital city had been fought over and much damage, some of it wanton, had been done by the invaders. Secondly, some of the British troops, and particularly the American loyalist units, had acted with unnecessary brutality. For the sake of historical accuracy it should be added that Banastre Tarleton, the British commander of the most dreaded legion of loyalist troops, was also a Middle Templar. Thirdly, there was little excuse for the long detention of the prisoners at St. Augustine. Fourthly, the British continued to exercise a stranglehold on shipping and commerce, which increased the hardship caused by the war. One instance of that hardship occurred in May 1786, when Edward Rutledge's supervisor asked Henry Laurens if he could let him have some food for his employer's slaves, as without it, they "won't have a bite after next Sunday." Laurens was fortunately able to scrape together a hundred bushels of corn, peas and rice to help out for some weeks.[27]

John Rutledge did not practice law again, but served as a judge in different jurisdictions. He started off in 1784 in the South Carolina Equity court he had planned and became its Chancellor. Both his brothers appeared as advocates in his court, Hugh having resigned his Admiralty court post.[28] On Washington's nomination John served briefly as a founder member of the United States Supreme Court, but resigned the post to take up that of Chief Justice of his home State. John Rutledge's last major

C.C. Pinckney
From the Collections of the South Carolina Historical Society

contribution on the national scene was earlier, at the Constitutional Convention in 1787, where "it was inevitable that he would lead the delegation sent from his state." He spoke on many issues and chaired the drafting committee that produced the original version of the Constitution. He was the first to describe the Constitution as "the supreme law of the land" and was responsible for other important suggestions.[29]

THE PINCKNEYS

The first Pinckney in South Carolina was the grandfather of the brothers C.C. and Thomas Pinckney, and their sister Harriott. He was also called Thomas, and had arrived from County Durham in 1692. The first Thomas had a successful career as a merchant and was able to send one of his two sons, Charles, to the Inner Temple to study law. Charles Pinckney I, as he is sometimes referred to, married his second wife, Elizabeth Lucas, the mother of the three children mentioned, in 1744. She was a remarkably able woman: born in the West Indies the daughter of an English army officer, at school in England and then brought to South Carolina by her father as a fifteen-year-old, she had successfully introduced indigo to that colony as a crop before her marriage.[30]

After practicing law for some time, and serving as Speaker of the Commons House of Assembly for a while, Charles Pinckney was first appointed a Chancery judge and then Chief Justice of South Carolina in 1752, by Governor James Glen. However, that appointment was never confirmed by the British government, which nominated an English placeman, Peter Leigh, in his stead. Leigh was a nonentity, who had held a minor post only, but fortunately turned out to be competent enough for his important new post. Before his arrival, Pinckney had acted as Chief Justice for six months, and so was entitled to feel indignant. His compatriots often referred to him as Chief Justice Pinckney (though sometimes as Colonel) until his death, even though he never again sat as a judge after what may accurately be called his disappointment.

The Chief Justice felt that his sons could not obtain a good enough education in South Carolina and decided to have them educated in England. His wife had wanted to return "home" to England for a visit for some time, and the loss of his post made it possible for him to accompany her and the three children. Pinckney was appointed commissioner of the colony in London as a consolation, but that job did not amount to much and took up very little of his time. After he had made adequate provision for their finances, which included letting their magnificent house to Governor Glen, the five Pinckneys sailed early in April 1753. The journey to England was very fast: twenty-five days from Charleston to Portsmouth. However, because of smallpox at the south coast ports, the parents abandoned the idea of landing there and sailed on to London, where they had the children inoculated at once.[31]

On 19 February 1753, Peter Manigault, the twenty-one-year-old in the last year of his legal studies in London, wrote home to his mother in South Carolina from his chambers at 2 Brick Court in the Middle Temple, mentioning his tutor. "I presume you have heard that Mr. Corbett has purchased the office of High Bailiff of Westminster. Mr. Leigh, the gentleman whom he bought it of, is made Chief Justice of Carolina. He is reckoned a sound lawyer and a merry companion." Three months later Manigault met his newly arrived compatriots and informed his mother: "Last night I had the pleasure of Mr. and Mrs. Pinckney, Mr. Corbett, Mr. and Mrs. Freeman to spend in the evening with me. Mr. Pinckney was just returned from seeing the ceremony of inoculation performed upon the children."[32] Gabriel Manigault, as one would have expected, seems to have responded to his son's earlier plea for a stock of madeira and rum for guests.

Shortly afterwards Manigault wrote to his father: "You will think it a little odd that I am writing to you from Westminster Hall, where 'tis reasonable to imagine I have matters of another kind to see to. To say the truth, we are at present hearing some very tedious affidavits read, which is the most disagreeable circumstance that waits upon an attendance at

Westminster Hall. Colonel Pinckney does us the honor of his company, and seems very fond of passing his time among the gentlemen of his own profession." There was confirmation of that fondness for the company of lawyers two years later, when his wife mentioned that Pinckney had attended the Surrey quarter sessions at Guildford.[33]

On 24 June 1753, Manigault reported to his mother: "We have a number of Carolinians in England at this time and some of them are bent upon settling here. What can induce any one to change Carolina for England I can't imagine, unless it be for the sake of their health. Colonel Pinckney has taken a house at Richmond."[34] The Pinckneys lived in Richmond, Surrey, for a while and then bought a house in Ripley, in the same county. However, they were anxious to have a home in the heart of London as well. Eliza wrote to a friend: "Would you believe that from Temple Bar to Westminster we could not get an unfurnished house but one and that at a hundred a year. The house we have taken is a very good one in a very good street. 'Tis the last but one on the left hand in Craven Street."

That short street off the Strand is best known for the man from Philadelphia who lived for many years in another house "last but one on the left hand": Benjamin Franklin. The only difference was that his house was in the first block of eight houses and the Pinckneys' in the only other one. At about the same time Eliza made an interesting comment about one aspect of London life: "The most disagreeable thing here to me is the perpetual card playing. It seems with many people here to be the business of life."[35]

Two other Pinckneys should be mentioned at this stage. The Chief Justice's nephew Charles, born in 1732 (Charles Pinckney II), was the son of his impoverished brother, William. He was fourteen years older than the elder son of the Chief Justice, who generously paid for him to have five years' education in England. The nephew, who studied law in South Carolina only, became a leading Charleston lawyer and was also sometimes known as Colonel Charles Pinckney. He in turn had a son named Charles, born in

1757. That Charles (Charles Pinckney III) was admitted to the Middle Temple in 1773, but never attended it because of the conflict; instead, he studied law with his father. After qualifying in South Carolina he had a most distinguished public career, some of which was discussed earlier.

In 1758 Charles and Eliza Pinckney, after five years in England, returned to Carolina, taking their nine-year-old daughter Harriott with them but leaving their boys, only twelve and seven, to finish their schooling. The parents' move back to America was not intended to be a permanent one. The Chief Justice, who was so worried about the danger of a French descent on South Carolina that he had written to William Pitt to express his concern, was hoping to wind up his affairs there. They could then return to England, where they would be able to live in safety, on his investments.

The plan went badly awry as Charles Pinckney died of malaria within weeks of his return to America. Shortly before his death he demonstrated both his love of the law and his preparedness to help a young man to learn it. His wife wrote to a friend: "But weak and low as Mr. Pinckney is, when he has an interval of ease he can't help interesting himself in the welfare of his friends." After referring to a disappointment suffered by the young man, Eliza Pinckney mentioned that she had offered to let him stay in their house as a member of the family, adding: "And Mr. Pinckney will put him into a course of reading law, which may be of use to him as a gentleman, though he may not intend to practice the law as a lawyer. Mr. P. desires me to say further he is sorry he can't make him the offer, in case of his liking the law and his parents approving his being of that profession, to take charge of him altogether for that purpose, on account of his bad health, as well as it being too late in life for him to enter into such an engagement."[36]

The widow had to stay in South Carolina to wind up her husband's estate, thinking that it would take her two years or so, but soon found that she had to run the family plantations, making it impracticable to return to England as planned. She remained in America, but decided that she had to leave the boys in England to continue their education. Her husband's will had specified that they were to "be virtuously, religiously and liberally brought up, and educated in the study and practice of the laws of England," and she shared that aspiration for their sons. That being so, she did not see them again until they returned home many years later.

As a result of their mother's decision, which cannot have been an easy one for her, C.C. and Thomas each received the same lengthy, rounded education: one that fitted them both admirably to serve the future needs of their country. It is probably true to say that no young American, with the possible exception of John Quincy Adams, received a better overall education for the tasks ahead, than the Pinckney brothers. They both attended preparatory school and then Westminster School. From Westminster both moved on to Oxford University and the Middle Temple—and while in Europe had some military training as well.

One fact that emerges very clearly from Eliza Pinckney's letters, apart from her devotion to her children, is the amount of help she obtained for her sons when widowed, from various friends in London, both American and English. A Mrs. R. Evance was formally the guardian of the boys, and she was regularly provided with funds by the mother's agent in London, George Morly, whose address was Somerset House, in the Strand. He occasionally visited the boys and reported back to their anxious mother. Among several others who looked them up was John Rutledge.[37]

In 1764 C.C. left school, started his studies at Christ Church College, Oxford and was admitted to the Middle Temple. He attended lectures given in Oxford by William Blackstone, and later applied himself to his studies at the Inn. He was in the thick of the Stamp Act crisis in London and clearly appreciated that he might one day be required to fight for his country, which, despite his long absence from it, was still South Carolina. While in England both he and Thomas were conscious of being South Carolinians and objected when Americans were spoken of in a slighting tone. In 1768 he found time to attend the Royal Military Academy, at Caen in Normandy, to learn something of military science. His knowledge of French was to prove

Thomas Heyward, Jr.
From the Collections of the South Carolina Historical Society

very useful for him later, both as a soldier and as a diplomat.

On 29 January 1769 C.C. Pinckney was called to Bar by the Middle Temple. Although one might have expected him to rush home after his lengthy absence, he not only went out on one circuit but also took a room in the Inn. A recently discovered document in the Middle Temple archive, dated 20 January 1769, records: "William Burke Esquire having surrendered all that chamber with its appurtenances situate in Elm Court No. 4 four pair of stairs high on the East side of the staircase Mr. Charles Cotesworth Pinckney is admitted thereunto to hold the said chamber and its appurtenance to the said Charles Cotesworth Pinckney for the term of his natural life And he give for a fine £2. (signed) Henry Hatsell, Treasurer." There was, fortunately, no obligation for Pinckney to remain there for life and shortly afterwards it was taken over by another newly called barrister, who was doubtless known to him. His successor was another bright student, Richard Pepper Arden, who became the English Attorney General, Master of the Rolls and Chief Justice of the Common Pleas.[38]

Six other documents found at the same time not only provide useful examples of the kind of exercises students undertook, but also show that Pinckney's study partner was Thomas Heyward from Charleston. Each of the documents drafted by the students, with the customary pinch of humor, states a hypothetical case on a different area of law, to be discussed and mooted. Each was signed by the six students in the syndicate. It is a strangely moving experience to handle these six small and trivial scraps of paper, bearing the signatures of the two lead students, far away from home: one a later signer of the Declaration of Independence (Heyward), the other a signer of the Constitution (Pinckney). The fact that those scraps are still in existence is testimony to the depth and value of the Middle Temple archive—and to its continuing relevance for a study of the Revolution.

One of the cases reads (roughly): "In an action of trespass the defendant pleads a parol submission to an award, and that the arbitrators awarded that the defendant should provide a couple of pullets to be eaten at his house in satisfaction of the trespass, and avers that he did provide a couple of pullets at his house, and the plaintiff did not come. The plaintiff replies [.....] another award. The defendant tenders issues upon it.

Query: Whether the defendant ought not to have pleaded that he gave the plaintiff notice of the time that the pullets were to be eaten?

Query: Whether the defendant ought not to have laid the evidence now whose the performance was?"

Another reads: "Special action of trespass and battery for a battery committed by the defendant upon the plaintiff and breaking his skull. The plaintiff declares of the battery and that he brought an action for it against the defendant, and recovered £55 and no more, and that after that recovery part of his skull by reason of the said battery came out of his head, *per quod se*. The defendant pleads the said recovery in bar. The plaintiff demurs.

Query: Whether the prior recovery in the action of assault can be a bar to the [claim?]

Query: Whether the jury could give damages for the main [injury?] before it happened?"[39]

After sixteen years in England, eleven of them since his parents had gone home, C.C.Pinckney returned to South Carolina in the summer of 1769. Thomas stayed behind to complete his education. As one of his last acts in England, C.C. had seen to it that his younger brother was admitted to the Inn on 16 December 1768, and he probably left him provided with law books. The separation of the brothers, who were very close and had supported each for eleven years, must have been difficult for them, even though they had the consolation that their widowed mother, who had never remarried, was getting one of her sons back to support her.

Thomas doubtless missed the steadying influence of his elder brother and on one occasion as a student got into a serious scrape. He was involved in an incident that might well have proved disastrous for his hopes of a legal career, had there not been a sensible plea bargain to conclude the affair, which also involved two other American students. One of them described the incident in the following light-hearted manner—"showing little remorse", to use the time-honored judicial phrase, which usually precedes a stiff sentence.

"We had supped at a fashionable place of resort in Covent Garden, the rendezvous for bucks and disorderly spirits, and after being prepared for adventures, kicked the waiters down the stairs and sallied forth, but the landlord gave a signal for his spies (who were always at hand) for the watchman at 2 o'clock in the morning, who attempted to arrest us. We drew our swords (which were more for show than service) and defended ourselves heroically, but were overpowered, disarmed and taken prisoners, with broken swords, black eyes and bruises, and conducted to the 'Round House', a secure place or cellar provided for such occasions which frequently occurred. Early in the morning we were indulged with a hackney coach and conducted to Sir John Fielding, the famous City magistrate, for examination." In short, they were taken to Bow Street magistrates' court.[40]

The miscreants were able to avoid a prosecution by agreeing to have supper at the landlord's establishment at the outrageous price of two guineas apiece. Fortunately for them, none of the three law students was foolish enough to argue that they were being illegally amerced, contrary to Magna Carta. Thomas Pinckney was the only Middle Templar involved, and must surely have been led into trouble by his two colleagues! They were members of two other Inns of Court, which shall remain nameless—but in fairness to the fourth Inn, Lincoln's, it should be added that none of *its* members played any part in that disgraceful scene. It was just as well that Pinckney was not convicted of any offence. After being elected governor of South Carolina in 1789, in 1792 he became the first minister to be sent by the Federal government to London—John Adams having earlier been dispatched by Congress only.

Unlike his brother, Thomas was able to make a trip home for eighteen months during his studies, which compensated him in some small measure for the extra years he had to spend in England on his own, at a time when conflict was becoming more and more likely.[41] While in London, Thomas participated in the political discussions involving the colonies, writing later to the son of a contemporary: "At this period American politics occupied much of the public mind in London, and the young Americans attended a meeting of their countrymen convened by Dr. Franklin, Mr. Arthur Lee, Mr. Ralph Izard, etc., for the purpose of framing petitions to the Legislature and the King, deprecating the acts of Parliament, then passing, to coerce our country. But the petitions not having the desired effect, and foreseeing that an appeal must probably be made to arms, we endeavored to qualify ourselves for the event and hired a sergeant of the royal guards to drill us at your father's lodgings. From him we obtained the knowledge in military service we could derive from a person of his rank."[42]

Thomas was one of thirty signatories to a petition in 1774, together with fifteen fellow South Carolinians, and at about that time wrote to ask C.C. to lend him the money for his call, as he was anxious not to be "obliged to stay here a day after I have an opportunity of leaving England."[43] He was called to the Bar on 25 November and sailed for home early in December 1774. He was seen off by John Laurens, who had traveled to Gravesend on the Thames with him. They were to meet again at the siege of Savannah and at the battle of Yorktown, fortunately on the same side.

Thomas Pinckney was admitted to the Charleston Bar shortly after his return home, at the age of twenty-four, and conducted his first case in February 1775. The closeness of his family is clear from the enthusiasm displayed on that great occasion. Eliza Pinckney wrote to her daughter Harriott, by then married and in her own home: "Your brother [C. C.] has been here; he just stepped in from court to let me know Tomm had spoken for the first time. They have gained the cause and ----- (I forget the client's name) presented Tomm with a couple of [gold] Joes as soon as he had done. I have seen nobody yet to know how he spoke but his brother, and he, you know, is very partial to him."

Eliza made some later additions to her letter: "Tomm is come in from court; he don't seem at all satisfied with himself; says he was confused. Mr. Ned Rutledge called in the evening; he is very friendly to Tomm. I told him I was sorry Tomm seemed so dissatisfied with himself. He said he had no cause. Your cousin Pinckney, has just been in. She says her husband [Charles Pinckney II] was extremely pleased to hear him; said he acquitted himself extraordinarily well, with great calmness and good sense, not at all confused or flustered."[44]

C.C.Pinckney and Edward (Ned) Rutledge remained friends until Rutledge's early death in 1800 and were involved in many joint ventures, including the law, the army and politics, both national and South Carolinian. Their closeness became known to Washington, who offered them the seat on the United Supreme bench vacated by John Rutledge, leaving the choice of who should accept the post to them. "Will either of you two gentlemen accept the office, and in that case, which of you?" Both declined on financial grounds: the years of service for their country had left them with a number of debts and other problems. By an unhappy coincidence, John Rutledge died in the same year as his brother Edward, and in tragic circumstances, as he had suffered a serious mental breakdown.

Once it became tolerably clear that an armed conflict with Britain could not be avoided, the Pinckney brothers embarked on their military careers, which ended with both of them eventually attaining the rank of major-general. One of their fellow captains in their early days in the militia was the South Carolinian, Thomas Lynch, who had been educated at Eton and Cambridge, and then at the Middle Temple with Edward Rutledge and Thomas Pinckney. When he was with C.C.Pinckney on a recruiting drive in North Carolina, Lynch went down with a bad fever, which left him handicapped for the short remainder of his life. However, he was just fit enough to replace his father, also Thomas, as a member of the South

Carolina delegation to the Continental Congress, when he died in 1776, on the way home from Congress.

Thomas Lynch, Jr., wrote on 7 July 1775 to Ralph Izard in England from Philadelphia: "Can the friends of old England find no way to stop this fatal war going on—to the certain destruction of that once great state? All America pants for reconciliation; they dread, what may be easily prevented by government, a total separation. Should war go on another year, a government must be formed here—it is unavoidable, and when once that is done, it will be, I fear, impossible to restore the connection."[45]

Lynch was a great admirer of C.C. Pinckney and wrote an introduction for him to General Washington, assuring him that "no man living had a higher spirit, a nicer sense of honor or a more incorruptible heart than he has." He added that he was confident Washington could use a man of high principles and military skills: "I will willingly engage my life that the friend I now venture to recommend to your favor, is such an one."[46] By his actions and letters, Washington later made it plain that he had found that Lynch had not exaggerated Pinckney's qualities in any way.

Although C.C. Pinckney was with Washington at the battles of Brandywine and Germantown, there is no evidence to support the suggestion, sometimes made, that he served on the general's staff, like his fellow Middle Templars, Joseph Reed and John Laurens. On being promoted to lieutenant-colonel he had asked for leave to observe the general at work, and was with him for that purpose. Of course, he may well have been requested to help out while at the headquarters as an observer, as he was by then an experienced soldier.

C.C. had been one of the defenders of Sullivan's Island. After that, both brothers were in several battles in the war, mainly in the South, and played their full part, with Major Thomas Pinckney regularly serving under Colonel C.C. Pinckney. While serving under General Moultrie's command, C.C. wrote him a number of letters, one of which illustrated the value of his broad education and his strength of character. On 3 February 1779, while in

Charleston, he expressed his concern about a plan in the South Carolina legislature to toughen up the terms of service for the militia, so as to include harsh military punishments. "It is not the danger, or apprehension of danger, that should oblige a patriot to part with essential rights. For my own part (who consider the present militia law as a very rigorous one, and one that would answer every purpose were it faithfully executed) I cannot, and will not, ever give my consent to part with the constitutional freedom, and liberty of the people, in the mode pointed out by this before unheard of militia Bill."[47]

Pinckney, good lawyer that he was, had appreciated the lesson that has continually to be relearned. When one is pursing decent objectives in times of strife, it is possible, with unthinking haste, to abandon or to dilute some of one's own hard-won liberties in the process.

Like many other South Carolinians, the Pinckneys suffered great personal losses as a result of the war being fought over their towns and plantations. On 17 May 1779 Thomas wrote to his mother about the destruction of his house by the British. After withdrawing from the approaches to Charleston, Prevost's men had taken "all the best horses they could find, burnt the dwelling-house and books, destroyed all the furniture, china etc., killed the sheep and poultry and drank the liquors." His mother also suffered losses and wrote to him about his brother's offer, "to divide what little remains to him among us; I am greatly affected, but not surprised at his liberality."[48]

When Charleston fell to the British in the following year, C.C. Pinckney was one of the many taken prisoner. Thomas Pinckney avoided capture at that stage as he had been dispatched from the city to get reinforcements. On 11 June 1780 Thomas wrote to his mother and sister that he had been able to go under a flag of truce to visit his captive brother. "I had the satisfaction of half an hour's conversation with my brother at Mr. Simpson's, in his presence. This gentleman behaved with the greatest politeness and indeed in a friendly way to me, offering to render me any service in his powers."[49]

James Simpson's story is worth a minor deviation. He had been the last Royal Attorney General of South Carolina and was replaced in March 1776 by the Middle Templar and patriot, Alexander Moultrie, a half-brother of the general. After the fall of the city, Simpson acted as the British intendant or mayor of Charleston and head of the police, later becoming secretary to General Sir Henry Clinton, the British Commander-in-Chief. His humanity was apparent once more when he pointed out to Clinton on 1 July 1780: "Numbers of families, who four years ago abounded in every convenience and luxury of life, are without food to live on, clothes to cover them, or the means to purchase either."[50] His shrewdness led him to understand the importance of the civil authorities, such as those headed by John Rutledge, and of the local militias which sustained them. He appreciated that is was "from their civil institutions that the rebels derive the whole of their strength".[51]

Simpson had entered his son William at the Middle Temple in May 1775 and, somewhat unusually, had joined the Inn himself only after his son, in November 1777. James Simpson was called to the Bar by the Inn on Independence Day in 1783 and his son three years later. Moultrie, his successor as Attorney General, may have been a patriot, but unfortunately turned out to be a crook. He was impeached for embezzling £60,000 of public funds and convicted by the South Carolina Senate in 1793.[52] These two successive Middle Temple Attorneys General illustrate the point that—as always in a civil war, or indeed any war—neither side had a monopoly of good, or of bad men.

Thomas Pinckney was able to report some further civilized behavior on the part of the enemy shortly after his encounter with Simpson. During the battle of Camden on 16 August 1780, which the British won, he had the tibia and fibula of one leg shattered by a musket ball, and nearly died from loss of blood. By a stroke of good fortune, one of the British captains, Charles McKenzie, had been at school with him in England and recognized the wounded prisoner. He got the British doctors to attend to Pinckney, and they managed to save the leg, which he had expected to lose. He then received nursing care from a woman who lived near the battlefield.[53]

On 7 September the patient wrote home to ask for "one article so essential to my health." He explained: "What I mean is good port wine, which, I believe, with the bark must be my main support this fall." The bark he referred to was the Peruvian bark, or quinine, which Arthur Lee had earlier discussed in his Edinburgh paper. The combination was needed to save Pinckney from the dangerous malaria mosquito, which had killed his father and thousands of others. Among the British officers treating him with kindness during his successful convalescence in captivity, was the dreaded Banastre Tarleton.

The British regularly tried to persuade American prisoners to change sides, and both Pinckneys were approached with the usual offers of a pardon and other benefits, notably freedom from captivity. Thomas Pinckney replied to one offer with the words: "I entered into this cause after reflection and through principle; my heart is altogether American, and neither severity, nor favor, nor poverty, nor affluence can ever induce me to swerve from it."[54] He was eventually exchanged and recovered from his injuries sufficiently to participate in the final battle at Yorktown with his friends, Lafayette and John Laurens.

His sister Harriott had married Daniel Horry, a member of the Inner Temple and a local planter, who served in the war as a cavalry commander, attaining the rank of colonel. After the fall of Charleston, he served for a while under Governor Rutledge, but once the British had control of his property and family, he sought their protection.[55] That step enabled him to take his twelve-year-old son, another Daniel, to England, where he placed him at his uncles' school, Westminster, and entered him at their Inn, the Middle Temple, in October 1781, rather than at his own.

After being educated in England, young Horry married a niece of Lafayette, his uncle Thomas' friend, and settled down in France. He never practiced law and never lived in the United States, but seems to have been proud of his heritage, as he changed his name to Charles Lucas Pinckney Horry—although he may have lengthened his name merely because his new uncle, the gallant Marquis, had so many of them (which the writers have studiously ignored).

Colonel Horry's case provides another illustration of the dilemmas caused by a civil war. It is not only at the outset that difficult choices have to be made, but also later, as when one's captors are exerting direct pressure or when one's family is, in effect, taken hostage. The change of sides could be in either direction. It is scarcely surprising, given the changing and sometimes intolerable pressures, "that there were many thousands who shifted allegiances as circumstances dictated on different occasions in the war."[56]

C.C. returned to Charleston at the end of the war, resuming both his legal practice and his political career, being elected to the Assembly. In 1787, together with his cousin, Charles Pinckney III, he attended the Constitutional Convention in Philadelphia. They both contributed significantly to the discussions, which were led by James Madison, Jefferson's Virginian ally and, in due course, successor as President of the United States. According to Bradford, "It is possible that, without Charles Cotesworth Pinckney, no Constitution could have been agreed upon in Philadelphia or approved in the lower South."[57] In the same year Thomas was elected Governor, with the help of his friend, Edward Rutledge, and chaired the ratification proceedings in South Carolina. All three Pinckneys were to be sent abroad as representatives of the United States—but their diplomatic missions will be discussed in a later chapter.

Eliza Pinckney had the great joy of seeing both her sons succeed in virtually everything they attempted. In 1793 she became very ill with cancer and traveled to Philadelphia with her daughter for treatment, but died there. Her elder son could not attend her funeral because he was in South Carolina; the younger was by then in London as the United States minister. However, in a remarkable tribute to an unusual woman and her sons,

President Washington insisted on acting as one of the pallbearers.

Charles Pinckney III, their cousin, who had been admitted to the Middle Temple, but prevented by the hostilities from attending, was exceptionally clever and very ambitious. At an early age he decided that the best way to see the world would be to do so as a representative of his country. Although he managed eventually to attain such a post, it was principally in South Carolina and in Philadelphia, after military service during the war, that his talents proved of greatest value to his countrymen. He was governor on four occasions, and proved to be a useful member of both the Congress and the Constitutional Convention. The fact that he was a Pinckney, and that his family was already linked with other leading families in the State, clearly did no harm, despite the fact that his own father sought British protection in 1780. In April 1788, he widened the magic circle when he married Mary Eleanor, the daughter of Henry Laurens. Four years later, Mary's brother, Henry, Jr., married John Rutledge's daughter, Elizabeth.[58] During his term as governor in 1796-98, Pinckney's younger brother, Miles, who had been admitted to the Middle Temple in February 1787, acted as his secretary.

Despite his youth, Charles Pinckney was one of the first members of Congress to appreciate that the out-dated Articles of Confederation were ham-stringing the future progress of the United States, and to make concrete proposals for a new Constitution. As discussed earlier, his proposals were carefully considered in the discussions in Philadelphia in 1787 as a delegate to the Constitutional Convention, where he played an important part.

The secretary of the Constitutional Convention was Major William Jackson from South Carolina, who had been appointed in preference to William Temple Franklin (much to his grandfather's disgust). Jackson had earlier been appointed as one of General Lincoln's aides, on the recommendation of C.C. Pinckney, and had been captured at Charleston with John Laurens. They were both fortunate enough to be paroled and then exchanged. In 1781, when Laurens was dispatched by Congress to France to obtain further military and financial help, he chose Jackson to accompany him as his official secretary—with Tom Paine as his unofficial one. As we are considering South Carolina's most distinguished Middle Templars, this is perhaps a convenient point at which to interpose a little more on John Laurens.

Laurens clearly made a considerable impression on many who encountered him. One of his colleagues on the staff of the Commander-in-Chief was James McHenry, who was to be one of the Maryland delegates at the Constitutional Convention, and who was later appointed Secretary for War by Washington, when C.C.Pinckney turned down his offer of the post. McHenry commented that Laurens "was surpassed by few men in genius, ability and gallantry." Their colleague, Alexander Hamilton also thought highly of him—though his judgment may have been clouded by the fact that he seems to have had a crush on Laurens, for he certainly sent him love letters, which Laurens, who had a wife back in England, ignored.[59]

That Washington had a good opinion of his aide is clear from the letter he wrote to Franklin when dispatching Laurens to Paris: "Justice to the character of this gentleman conspiring with motives of friendship will not permit me to let him depart without testifying to you the high opinion I entertain of his worth as a citizen and as a soldier." Whiteley was probably correct when she wrote, in her interesting study of the general's military family, "Undoubtedly he loved John Laurens." Joseph Ellis has recently written: "His most trusted aides—Joseph Reed was the first, followed by Alexander Hamilton and John Laurens later in the war—became surrogate sons."[60] Laurens returned from his mission to Paris just in time to participate effectively in the assault on Yorktown in October 1781, together with his former colleagues on Washington's staff, Lafayette and Hamilton.

When the British commander, General Earl Cornwallis, offered to surrender, Washington nominated Laurens to negotiate the terms on his behalf. And so it was that a twenty-six-year-old student member of the Middle Temple had the great honor of representing his revered Commander-in-Chief in the surrender negotiations. Washington had instructed him to insist that the British surrender on humiliating terms, similar to those they had imposed on the Americans at the surrender of Charleston. When the British representative protested that Cornwallis had not been there, Laurens pointed out that he himself had been one of those prisoners. However, he recollected his role and gave the famous impersonal answer: "It is not the individual that is considered. It is the Nation."

After the surrender, Laurens was placed in charge of all the prisoners. Cornwallis was formally still the Constable of the Tower of London, where the most distinguished American prisoner of the war was detained at the time, charged with treason. The prisoner was Henry Laurens, John's father, the former President of Congress, who had been captured in the previous year by a British ship when on passage to the Netherlands to obtain help for the United States. John Laurens suggested that the Constable might like to be exchanged for one of his prisoners in the Tower. Some weeks later, after Edmund Burke had gleefully drawn attention to the situation in the House of Commons, that unique exchange took place.

After his release on 31 December 1781 from his fifteen months' captivity, Henry Laurens was befriended by his son's Middle Temple colleagues, notably Thomas Day and William Jones, firm supporters of America throughout. Apart from other common interests, Day and John Laurens had shared a detestation of slavery, and had both expressed their strong views in writing: Day in print and John in his correspondence. For example, on 30 September 1776, while he was still attending the Middle Temple, John had written to Francis Kinloch, a Carolinian friend studying at Lincoln's Inn: "I think that we Americans, at least in the Southern colonies, cannot contend with *a good grace* for liberty, until we shall have enfranchised our slaves. How can we reconcile to our spirited assertion of the rights of mankind, the galling abject slavery of our negroes?"[61] On 1 March 1782, after Yorktown but before a peace had been agreed, Jones wrote to Viscount Althorp, who had been his pupil, about the former prisoner in the Tower. "Mr. Laurens was with me yesterday for two hours: he talks divinely. Did you know that the Americans had settlements *seven hundred* miles from the coast? Subdue such a people! The King may as easily conquer the moon or wear it in his sleeve."[62]

Sadly, John Laurens was killed in a skirmish with a British foraging party on 27 August 1782, at a time when his father was one of the four American peace commissioners, who were to sign the preliminary Peace Treaty shortly after receiving the news. The grieving father asked Day, who was a poet and an author as well as a barrister, to write the epitaph for his son. Day complied with his request, and then introduced Henry Laurens to his own bookseller/publisher, John Stockdale, who had learned the trade from John Almon, and had taken over his American business. As a result, Laurens stayed over Stockdale's bookshop in Piccadilly on at least four occasions and recommended it to John Adams, who took the same lodgings (with his son, John Quincy) for two months, after signing the final Peace Treaty in Paris in September 1783. Adams later introduced Jefferson to the bookseller, who published his only book, *Notes on the State of Virginia*, in 1787, as well as works by both John and John Quincy Adams.[63] None of that would have happened but for John Laurens' membership of the Middle Temple, and the good impression he had made there as a spirited young man.

Chapter 7
THE DULANYS AND CARROLLS OF MARYLAND

The contribution of the Maryland members of the Middle Temple to the Revolution was significantly less than that of their brethren from South Carolina, Virginia and Pennsylvania. However, they merit a brief discussion as Maryland was not only the fourth most populous of the colonies at the time, but also the one which sent the fourth largest number of its inhabitants to the Inn, after the three mentioned. While they may not have contributed greatly on the national scene (other than John Dickinson, who was born in Maryland but left it at an early age), they were active in the setting up of the new State of Maryland as a part of the new United States of America. Maryland also provides a rare example of religious discrimination, and how it could spur on a gifted individual into overcoming some of the resultant handicaps.

Daniel Dulany, Sr., was born in Ireland in 1685 but moved to Maryland early in the new century. In 1710 he became a member of the local Bar in

Annapolis and in February 1717 was admitted to Gray's Inn. He was appointed Attorney General of the province in 1720 and later served in the legislature and on the Proprietor's council. In 1728 his pamphlet, *The Right of the Inhabitants of Maryland to the Benefit of the English Laws*, was well received. He died in 1753, leaving four sons, the eldest and youngest of whom attended Cambridge University and were Middle Templars. Daniel Dulany, Jr., born in 1721, had been admitted in March 1742 and called to the Bar in June 1746. Lloyd joined the Inn only after his father's death, in October 1761, but was never called to the Bar in England.

The younger Daniel inherited three interests from his father, which helped to make him a leading figure in the run-up to Independence. Like his father, he had an interest both in law and politics. Like him, he was able to wield a pen to advantage and to write an important political pamphlet, as well as letters to a newspaper—a talent that led to an inky duel with a member of the Carroll family, also originally from Ireland. After returning to Maryland from England, Daniel followed in his father's footsteps by joining the local Bar and becoming a member of the Proprietor's council. He was soon one of the foremost lawyers of Maryland.

The Stamp Act led to his influential pamphlet *Considerations on the Propriety of Taxing America*. The British government had put forward the spurious argument that the colonists had virtual representation, as English members took care of their interests. The falsity of this line was exposed by Daniel Dulany, Jr., who pointed out that those members had done little or nothing to safeguard the interests of the Britons residing in America. The pamphlet was re-published in London by John Almon, the pro-American bookseller and publisher, who also published John Dickinson's work, and so copies were readily available for the colonists' English friends. William Pitt was so impressed by Dulany's pamphlet, that he relied on it when speaking in a debate in Parliament, during which he held it up for emphasis. When the delegates from Maryland attended the New York Stamp Act Congress, they were armed with instructions that had been prepared for them by a committee of the Lower House of Assembly, doubtless inspired by Dulany's lead. Three of those committee members were fellow members of the Middle Temple: James Hollyday, John Hammond and Edmund Key.[1]

Like many other bitter opponents of the British government's taxation measures, when the time came for a decision on which side to take, Dulany chose to be loyal to the Crown. It may well be that his "cold and distant" response to the approach by the young Virginian revolutionary, Arthur Lee, referred to earlier, was attributable to his recognition of fact that he and patriots such as Lee were going to have to part company before long. On the other hand, Dulany's attitude could equally well have been due to the fact that he was a rather unpleasant man, who looked down his nose at those he considered to be inferior: a rather large body of fellow citizens, which possibly included all Catholics.

The Catholic Carroll family was founded in Maryland by Charles Carroll, who had left Ireland for London, where he had joined the Inner Temple in 1685. He is sometimes referred to as Charles Carroll the Settler. At the age of twenty-seven he was appointed as Attorney General and traveled to the province, which had been founded as a safe haven for his co-religionists. Unfortunately for him, he arrived at about the time of the Bloodless Revolution of 1688, which saw off King James II and his Catholic wife, followed by the installation of the Protestant joint monarchs, William and Mary. A Protestant coup in Maryland brought the Catholic dominance there to an end at about the same time, so Carroll lost his job within days of his arrival.

His eldest son Henry joined and attended Gray's Inn, but was drowned on the way home from England. Charles Carroll died in the following year, 1720, leaving his eighteen-year-old son Charles as head of the family; he is sometimes called Charles Carroll of Annapolis. Young Charles was bitter about not being able to follow his own ambition of studying law. During a fit of temper one day he challenged the Middle Templar, James Hollyday, to a duel. He had made the mistake of challenging a member of the Assembly, and found himself committed for contempt.[2]

Somewhat confusingly, like the Pinckneys, the Carrolls kept on calling their male offspring Charles. The second Charles Carroll also had a son named Charles, who as an adult made a point of calling himself Charles Carroll of Carrollton, and even signed the Declaration of Independence with that name in full. For a reason that is well known (a pretended concern that King George should not strain his eyes), John Hancock, the President of Congress, appended the tallest signature to the Declaration, but Carrollton certainly provided the longest. He established another record by living the longest of all the signers: he was the last one to die, in 1832. He chose his long name so that he would not be confused with his father or grandfather—or with his older cousin, Charles. That cousin was a member of the Protestant family of Maryland Carrolls and had been called to the Bar by the Middle Temple in November 1754; he was usually referred to with the suffix Barrister. To simplify matters, we shall refer to Charles Carroll of Carrolton as Carrollton.

Carrollton had a sound Catholic schooling in France, before turning to a study of the civil law there. He came to London in September 1759 to study the common law, which would be far more useful in Maryland. He moved at once into chambers in the Temple, which had been obtained for him by a friend of his father. He liked London and wrote home: "My chambers are genteel and convenient and in the most wholesome part of the Temple." Unfortunately, he felt obliged to add: "The choice of good company is the most difficult and yet the most important article, in which the Temple appears to be deficient, though extremely convenient in every other point. Few young gentlemen are here to be found of sound morals."[3] Carrollton soon decided that the common law was only marginally more interesting than the civil law, and such limited enthusiasm as he had had for a career in the law swiftly evaporated. His father liked the idea of Carrollton studying at his grandfather's Inn, the Inner Temple, but the young man could not see much point in that.

He wrote to his father in November 1759: "I should be glad to know whether you would have me entered of the Temple, as the Roman Catholic religion is an obstacle to my being called to the Bar. I don't see the necessity or need of it, especially as I cannot be entered under twenty pounds." That letter crossed with one his father had written in October, in which he stated out that he could still make a good living in the law, without being called to the English bar. In any event, the father pointed out, competence in law was "absolutely necessary to every private gentleman of fortune who has the least idea of being independent."[4] Fortunately for Carrollton, he was able to lead the life of a private gentleman of fortune and did not need to earn a living. The prejudice that he met with in London was shocking but was also to be found back home in Maryland, despite the fact that it had been founded for Catholics. By the eighteenth century "political control throughout the colony rested firmly in the hands of a Protestant elite of English descent: even rich Catholics like the Carroll family could not exercise the political influence that they might have expected because they were excluded from voting and holding office."[5]

The young man clearly had a wise head on his shoulders. As early as 12 November 1763 he wrote to his father from London: "America is a growing country: in time must and will be independent." Ten years later he forecast that migration would make "British America in a century or two the most populous and of course the most potent part of the world."[6]

Carroll encouraged his son to remain in England and he stayed for five years, during which time he interested himself in various subjects, including politics. One of the reasons his father suggested Carrollton should stay away from Maryland, was that during the Seven Years' War against France, the Catholics there had an outrageous double tax imposed on them, which was only repealed after the end of the war in 1763.[7] After his return home, given that Catholics were debarred from holding public office, Carrollton might have remained out of politics altogether, had it not been for the fact that he was stung into activity by the hostility of the Dulany family toward the Carrolls, and especially that of the Middle Templar, Daniel Dulany, Jr. Apart from anything else, he had made offensive remarks about Carrollton's father.

Like some other colonies, Maryland underwent the experience of having a British governor who decided that his own powers justified his overruling of the local legislature's decision and wishes. Governor Robert Eden, an appointee of the Proprietor rather than of the Crown, insisted on fixing certain officers' fees at a level disapproved of by the Assembly. His arrogance was one of the major factors in awakening opposition to the proprietary interest and in the increasing success of the patriot party. Dulany, who was a member of the Governor's Council and Provincial Secretary, inspired by the success of his earlier Stamp Act pamphlet, decided to write once more— but this time in support of the governor and the establishment, and therefore contrary to the wishes of the patriots.

Dulany wrote a fictitious dialogue between two citizens for the *Maryland Gazette* of 7 January 1773. The First Citizen asked a number of slanted questions, which the Second answered, putting the governor's case each time. Carrollton had no difficulty in identifying the author and decided to challenge his arguments. Very cleverly, he wrote to the editor as though he were the wronged First Citizen, who had been misquoted, and followed that complaint up with various corrections. He wrote: "The sentiments of the First Citizen are so miserably mangled and disfigured, that he scarce can trace the smallest likeness between those, which really fell from him in the course of that conversation, and what has been put in his mouth." He also referred neatly to his opponent's earlier work, before demolishing his case: "On this occasion I cannot forbear citing a sentence or two from the justly admired author of *Considerations*, which have made a deep impression on my memory."

Dulany responded, using the name of Antilon for the Second Citizen, and Carrollton replied as the First Citizen, until each had written four letters. Many people preferred the arguments put forward by Carrollton.

Dulany, a leading lawyer in Maryland, was not used to being outclassed and never recovered from the loss of face involved. He claimed to be neutral rather than loyal to the Crown, and disappeared from the political scene. He had the fortitude, or perhaps arrogance, to remain in Maryland for the rest of his days, suffering from some degree of patriot maltreatment during the war. After the war he practiced law again, so presumably was prepared to swear the required new oath of allegiance.[8]

Dulany's equally arrogant brother, Lloyd, was also a loyalist but chose to go to England. The high point of his life was probably attained in 1771 when, as chairman of the Jockey Club in Annapolis, he several times entertained Colonel George Washington, who used to come over from Virginia at the time of the races.[9] When living in London Lloyd Dulany felt his family insulted by an article in the *Evening Post* for 29 January 1779, written anonymously by another loyalist from Maryland: an obnoxious, boastful cleric, Bennet Allen. Allen suggested that the Dulanys were backing both sides and that Daniel had deliberately stayed behind in Maryland to look after their interest there. Lloyd Dulany only discovered the identity of the author three years later and challenged him to an immediate duel when encountering him in Hyde Park. The cleric was the better shot. Dulany died of his injuries; his opponent went to Newgate prison for six months for manslaughter.[10]

Although the double taxation rule had been lifted, Catholics could still not stand for office in 1773. However, Carrolton's runaway success in the printed debate greatly influenced the outcome of the next election, which followed it almost immediately. The patriots won it hands down. "Every county sent to the Assembly representatives who could be counted on to oppose Governor Eden's policies."[11]

Some of the more responsible and less bigoted Protestant politicians realized that it would be foolish not to make use of Carrollton's obvious talents. When the First Continental Congress was summoned in the following year, he was invited to accompany the Maryland delegates to

Philadelphia. Fortunately, Carrollton did not stand on his dignity and say, "Either I go as a delegate, or not at all," but accepted the invitation. The leader of the delegation was Matthew Tilghman, the Speaker of the Lower House. One of the official delegates was Robert Goldsborough, Dickinson's relation, who had generously shared not only his chambers but even his bed with him, when he arrived in London to join him as a student at the Middle Temple. Goldsborough, who had been Attorney General for two years, was one of the many lawyers who weighed the pros and cons of the arguments of both sides carefully and took their time before backing Independence.

Carrollton's contribution at the First Congress was so sound that he was invited to the Second Congress in 1775 as an adviser to the delegation. Together with Benjamin Franklin, and fellow Marylander Samuel Chase, later a United States Supreme Court justice, he was appointed by the Congress to go to Canada to try and persuade that province, sometimes called "the fourteenth colony" by optimists, to join the thirteen in their opposition to the Crown. Carrollton was chosen partly because it was thought that his persuasive and linguistic powers might be useful in the mission's dealings with the French Catholic population. Although the mission was unsuccessful, the respect which Carrollton had earned, and the hard work he had undertaken for the patriot cause together with Chase, led to his being appointed as one of the Maryland delegates to the Congress in 1776.

On 28 June 1776 the Maryland Convention voted in favor of Independence and instructed its delegates to vote accordingly at the Congress. Carrollton arrived too late to participate in the Independence debates and voting, but was able to sign the Declaration. He had the distinction of being the only Catholic to do so. Despite his late arrival, Carrollton was not the last to sign; the signing by the various delegates was spread out over several months. The last signature was not appended until January and, as so often happens when many people come from afar for an event, was that of a local man: Thomas McKean. The only member of the

Inner Temple to sign the great document was William Paca, another delegate from Maryland. (Had Carrollton been a Protestant, the Inner Temple might well have had double the numbers of signers.)

Charles Carroll, the Middle Temple barrister, was not as influential in the revolutionary movement as his cousin Carrollton, but nevertheless played his part. While Carrollton was attending the First Continental Congress in October 1774, Carroll was involved in Maryland's equivalent of the Boston Tea Party. A cargo of tea had arrived on board the *Peggy Stewart* and some indignant patriots were in favor of burning the ship, complete with its cargo. Carroll addressed the dockside crowd and called for moderation. He succeeded in persuading the assembled patriots to burn the cargo only, but two firebrands were already aboard and set the ship on fire, so that it was completely destroyed. Hoffman commented, a little unfairly: "As a result the barrister won the argument but lost the ship." He also wrote: "No other single act in Maryland played a greater role in shaping the attitudes individuals adopted toward the political conflicts both within the empire and at home."[12]

Both Carrollton and his barrister cousin were elected to the committee, chaired by Matthew Tilghman, which was charged to produce a Constitution and a Bill of Rights. Robert Goldsborough, William Paca and Samuel Chase were three other lawyer members. Carroll the barrister made his major contribution when he produced the first draft of the Maryland Declaration of Rights. Carrollton was responsible for a significant part of the Constitution, which, like that of South Carolina, has been described as "profoundly conservative".[13] Carrollton and the barrister were rewarded for their efforts when they were elected to the new State Senate, where they were joined by Tilghman, Goldsborough and Paca.[14] Once the United States Constitution came into effect, Carrollton became one of the first two Senators from Maryland, together with his kinsman, Daniel Carroll, who had been one of the two Catholic signers of the Constitution. The fact that both of the first two Senators from Maryland were Catholics, may be said to have underlined the fact that one form of discrimination, at any rate, had officially become a thing of the past.

William Vans Murray, another member of the Middle Temple and of the local legislature, thought it wrong that Carrollton should be a member of both the United States and the Maryland Senate simultaneously, as he was concerned about a possible conflict of interest. He accordingly introduced legislation barring such double service, which led to Carrollton choosing to serve in his home Senate rather than the Federal one.[15]

Maryland, together with Virginia, provided the site for the District of Columbia, the exact location having been determined by three commissioners appointed by President Washington, of whom Daniel Carroll was one. He turned out to be extremely lucky: once the site boundaries had been fixed, he was able to profit from his extensive land holdings within them.[16]

Matthew Tilghman and his extended family members repay a brief study, partly because they spanned two provinces and States, Maryland and Pennsylvania, and partly because they were divided, some being patriots, others loyalists. Of course, the larger a family, the greater the chance of opposing views within it. Matthew Tilghman has been called "the Patriarch of Maryland", as he was the most important patriot leader there, chairing every Convention and leading the delegation to the Continental Congress. Charles Carroll the barrister was his son-in-law and helped to cement links with his cousin, Carrollton. He also helped to bring Samuel Chase into the patriot grouping. "Chase personally liked Charles Carroll the barrister, for the role he had played in aiding him and his Annapolis followers in their rise to political prominence."[17]

In Pennsylvania Matthew's brother, James Tilghman, was a loyalist, despite a close friendship with George Washington before Independence. He had married a daughter of Tench Francis, his law teacher, one of Philadelphia's most distinguished lawyers, who served as Attorney General of Pennsylvania from 1744 to 1752, and they called their first son Tench in his honor. At different times, James Tilghman practiced law in both provinces and became a close associate of Dulany. Tench was born in Maryland in 1744 and lived there until 1758, when his grandfather Francis took him to Philadelphia for his education. As an adult, Tench Tilghman was not only a patriot like his uncle Matthew but, as mentioned earlier, was one of Washington's closest aides. The embarrassment that the aide was caused by his loyalist relatives, who included his brother William, later Chief Justice of Pennsylvania, must at times have been excruciating. William also straddled the two provinces, for he had studied with his father at Chestertown on the Eastern Shore and had been admitted to the Maryland Bar. Their brother Richard studied law with Dulany and joined the Middle Temple in July 1769. He became a loyalist and left Maryland for England with the last Royal governor, Robert Eden, who had been invited to depart by the sixth Convention, chaired by Carroll the barrister.[18] Richard Tilghman went further afield than most loyalists: he practiced in India until he had the misfortune to drown while on a sea voyage.

Reference has earlier been made to the network of relationships brought about by the intermarriage of leading families as, for example, in South Carolina. The Tilghmans provide one of the extreme examples of such a network. Tench Tilghman's mother was one of the nine children of the great Tench Francis, eight of whom married and had issue: forty-nine children, to be precise. As a result, Tench Tilghman was related to many leading men in the two colonies and States, including the four successive Chief Justices of Pennsylvania: Allen, Chew, Shippen and his own brother, William.[19] One of his many cousins was Edward Tilghman, Chew's nephew and son-in-law, who had attended the Inn with the encouragement of that Chief Justice.

The further contributions made by William Vans Murray will be considered in the chapter dealing with the ambassadors of the United States. We shall also discuss the Middle Templar who became Washington's first ambassador in London. However, a discreet veil will be drawn over the career of Joshua Johnson, a merchant from Maryland, who was the first American consul in England. He was a generous host in London to American students like Murray and his close friend, John Quincy Adams, but managed that generosity by being recklessly extravagant.

Immediately after his daughter Louisa had married the future sixth President in London in 1797, Johnson made a hasty departure from England, leaving not only many unsatisfied creditors, but also a dowry unpaid. The newly-weds found themselves "hounded by bill collectors who had discovered that Joshua had left town." The father of the groom, President John Adams, nevertheless later thought Johnson fit enough to be appointed Postmaster for the District of Columbia.[20] Johnson's brother Thomas was rather more meritorious: he was a leading patriot and served as the first post-Revolution governor of Maryland before being appointed to the United States Supreme Court.

Chapter 8
THE AMBASSADORS

One after another, the original United States commissioners and ministers in Europe returned home. A reasonably optimistic forecaster might have hazarded the guess that the really difficult stages of diplomacy had been overcome. The United States had been recognized as an independent state and the new country was at peace with the world. However, it was not long before the infant republic was at loggerheads not only with its former enemy, Britain, but also with its allies, France and Spain. The relationship with France reached such a low point that it was called the Quasi or Half War.[1] New ministers (loosely referred to as ambassadors, whatever their actual rank) were appointed with the important task of making up any existing disputes and then of securing a permanent peace with the countries to which they were dispatched.

No less than five of the new ambassadors of the United States were Middle Templars. They were the three Pinckneys: first, Thomas, the younger brother; then the elder one, Charles Cotesworth (C.C.); and finally their cousin, Charles Pinckney III. In addition, there was William Vans Murray, who had become friendly, while in London attending the Inn, with John Quincy Adams; and William Loughton Smith. The only one of the five who was not from South Carolina was Murray, from Maryland.

Congress ratified the Peace Treaty with Britain, which had been signed in Paris on 3 September 1783, and the formal document arrived in Paris in March 1784. David Hartley, the British commissioner, came over for the final step of the peacemaking process: the exchange of the ratifications on 12 May. Next day, Benjamin Franklin reported to the secretary of Congress, Charles Thomson: "The great and hazardous enterprise we have been engaged in is, God be praised, happily completed." But not quite, as it happened.

Franklin's three fellow peace commissioners had been John Jay, Henry Laurens and John Adams. Before braving the Atlantic for their westbound passage, all three of those colleagues first made separate visits to the Roman bath at Bath to improve their health. Jay then returned home to his new post as Secretary for Foreign Affairs of Congress. Laurens went back to South Carolina, and later declined the opportunity to attend the Constitutional Convention in Philadelphia, despite being elected as one of the five delegates for that State. Franklin handed over his Paris post in time to attend the Convention in his home city. His successor in Paris was Thomas Jefferson, who was there long enough to be an enthusiastic spectator at the gory birth of the French Revolution.

The only peace commissioner to remain abroad was John Adams, who became increasingly frustrated and anxious to return home. Even before his appointment as minister to London, he had been yearning to see Massachusetts again and had been getting ready to pack. On 6 June 1784, Adams wrote from The Hague to his sixteen-year-old son, John Quincy, then in London,: "You say nothing of our books at Stockdale's, have you shipped them? And by whom? I am impatient to collect together here all the little things which belong to me, that I too may be in a condition to return home, upon occasion. My best respects to Mr. Laurens. Happy Mr. Jay! Happy Mr. Laurens! in their prospects of seeing home."[2] Unhappy Mr. Adams! On 31 January 1785, Congress voted in favor of a motion to send a minister plenipotentiary to London. The seconder of the motion was the youngest of the Pinckneys, Cousin Charles, who was already beginning to think of a diplomatic career for himself.[3] On 24 February John Adams, who was still serving in Europe, was chosen—and he was not a man to decline a job when his country needed him, whatever the cost to himself and his family.

Adams was required by Congress to serve as the minister to the Court of St. James in the period from May 1785 to March 1788, during which he had a frustrating time. The Peace Treaty he had helped to negotiate was not fully implemented and no trade treaty was ever embarked on while he occupied the post, though there was a pressing need for one. Worst of all, Britain's Orders in Council placed grave restrictions on American trade with the British Isles, Canada and the West Indies, with serious consequences for many Americans.

The eighteenth century provided several instances of peace treaties and surrender terms that were considered by many critics to be too generous to the enemy, among them the treaty concluding the Seven Years' War and the Saratoga surrender agreement. Benjamin Franklin made the comment: "I have never yet known of a peace made that did not occasion a great deal of popular discontent, clamor and censure on both sides. The populace on each side expect better terms than really can be offered; and are apt to ascribe their disappointment to treachery."[4] Another such document was the 1783 Peace Treaty, which, to many English eyes, was too favorable to the United States, partly because Lord Shelburne, a friend of America's, had wanted it that way. A substantial number of Members of Parliament objected to what they regarded as the excessive concessions granted and the backlash had two important effects.

The first was that Shelburne lost office; the second, that the new nation was deprived by the new British government and Parliament of its fair share of international trade. There was a peace treaty and an end to the fighting, but no real peace. A dispassionate observer might well have commented: *"C'est magnifique, mais ce n'est pas la paix."* However, as David McCullough wrote of Adams, "If the years and effort at London had come to naught, he at least knew he had given devoted service, conducting himself with aplomb and dedication. No one could fault him for a false step. Nor could it be imagined that another of his countrymen in the same role could have done better."[5]

Between the time of his release from the Tower of London at the end of 1781 and his departure from the city in June 1784, Henry Laurens—except when visiting France—had acted as an unofficial ambassador, negotiating with the British government and trying to help the imprisoned American sailors and other citizens. On at least one of his prison visits he was accompanied by his son's English friend from the Middle Temple, Thomas Day, who acted as his unofficial secretary. Incidentally, one remarkable fact about the sailors who were taken prisoner is that, despite their suffering, surprisingly few of them switched their allegiance to the British during the war, when compared with the men serving in Washington's army.[6] When Adams was recalled early in 1788, he was not replaced until Thomas Pinckney arrived in January 1792, as the first minister to be dispatched to London by the Federal government of the United States. In the interim period there had briefly been another unofficial ambassador, the dynamic Gouverneur Morris, who had been sent by President Washington with a specific task.

Morris was a very talented lawyer, with financial and business skills, whose abilities had become apparent to Washington, both at the Continental Congress, which he attended as a delegate of New York, and at the Constitutional Convention, where together with Middle Templar, Jared Ingersoll, Jr., and others, he represented Pennsylvania. In early 1778, together with Joseph Reed and other colleagues, he was very active on the committee of Congress, which did its utmost to help Washington's long-suffering army at Valley Forge but, like Edward Rutledge, he was a hard-working member of several other committees as well. He found himself acting as a virtual Foreign Secretary for Congress and laid down some of its foreign policy guidelines.[7]

Although Morris had amply demonstrated his abilities, he had to wait for some time being called upon to use his talents abroad as an official minister. In the meantime, he had traveled to France and England on business in 1788. In Paris, Morris gave the term International Relations a fairly broad interpretation and seems to have thought that it covered sharing a mistress with Charles de Talleyrand-Perigord, the impious Bishop of Autun, soon to be the French Foreign Minister. The known existence of a dangerous rival apparently did not have any chilling effect on Morris' ardor—but possibly the opposite.

In October 1789 Washington asked Morris to go to London to explore with the British government the implementation of the outstanding terms of the Paris Peace Treaty. Each country was becoming increasingly irritated by the other's failure to comply with those terms. The continued British occupation of American frontier posts was the most serious matter for one side; the Americans' failure to pay their pre-war debts due to British creditors for the other. Morris tried to negotiate a settlement of outstanding matters with the Duke of Leeds, the Foreign Secretary, and also with William Pitt, the Prime Minister, but repeatedly drew a blank, mainly because they were not particularly concerned about American concerns. Morris managed one minor success. The British were preparing to go to war with Spain, if it maintained its claim to the Nootka Sound (Vancouver), and reinforced the navy with the help of the press gang. Morris was able to secure the release of some of its American victims.[8]

There was possibly one other useful result of his mission. Washington authorized Morris to refer to America's disappointment that no British minister had been sent over to reciprocate the appointment of John Adams to London in 1785. By early 1791 the British government at last decided that it was time to send a minister to the United States, and George Hammond was chosen; he had been David Hartley's secretary in Paris during the peace negotiations. "The presence of George Hammond as British minister at Philadelphia in 1791 was, in fact, the first marked success of Washington's new administration in the field of foreign affairs."[9] Hammond settled in so well that after two years he married Margaret Allen, the daughter of Andrew Allen, the former Attorney General, and granddaughter of Chief Justice Allen.

After Jefferson's departure from Paris, William Short, who had been his secretary, coveted the post there, but in 1792 it went to Morris, who bravely served as the only foreign minister in the city during the worst days of the Terror. Unlike his predecessor, Jefferson, he did not approve of what he witnessed; once his disapproval became clear to the French authorities, they requested his recall in 1794. James Monroe, the future fifth President, was his successor, but lasted only two years before he, too, was recalled. His obvious sympathy with the French fitted ill with Washington's and Adams' plan for a neutral stance on the part of the United States.

THOMAS PINCKNEY IN LONDON AND MADRID

At the time Thomas Pinckney was chosen by Washington as the first Federal minister for London in November 1791, he had, thanks largely to Edward Rutledge's help, been governor of South Carolina for two years and had been instrumental in getting the new United States Constitution ratified there. However, unlike Rutledge, he was not known on the national scene. He was a meritorious, wounded major, with a residual limp, but there were plenty of those around. His excellent education was probably something only a few friends knew about. And yet, although he turned out to be an adequate rather than a brilliant representative in England, thanks to several strokes of luck, his four years of diplomatic service in Europe nearly made him President or Vice-President of the United States.

Pinckney was not sure whether he should accept the post to the country where he had lived, with one short break only, from the age of three until twenty-four, and where he had received the whole of his education. Pinckney was so close to Edward Rutledge that their friendship has been described as one that was "warmed and cemented by a thousand affectionate actions", and that had led to their children having "grown up together as if they were the children of the same parents".[10] It was understandable that Pinckney should have wanted his friend's advice.

On 24 November 1791 he wrote to Rutledge: "Almost every private consideration appears to me to be against this determination, but every public one (my inability excepted) in favor of it. Pray let me have your thoughts—as you made me a governor and now insist upon my being a minister, you must advise me in this situation, as you supported me in that former."[11] Rutledge clearly had confidence in Pinckney's abilities and allayed any feelings of inadequacy that he might have had, so on 29 November Pinckney wrote to Thomas Jefferson, the first Secretary of State, accepting the offer. Jefferson had recommended Pinckney for the post in Paris, but President Washington preferred to send him to London.[12] Jefferson, who admired France and disliked Britain, must have gritted his teeth when he instructed the new minister that his principal task was to express "that spirit of sincere friendship which we bear to the English nation."[13]

Pinckney's departure was delayed for some months but he eventually arrived in London in July 1792. During his mission John Adams had rented a house in Grosvenor Square, but it was to be some time before the United States could afford to buy one there, so Pinckney leased 1 Great Cumberland Place, near the junction of Oxford Street and Hyde Park, for the next four years. Just as Adams was finding, to his dismay, that being Vice-President was only half a job at best, so Pinckney soon realized that he was a minister with only limited functions. The main discussions between the two countries were being conducted by Jefferson and Hammond face to face in

Philadelphia—not that they were able to agree on much. As though to make it clear to him that his post was a minor one, Pinckney was not even provided with a secretary and had to make his own arrangements. He asked Edward Rutledge to sound out William Allen Deas, who came and joined him in London. Deas, as might be expected by the perceptive reader by now, was from Charleston and, like the two friends, a member of the Middle Temple, having been admitted in November 1786.[14]

Pinckney's principal task in England was to deal with the problems of American ships, their crews and their cargoes, especially after Revolutionary France declared war on Britain on 1 February 1793. The British navy, on the orders of the government, was detaining ships, their cargoes were deemed to be contraband, and many American sailors were being seized as British citizens or as alleged deserters. Some were sent to prison, others to sea to crew British warships. Pinckney was also concerned to try and save Americans from the press gangs, a task that was very difficult—despite Morris' limited success in that field—given that many British people were unable to save their own employees or loved ones from their tender mercies.

The scale of the problem was well summarized by Pinckney's grandson: "There are letters to Mr. Pinckney from prisons all over England, and from prison ships along her coasts, complaining of illegal imprisonment and imploring his efforts for their release. Lord Castlereagh admitted, at a later period, that '3500 seamen in the British navy claimed their discharge as American citizens, of whom 1700 were probably entitled to it'."[15]

Pinckney received a friendly welcome in England, where he met some former companions from school, university and Inn. The British Under-Secretary for Foreign Affairs, J.B.Burges, wrote to the minister at The Hague: "We have a new American Minister, Mr. Pinckney, an old friend and brother-Westminster of mine, whose manners and temper exactly qualify him for the place he has taken. I have known him about thirty years and do not know a more worthy and excellent man." John Adams wrote at about the same time of an encounter with Pitt's Foreign Secretary, better known by his earlier courtesy title of Lord Carmarthen. "The Duke of Leeds once inquired of me very kindly after his classmates at Westminster school, the two Mr. Pinckneys, which induces me to conclude that our new ambassador has many powerful old friends in England."[16]

In February 1793 the Foreign Secretary, Lord Grenville, put Pinckney in touch with Phineas Bond, the British consul who was in England on leave from Philadelphia, so that the two of them could discuss the maritime problems and try to find solutions. The problems were likely to worsen, as the war with France was making Britain's need for ship's crews daily more pressing, which in turn led to more pressing daily on the high seas and highways. Bond suggested the reintroduction of certificates of nationality for American seamen, but that idea did not appeal to Pinckney, who foresaw the difficulties that could arise. Unfortunately, Bond returned to America as consul-general before they could reach any agreement.

Bond was another Middle Templar, with an interesting history that fits well into this chapter, not only because of his consular activities, but because he acted for a while as the British chargé d'affaires in Philadelphia and might have become the second British ambassador, on Hammond's promotion out of the job. Born in July 1749, the son of a well-known Philadelphia doctor, Bond arrived in England towards the end of 1770, with a letter of introduction from Deborah Franklin to her husband Benjamin and another from one of his father's lawyer patients, Joseph Galloway. He was admitted to the Inn in the following April, and greatly appreciated being in London, and especially in the Temple. He loved the freedom of student life, writing with much the same enthusiasm as that shown by Peter Manigault and John Dickinson in their letters home: "A Templar keeps what hours he pleases, has no one to call him to account for any malpractices he may be guilty of, beyond the breach of the peace."[17]

While still a student, Bond found that, thanks to his contacts on both sides of the Atlantic, he was able to help a number of British merchants to recover their debts from some of their American debtors. In 1773 he was obliged to return home, without being called to the Bar in England, as his father was dying. Once home, he was admitted to the local Bar and became a very successful lawyer. Like many others, he found himself opposed to the British taxation measures, but against Independence. However, he became an undoubted loyalist. In August 1777 Bond was one of the leading Tories placed on the parole list and in September he was jailed. When about to be deported to Virginia, he managed to escape to the British lines and soon afterwards guided the leading invaders into Philadelphia. Not surprisingly, he was later charged with high treason by his fellow Middle Templar, Joseph Reed, when President of the State. In the meantime he had returned to England and his studies at the Inn. He was called to the English Bar in June 1779, moving into chambers at 5 Brick Court (second floor west) shortly afterwards.[18]

Once qualified in England, Bond built up his earlier connections with the British merchants who had business dealings with America. After Sir John Temple, another loyalist, had been appointed as the first British consul in America, Bond and some of his clients thought that he would make an admirable second one. After considerable lobbying and delay, he was duly appointed as consul for five States, including Pennsylvania. That meant that he was free to go home—albeit apprehensively—to see his family in Philadelphia, the city that became his base in the fall of 1787. When Hammond arrived in October 1791 as the first British minister, Bond handed over his accommodation to him and helped him to settle into his new post.[19]

On 8 May 1797, William Eldred, the Under-Treasurer of the Middle Temple, wrote to Bond in America that he was indebted to the Inn for outstanding dues of some £10, and additionally as the surety for the similar amounts due from two fellow Philadelphian members. The first was William Rawle, who had moved from Philadelphia to New York with his loyalist stepfather, Samuel Shoemaker, and then studied law in that city before sailing for England and the Middle Temple in 1781.[20] He returned to Philadelphia in 1783, practiced successfully at the Bar, served as a member of the State legislature and later turned down Washington's offers of the post of Attorney General of the United States. The second was Benjamin Chew, Jr., son of the Chief Justice, who also practiced law in Philadelphia. Unlike Bond, neither of them had been called to the Bar by the Middle Temple, though both had attended the Inn. Chew wrote to Eldred on 28 August: "Previous to my leaving England in April 1786 I appeared at the office of the Middle Temple and discharged the amount due for my commons."

However, Bond, who had made a living out of collecting debts due from American debtors to British creditors, was satisfied that the amounts claimed were outstanding and paid all three together. The Inn's Parliament minutes show that he explained that neither Rawle nor Chew had intended to be called to the Bar by the Inn. "They were merely admitted for the purpose of deriving that benefit from an intercourse with professional men to which an induction into an Inn of Court naturally introduced them." Eldred wrote to Bond on 16 November, indicating that there was no problem about the two student members withdrawing from the Inn, as they wished to do, but pointed out that Bond, as a barrister, was in a different position. The advice that he gave was clearly followed by Bond and proved to be very useful to him later.

Eldred wrote: "I believe you are aware that you will be liable to an annual duty of 16/2d so long as you continue to be a barrister of the Society but I think it is probable you may not be aware that if you take a certificate of your being called to the Bar &c. your account will be suspended, and according to custom any gentleman taking such a certificate is not liable to duties unless he returns; but should you take such a certificate and not return again to the Society before it comes to your turn to receive an invitation to the Bench, your name would not appear on the list of senior barristers, and you would be utterly precluded from coming to the Bench." The Bench referred to was not the judicial bench, but the bench of Masters of the Inn, or Benchers.[21]

Bond did not return to England again until shortly before the 1812 war broke out between the two countries he loved, when he attracted hostility in Philadelphia once more for his friendly feelings towards Britain. He remained in England and became a Fellow of the Royal Society. He was elected a Bencher of the Middle Temple in 1812 and Autumn Reader in 1815, the year in which he was also awarded degree of Doctor of Civil Law by Oxford University. His appointment as Reader came just in time, for he died on 29 December and was interred in the Middle Temple vault in the Temple Church.[22]

Alexander Hamilton, the first Secretary of the Treasury, regarded a trade agreement with Britain as essential for the financial health and expansion of the United States. In 1794 Washington, rather than leaving that task to his resident minister there, sent Chief Justice John Jay to London to negotiate with the British government, with a view to ending all outstanding disputes. Thomas Pinckney had no experience of high-powered negotiation, whereas Jay had impeccable qualifications for the task. He had succeeded Henry Laurens as President of Congress in December 1778, before being sent to Spain. It is true that the two years he had spent as his country's representative there had proved almost completely fruitless; that was not his fault, but that of the obstructive Spanish government. When in April 1782 Franklin had sent for Jay to help him with the peace negotiations in Paris, writing, "Here you are greatly wanted", Jay had happily shaken the dust of Spain off his feet. He and fellow-lawyer John Adams then played an important part in the successful negotiations with Britain.

After his spell as the Foreign Secretary of Congress, the newly elected President Washington had offered Jay a choice of posts, and he had chosen that of Chief Justice—it was then that John Rutledge was appointed as his senior Associate Justice in the Supreme Court of the United States. Another Justice appointed at the same time was the Virginian, John Blair, who had been called to the Bar by the Middle Temple in 1760, had served as Chief Justice of Virginia from 1779 and had been one of the seven Middle Templars to sign the Constitution in 1787, John Rutledge being another.

Washington made it clear that he was content with Pinckney, when he wrote to Jay: "My confidence in our minister plenipotentiary in London continues undiminished. But a mission like this, while it corresponds with the solemnity of the occasion, will announce to the world a solicitude for a friendly adjustment of our complaints, and a reluctance to hostility." Pinckney was disappointed not to be offered Jay's task, but accepted the decision philosophically, writing to his brother: "I will cheerfully aid the objects of Mr. Jay's mission, and render his residence here agreeable. I ought to add that Mr. Randolph's letter to me and Mr. Jay's instructions are very friendly and calculated to prevent my feelings from being wounded by the measure."[23] Edmund Randolph, as related earlier, had been Washington's first Attorney General and had then become his second Secretary of State on the resignation of his cousin, Thomas Jefferson, from that post.

C.C.Pinckney made a good point about the Separation of Powers, when he wrote to his brother Thomas about Jay's diplomatic post: "I dare say the President is sincere in his declarations; but the appointment of a judge to that office has been deemed generally inconsistent with the spirit of our Constitution."[24]

During Jay's negotiations in London, he received hospitality from Pinckney, despite the recent loss of his wife, and also received some assistance from him. "The evidence in the official files supports the fact that the two men did work in close harmony."[25] Jay also had some help from the new young minister appointed to the Netherlands, John Quincy Adams, who had been asked to travel via London so that he could deliver some additional papers to Jay and Pinckney. He later returned from The Hague so that he could help with the treaty, by then in draft form. "London's greatest satisfaction, however, was the heady experience that came when Adams was called to share in talks between Jay and Thomas Pinckney, as the two older statesmen reviewed, article by article, the treaty Jay was concluding with the British government. These discussions, which frequently adjourned for dining and theater, greatly heartened young Adams. Only weeks before, he had complained of being an obscure attorney."[26]

The Jay Treaty was signed on 19 November 1794. It dealt with most of the outstanding disputes, but was howled down in the United States as being far too much in Britain's favor. When it turned out to be extremely unpopular, including with his friends, the Rutledges, and with his cousin Charles, Thomas Pinckney successfully distanced himself from it, by minimizing his own contributions. On 26 February 1796, he wrote to Jefferson, pointing out that while Jay had consulted with him at all stages, he personally had not been present at any of the meetings with the British Foreign Secretary.[27] In other words, "Don't blame me!" Pinckney was fortunate that all the brickbats being flung around were aimed at the Chief Justice. (Lawyers are not often that lucky.)

Pinckney's next stroke of luck was being asked to go to Madrid as a special envoy—and at a time when the Spanish government was anxious to improve relations with America. The Madrid authorities made it clear that they did not consider the two junior diplomats, William Carmichael and William Short, up to the task of concluding the important negotiations. Apart from other character flaws, Carmichael was a notorious alcoholic with the shakes, who ought to have been recalled much earlier.[28] The Spaniards were anxious to have a more senior minister designated, even though Short, who had been sent to assist the incompetent Carmichael, had made good progress. The task might well have been assigned to David Humphreys, the minister conveniently close by in Lisbon, but his hands were full, negotiating with the North African pirates preying on American ships in the Mediterranean, so he could not be spared.

Since his limited ambassadorial functions in London could be attended to by Deas, his secretary, Pinckney was dispatched to Madrid, leaving London in the spring of 1795. Bemis, the historian of both Jay's and Pinckney's Treaty (a name that he coined for the Treaty of San Lorenzo), described Pinckney's next stroke of good fortune. "He arrived in Madrid at the psychological moment, so opportune for gathering the laurels which might well have gone to the capable Short, but which by luck were to fall upon the brow of the elegant South Carolinian, who, through no fault of his own, crowded an able and faithful public servant off the stage of public notice." He added that Pinckney had more luck when bad weather held up a copy of Jay's Treaty, so that its terms were not known to the Spanish government, which would have resented them.[29] As a result, Pinckney found himself pushing against an open door, and obtained a favorable settlement with Spain, which included full rights over the Mississippi and resolved the southern frontier disputes.

The Treaty of San Lorenzo was acclaimed in the United States, in marked contrast to the reception of Jay's Treaty. Similarly, Pinckney was the hero of the hour, while Jay was perceived by many as the man who had sold out to Britain. Both extreme views were misguided: Pinckney had been confronted with a relatively easy task, while Jay had a far harder one, and had achieved as much as was reasonably possible.

Pinckney went back to London, but asked to be recalled and returned home in September 1796. The comment of his grandson, about his departure from England, may well be justified. "Many expressions of warm regard, both from Whigs and Tories, assured him that his dignified course during his mission had borne abundant fruit, and raised greatly the public estimation of his country."[30]

Pinckney recommended that his fellow Middle Templar, Deas, should be given the post of permanent secretary in London. The fact that shortly before coming to London, Deas had killed a man in a duel, probably did not count against him, as dueling was still considered by many to be acceptable. Henry and John Laurens each had more than one duel. Alexander Hamilton, who had acted as second to John Laurens in his famous duel with General Lee for insulting General Washington, was to be killed in a duel with Jefferson's Vice-President, Aaron Burr. As related earlier, Lloyd Dulany, a Maryland Middle Templar, was killed in a duel in London with a fellow loyalist. Even the sensible C.C.Pinckney took part in a duel, though he later tried to get the practice outlawed. However, Deas had made a number of ill-chosen and undiplomatic remarks while in England and was considered unsuitable for the London post for that reason.[31]

Once Pinckney had left Madrid, there was clearly a need for a senior American minister there, so Washington decided to switch Humphreys from neighboring Portugal, and to move John Quincy Adams from The Hague to Lisbon. Young Adams was all set to move, when his father became President and decided to send him to Berlin, as he regarded Prussia as more important than Portugal, and was well aware of his son's abilities. That left vacancies at Lisbon and The Hague, which were filled by the Middle Templars, William Loughton Smith and William Vans Murray.

Page Smith commented: "It might well be argued that the election of 1796 was the most important in our history. Washington's unanimous election to the Presidency in 1789 was, of course, a foregone conclusion, as was his re-election in 1792. Could the office of President devolve from the god-like Washington to an ordinary mortal and do this in a time of bitter factionalism?" One of the ordinary mortals whose name was put forward was Pinckney. Smith continued: "In a move to draw southern support away from Jefferson, the Federalists prevailed on Thomas Pinckney to run on the ticket with Adams. Pinckney's name on the ballot might also attract some votes in Pennsylvania and Maryland. With Thomas Pinckney, who was enjoying a modest fame as the author of an advantageous treaty with Spain, as Adams' running mate, the Republicans settled on Aaron Burr."[32]

The result was very close: Adams received seventy-one electoral votes, Jefferson sixty-eight and Pinckney a creditable fifty-nine. Under the rules of the Constitution, which applied until later amended, Jefferson, as runner-up, became the Vice-President of his main rival, Adams. Had a plot hatched by Alexander Hamilton succeeded, Pinckney might well have taken a crucial number of votes away from Adams. With ten more of Adams' votes, Pinckney would have been President; with seven, Vice-President. As it was, he received a consolation prize. When William Loughton Smith was appointed minister in Lisbon, Pinckney took over his Charleston seat in Congress, serving there as one of the best-qualified Representatives until 1801. Pinckney's elder brother, Charles Cotesworth, was a Vice-Presidential candidate in 1800 and a Presidential candidate in 1804 and 1808, but on none of those occasions did his share of the votes cast come near the number obtained by Thomas in 1796.

C.C. PINCKNEY AND WILLIAM VANS MURRAY IN PARIS AND THE HAGUE

As Thomas Pinckney was sailing home across the Atlantic after his successful mission to England and Spain, his brother was crossing in the opposite direction, heading for his unsuccessful—and unhappy—mission to France. Both Morris and Monroe had been criticized for their approach to the government in Paris ("Morris too hostile", "Monroe too friendly"), so Washington was anxious to appoint a neutral, dispassionate minister, who would be acceptable both at home and in France. The matter was of considerable importance, as there was a real danger of hostilities erupting between the two countries, despite the fact that they were still legally allied. C.C.Pinckney, who spoke French and knew something of the country, seemed the most appropriate choice. He had turned down offers of an appointment from the President before, despite his warm and friendly letters, in much the same vein as those he had written to Joseph Reed. For example, on 24 August 1795 Washington had written to C.C.: "It is unnecessary for me to repeat sentiments which you have so often heard me express; respecting my wishes to see you in the Administration of the general government; the sincerity of which you can have no doubt."[33] Finally, in 1796 Pinckney succumbed to his blandishments and accepted the President's offer of the challenging post in Paris.

Pinckney decided to take his nephew, Henry Rutledge, as his secretary. On 2 August 1796, Edward Rutledge wrote a letter to his son, pointing out the opportunities afforded by his appointment. He may well have recalled

William Vans Murray

his brother's long letter of advice when he was on his way to the Temple to study law. He listed the factors, including "the long and steady attachment of your uncle Pinckney towards you", which pointed to public service. He added: "It is under his direction, and his roof that you are to pursue and finish, I hope, your legal studies. A knowledge of the law will not of itself be sufficient. You must be logical, and eloquent, as well as learned; the first will enable you to reason clearly, the second will adorn your argument; each of these qualities will indeed enable you to do much good, for they are valuable, but when united, and united in a good cause, they become irresistible."[34]

C.C.Pinckney considered himself to be non-partisan, though a friend of France, but the Directory regarded him as tarred with the same brush as the unacceptable Federalists, Washington and Hamilton. "In the view of the French government, Pinckney's identification with the Federalist party was probably proved conclusively when his brother Thomas became John Adams' running mate in 1796."[35] As a result, the Directory refused to receive him until the United States government had made adequate reparation for a number of slights. One of the principal grievances was that the United States had entered into the Jay Treaty, which appeared to abrogate the existing treaties with France. There was something to be said for this French objection. One author has recently commented: "The true end of the war came in 1794, when to avoid a renewal of hostilities Chief Justice Jay negotiated a treaty with Britain that buried the French alliance of 1778."[36]

During Pinckney's early days in Paris no specific demands were made on the United States, so he was left in a state of limbo until ordered by the Directory to leave France. He left Paris in February 1797 and went to the Netherlands, by then the French puppet state of Batavia. He awaited instructions from home for nearly six months, conferring from time to time with John Quincy Adams, the minister there, and later with his replacement, William Vans Murray, who arrived in June. On his arrival at The Hague, Pinckney had been "completely bewildered" by the hostility shown by the

French. Young Adams explained that it was a case of transferred malice: they had shifted their anger to him from his brother Thomas, who had declined to disclose the terms of the Jay Treaty, when passing through Paris on his way to Spain.[37]

The newly elected President Adams was appalled to learn of the refusal of the Directory to receive Pinckney, and further alarmed by the news that it had, "in effect, launched an undeclared war on American shipping everywhere. The crisis had come to a head. Adams faced the threat of all-out war."[38] A number of hawks in America, such as Hamilton, wanted to go to war with France, but Adams was determined to try to avoid such a terrible step. He appointed two men to join Pinckney's mission: John Marshall, from Virginia, the future great Chief Justice, and Elbridge Gerry, a signer of the Declaration of Independence and future Vice-President—nowadays perhaps better remembered as the governor of Massachusetts who gave his name to "gerrymandering".

Murray assured Marshall about Pinckney: "You will find him a clear-sighted and honorable man, and of pleasing friendly manners." Incidentally, the mission to Europe may well have helped Marshall on his way to the Supreme Court. "John Marshall's acceptance of the position of special envoy to France marked his emergence as a national political leader. Before his appointment he had been content to remain in Richmond tending his burgeoning law practice. On his return from France he was admired by Federalists in every section of the country."[39] President John Adams made him Secretary of State in 1800 and Chief Justice of the United States in the following year, in succession to Oliver Ellsworth.

Once back in Paris, Pinckney, together with his two companions, found the situation much the same. A Swiss spokesman for the Directory and for Talleyrand, the new Foreign Minister, demanded compensation, or a "sweetener", of $250,000, together with a large loan. If they were not forthcoming, France would consider declaring war. Two further messengers made similar demands and threats. Pinckney's famous answer was, "No, no, not a sixpence." He and his colleagues reported back and Adams placed their correspondence before an indignant Congress on 3 April 1798. It was soon published, with the three blackmailers named as X, Y and Z—although it is usually only the victims of blackmail who are granted anonymity, and not the villains of the piece.

Gerry decided to stay in France, as a kind of hostage, as Talleyrand had claimed that his departure would lead to war, but Pinckney and Marshall returned home, to find preparations being made for an outbreak of hostilities. Washington had been appointed Commander-in-Chief once more and had then insisted on the ambitious Hamilton, his former aide, becoming Inspector-General. C.C.Pinckney was promoted to major-general and for the next two years help to prepare the army for a possible war with France. Incidentally, his brother Thomas, then in the House of Representatives, was not promoted to that rank until the 1812 War. Fortunately, neither Pinckney was ever required to fire a shot in anger after the end of the Revolutionary War. (One can exclude C.C. Pinckney's duel: though his shot may have been fired in anger, nobody had required him to fire it.) At the Constitutional Convention in 1787, when Gerry had proposed a limit on the numbers for a peacetime army, C.C.Pinckney had been one of the veterans who had successfully opposed such a provision. He had strongly believed that the way to deter a potential aggressor was to be prepared in peacetime. Having regard to what had happened to Gerry and him in Paris in 1798, Pinckney must have been delighted to put his theory into practice.

In November 1798 Washington traveled to Philadelphia to discuss with Hamilton and C.C.Pinckney the rebuilding of the military arm. The three generals "spent ten hours a day for six weeks huddled over lists of candidates for the new officers' corps. It quickly became clear that the Continental army would be the model for the new army and that previous service in the old army would be the chief criterion for inclusion in the new one." On his return journey home Pinckney, together with his wife, spent Christmas with Washington at Mount Vernon, and New Year's Day with Marshall in

Richmond.[40]

The heavyweights had failed to make any progress with the French; it was now the turn of the untried lightweight, William Vans Murray. He was born in Cambridge, Maryland in 1760 and in 1784 was admitted to the Middle Temple, where he became friendly with John Leeds Bozman, who later served as deputy Attorney General of Maryland. Murray regarded his own attendance at the Inn as almost a waste of time, so he clearly did not take full advantage of the opportunities that were afforded by contact with members of the profession and regular visits to the courts.[41]

Murray was one of the first students to attend after the war had been won, but he was nevertheless interested in politics, spurred on by a friendship that he formed in London with the bright and much traveled teenager, John Quincy Adams. It was a friendship that was to last for the rest of his life. Murray suffered from ill-health a great deal and when he died at the early age of forty-three, Adams wrote a generous obituary. One of the points that Adams made was that his friend and fellow-diplomat may not have wholly wasted his time while at the Middle Temple. "Here he became acquainted with, and enjoyed the society of several English gentlemen, then upon the same establishment, and who have since become very eminent characters in that nation, as statesmen and in the republic of letters as men of genius and science." Despite the temptations of city life, "he retained the firmness and resolution of devoting his time and attention to those objects, which were to mark the usefulness of his future life."[42]

Americans in London tended to meet at a few places in the city, prominent among them being the Carolina Coffee House in Birchin Lane, off Cornhill. However, they were also able to meet at the houses of American and English families. The hospitality shown by the Hanburys and the DeBerdts has been referred to earlier. Other meeting places included the homes of the first American consul in London, Joshua Johnson; of Benjamin Vaughan, Benjamin's Franklin's friend and the first compiler of his works; and of William Manning, the London mercantile associate of Henry

Laurens. Apart from hospitality and conversation, the students could there find the company of young women, as some small consolation for their absence from the potential brides back home. John Quincy Adams, as mentioned earlier, was to marry Johnson's daughter, Louisa, while John Laurens, like Vaughan, married one of Manning's daughters. Murray was especially welcome at Johnson's house as they were both from Maryland; he, too, met his future wife, Charlotte Hughens, in England, possibly there.

Young Adams and Murray could not agree on whether they had met at the home of Johnson or that of Vaughan. John Adams, who got to know Murray quite well, thought the two young men had first met in the Netherlands, when Murray was seeing something of Europe and called on the Adams family. Inspired by the three-volume *A Defence of the Constitutions of Government of the United States of America*, which John Adams wrote and had published in London in 1786 and 1787, the young Maryland law student wrote a booklet of six political sketches. It was also published in London in 1787 and dedicated to John Adams, the resident minister.

In the same year Murray returned home, without being called to the Bar in London, as his father had died—a not uncommon reason for a premature return to America. He was followed by Charlotte Hughens, who married him as soon as he was settled in the legal profession in Cambridge, Maryland. He was elected to the State legislature almost at once and then to Congress, where he served from 1791 to 1797. At the end of Washington's second term Murray campaigned for John Adams in the Presidential election. Hill, his biographer, made an interesting point about Murray and a fellow Middle Templar: "He might not have plunged so vigorously into a newspaper campaign in Adams' behalf had not William Loughton Smith, Adams' supposed defender, so badly bungled the job. Smith's 'Phocion' articles dwelt more on Jefferson's inadequacies than on Adams' merits." Murray did not know that Alexander Hamilton was plotting to rig the election so that Thomas Pinckney would be elected as the Federalist

President instead of Adams, but he appreciated the danger of such an outcome and worked hard to prevent it.[43]

Shortly before Adams became President, Washington appointed Murray as minister to The Hague, to replace John Quincy Adams. The friends were able to have a brief reunion in the Netherlands and thereafter kept up a regular correspondence between The Hague and Berlin. Despite his youth, Adams was becoming one of the most impressive diplomats of the infant United States, and his advice by letter must have been of considerable help to the new minister. As the United States had no minister in Paris, Murray proved a useful source of information about French affairs.

By the time that John Quincy Adams wrote Murray's obituary, he was an experienced diplomat and beginning to lay the foundations of United States foreign policy, so that his summary of his friend's achievements may be taken as accurate. "He arrived at The Hague at a very critical period of affairs. The misunderstandings and disputes between the United States and France were festering to a rupture. When the French government, listening to wiser suggestions than those which had almost precipitated them into a war with America, became sensible that the true interest of both nations dictated peace and reconciliation, their first step was to send to the Hague a negotiator calculated by his personal character, by his patriotism as a Frenchman, and by his friendly disposition towards the Americans, to second the congenial views and intentions of the American minister at that place. The first advances towards a restoration of harmony were thus made, by conferences between William Murray and [Louis-André] Pichou, then chargé d'affaires of France at The Hague; these led to certain propositions for a renewal of direct negotiations, made by France, which Mr. Murray transmitted to his government."

In fact, Murray very sensibly did *not* pass the message on to the Secretary of State, but communicated directly with President Adams, because he appreciated the importance of the French approach and knew John Adams well enough not to fear a rebuke for his shortcut. It was also on Murray's initiative that the Dutch offered to mediate—an idea that appealed to the French. Thomas Boylston Adams, who had been acting as his brother's secretary in Berlin, returned home in January 1799 and told his father that both John Quincy and Murray were convinced that the attitude of the French had changed for the better. He stressed that his brother accepted Murray's judgments without reservation.[44]

On 18 February 1799, John Adams took, what McCullough called, "the most decisive action of his presidency", adding that "of all the brave acts of his career, one brief message sent to the United States Senate was perhaps the bravest."[45] That praise was perhaps a little extravagant, as Adams knew his candidate and his talents personally and was helped by knowing of John Quincy's respect for him. The message began: "Always disposed and ready to embrace every plausible appearance of probability of preserving or restoring tranquillity, I nominate William Vans Murray, our minister resident at The Hague, to be minister plenipotentiary of the United States to the French Republic."

There was a great deal of opposition to the appointment of such a junior man as minister, but Adams insisted that he was best man for the job. However, he was prepared to compromise and, once more, to see two others appointed to join the selected minister. This time the two additional envoys were the Chief Justice of the United States, Oliver Ellsworth, from Connecticut (Jay having resigned the office on being elected Governor of New York), and Governor William Davie of North Carolina. Ellsworth had obtained the post of Chief Justice after the Senate had declined to confirm Washington's choice of John Rutledge, because of a very intemperate public attack he had made on the Jay Treaty.[46] The two additional representatives eventually set sail on 15 November, knowing that Talleyrand had promised that the French government would receive them.

They were joined in Paris by Murray, and their mission was received by Napoleon Bonaparte, who was keen to see an end to the Quasi War, partly because Admiral Horatio Nelson's ships had done so much damage to his navy at the battle of the Nile.[47] The three Americans found that they were able to work together effectively. The outcome of their efforts was the Convention of Mortefontaine, signed on 30 September 1800, averting war between France and the United States for all time. The Secretary of State by then was John Marshall, who must have been gratified to see a successful conclusion to the lengthy negotiations, in which he, like C.C.Pinckney and others, had played a frustrating and exasperating part.

President Jefferson decided that there was no need any longer for a minister in The Hague, so Murray was recalled in the following year and not replaced until 1814. After returning to Maryland, Murray wrote to John Quincy: "We had a long passage from Rotterdam—eleven weeks. Driven in by head winds to Falmouth I had the rare luck and consolation of meeting a brother in disgrace, my friend Smith from Lisbon, who had arrived an hour before in the Lisbon packet."[48] There was no disgrace, as Murray must have appreciated: the new President was recalling ministers appointed by his predecessors and closing both the Dutch and the Portuguese mission to save costs. Murray had been a successful diplomat at a difficult time, as John Quincy Adams later acknowledged.

WILLIAM LOUGHTON SMITH AND CHARLES PINCKNEY IN IBERIA

The diplomatic careers of William Loughton Smith and Charles Pinckney can be dealt with quite shortly as, fortunately, unlike their colleagues who have already been discussed, neither of them was required to try and prevent a war between the United States and the country to which he was dispatched: Portugal and Spain respectively.[49]

Smith, like the Pinckney brothers before him, spent many years abroad for his education, including a period at the Middle Temple. The difference between them was that his fourteen-year absence, from early 1770 to the end of 1783, meant that he missed the whole of the war, returning home only at the age of twenty-five. It also meant that he was one of the few Americans, who attended the Inn during the war.

Smith's father died shortly after his departure for England at the age of eleven, but he was fortunate enough to have Henry Laurens, a family friend, to keep an eye on him in London for a while—Laurens, the mainstay of the South Carolinian support network at the time. Smith had started at the small Islington school of Revd. Richard Clarke, who had moved from South Carolina. After a few months he was joined there by the three Laurens boys, John, Henry, Jr., and James, but it soon became clear to John Laurens and his father that Clarke had lost his ability to provide a sound education. Henry Laurens moved his elder two boys to a school in Geneva and later arranged for Smith to attend there also.[50] They were joined in Geneva by Gabriel (Gay) Manigault, who had been brought over from South Carolina by James Laurens, Henry's brother.

John Laurens was the first of the group of boys at school in Geneva to come to the Middle Temple and finally left the Inn in January 1777 to join in the war, becoming a member of General Washington's family of aides later that year. In the summer Manigault arrived in London to start studying at Lincoln's Inn. "Manigault took lodgings at the Carolina Coffee House, but he got his news that summer at the home of his fellow Carolinian Ralph Izard, which was a bee-hive of comings and goings."[51] Izard, a close associate of Arthur Lee, was soon to move to Paris to join him as a commissioner, so that news center closed down. Smith left Geneva at the end of 1778, visiting Franklin, Adams and Lee in Paris on the way to London, where he joined both Gay Manigault and the Middle Temple in January 1779, at the age of twenty.

On 30 September 1780 Smith wrote to Manigault, who had returned home just in time for the siege of Charleston: "I commenced my law campaign last November—as ignorant of the technical part of the law as any country clown, and provided with a most insignificant quantity of the theoretical part of it. I launched forth, resolved to seize upon all I could; but must say, with truth, that for the first term I understood almost as little of what was going on as the gaping crowd, who go to Westminster Hall for the sake of seeing two men in great wigs and black gowns abuse one another." Fortunately, by the third term, "The divine light of the law began to shine upon me with its benign rays, and I thanked myself for having persevered long enough to get over the most perplexing part of it." He was humble enough to add: "All I have learnt only serves to convince me that I still know but very little, particularly for a person who intends to make it a profession and not a matter of curiosity."[52]

Smith attended many trials and filled six notebooks as a record. One of the trials he was fortunate to be able to attend was that of Lord George Gordon, who was acquitted (shortly before 6 a.m. on 6 February 1781) of any involvement in the riots to which has name had been attached. Lord Campbell, a later Chief Justice and Lord Chancellor, wrote of Gordon, "Luckily for him, he was defended by an advocate who on this occasion gave full proof of those wonderful powers which afterwards rendered his name so illustrious."[53] Smith could not have heard a better advocate in action than the great Thomas Erskine, whose final speech for the defense must have been something to remember and to inspire any lawyer or law student present.

At the end of 1782, having gone on circuit a few times, Smith decided to return home. It was not until the November of 1783 that he got there, his being shipwrecked off the coast of England providing only a partial explanation for the time he took. He had taken his time with his studies and had displayed little zeal to get involved in the war back home. When he was eventually elected to Congress in 1789, his eligibility to take his seat as a qualified United States national was questioned by David Ramsay, because of his lengthy absence. The statement he made, successfully, to the House of Representatives on 22 May gave an explanation of sorts, but it does not make very convincing reading.[54] However, we need not pursue that matter here.

Once home, the leisurely student turned into a hard-working, serious politician. In 1786 he married Charlotte, the daughter of Ralph Izard. When the new Constitution came into force, Izard became one of South Carolina's two United States Senators, and Smith one of the first Congressmen, serving as such from 1789 to 1797. (Izard's fellow Senator was Pierce Butler, one of the four South Carolina delegates to the Constitutional Convention, and the only member of the delegation who was not a Middle Templar.) Izard and his son-in-law were able to work together in the Federalist interest and Smith became a supporter of Alexander Hamilton, the Secretary of the Treasury. Within a year of arriving in Congress, Smith "had become a figure of national prominence—a companion of Washington and the confidant of northern Federalist leaders."[55] In August 1790, Washington invited Smith to join him on a visit to Rhode Island.

The Presidential party was made up of a distinguished cross-section of government, and included Thomas Jefferson, then still Secretary of State, Justice John Blair of the Supreme Court and Colonel David Humphreys, Washington's long-serving aide, who had worked for Jefferson in Paris. Smith was probably not aware of their plan, but Washington and Jefferson were just about to send Humphreys to Europe to establish the post that Smith was to get in due course as his successor.

In 1790 it had become clear to Washington that Portugal was willing to enter into closer relations with the United States and that it might be possible to exchange diplomatic representatives. In August, he decided to send Humphreys as a secret agent to take soundings in Europe, in particular, in England, Portugal and Spain. He was to assess the danger of war between Spain and Great Britain over the Nootka Sound dispute, which carried with it the risk that France might join in on Spain's side. After a secret visit to England, he was to go on to Portugal to discuss the appropriate rank for the ministers to be exchanged.

On 11 August 1790 Jefferson sent Humphreys his instructions, which included the following in respect of his time in England: "When there you will be pleased to deliver to Mr. [Gouverneur] Morris and to Mr. [Joshua] Johnson the letters and papers you will have in charge for them; to communicate from thence any interesting public intelligence you may be able to obtain, and then to take as early passage as possible to Lisbon." Humphreys traveled incognito and made discreet inquiries in London. One calling place was the Piccadilly bookshop that was known to Humphreys, from his days as Jefferson's secretary in Paris, as being a valuable information center. It was also well known as such to Henry Laurens, John and John Quincy Adams, and the Secretary of State himself, whose only book, *Notes on the State of Virginia*, had been published there in 1787. On 20 October Humphreys reported to Jefferson about the risk of war over the Nootka Sound: "The business of the Cabinet has at least been conducted with great secrecy, during the course of the whole affair. Stockdale, the political bookseller, however informed me today, that he had just been assured by a person very high in office, that no war would happen."[56] That information fortunately turned out to be true.

Humphreys left England for Portugal, and on 18 February 1791, Washington informed the Senate of his mission, adding: "It happened, however, that previous to his arrival at Lisbon, the Queen had appointed a minister resident to the United States. I have, therefore, nominated David Humphreys minister resident from the United States to Her Most Faithful Majesty the Queen of Portugal." The Senate consented, so Humphreys had the honor of being the first minister to be appointed to represent the United States in Portugal. As discussed earlier, after Thomas Pinckney's departure from Spain, on the successful completion of his mission, Washington sent Humphreys to fill the important post in Madrid.

The vacancy then created in Lisbon was filled in 1797,when the newly elected President Adams appointed the reliable Federalist Congressman, William Loughton Smith, as Humphreys' successor. Apart from other points in his favor, he had bravely supported the Jay Treaty in South Carolina, despite the great hostility to it shown by many of his friends. Furthermore, in his eight years in the House of Representatives, "he had successfully led the Federalist forces in a long fight for the *rapprochement* with Great

Britain, which would endure for a decade."[57]

The new minister's task was not an onerous one: war between Portugal and the United States was not considered to be a danger. Smith found that, as well as having their long-standing treaty of alliance with Britain, the Portuguese were surprisingly close to their allies, with many naval, commercial and personal links. He personally continued to favor the development of better relations with London. He was not the only American to see the benefit of the British navy defeating that of Napoleon, while Britain adopted a friendly posture toward the United States, at a time when the fleet of the United States was being built up, almost from scratch.

Smith enjoyed his life in Portugal and the opportunities for travel that it afforded, but he became increasingly restive and requested a transfer to another capital—which never materialized. As minister in Lisbon, Smith was required to deal with the problem of the Barbary pirates, whose exit into the Atlantic was inhibited, to some degree, by the Portuguese navy, thus adding to their menace in the Mediterranean. After a while he suggested that the problem could be much better dealt with by his colleague in Madrid, a point that may have contributed to President Jefferson's decision to close the Lisbon embassy at the same time as recalling Smith. After his return home, Smith made three unsuccessful attempts to get back into Congress.

The new President also recalled David Humphreys from Spain. However, Jefferson appreciated that, while the Netherlands and Portugal could be left without a resident United States minister, Spain could not be neglected in the same way. Charles Pinckney III was a United States Senator from 1798 until 1801, when Jefferson rewarded him for his support—and for his abandonment of the Federalist cause—with the post in Madrid, where there was still important work to be done. The three major tasks for Pinckney were to get Spanish acceptance of the Louisiana Purchase from France; to settle all outstanding claims of the United States; and to attempt to win Florida from Spain. He succeeded with the first two, but his country had to wait for another fifteen years before acquiring Florida.[58]

Pinckney served in Spain from 1801 to 1805. In the year after his return he was elected for a fourth term as Governor of South Carolina, and in 1818 as a Representative in the United States Congress—an unusual move for a man who had been both an ambassador and a Senator. Bradford has suggested that he was driven on by his wish to make up for his father's defection to the British. Because of that, he "spent the remainder of his life being more visibly loyal to South Carolina, the nation, and the values of his class than anyone could rightfully expect him to be, in order to live down the shame of his father's public disgrace."[59] All three of the younger Pinckneys could certainly look back with justifiable pride on their own achievements on behalf of their country and State, not least of which were their services abroad.

Ralph Izard deserves a slightly frivolous footnote. Although not a member of the Middle Temple himself, he may almost be considered an honorary member. We have seen that two of his daughters became the wives of two diplomatic Middle Templars: Anne married William Allen Deas, while Charlotte married William Loughton Smith. After the war Izard sent his son Henry to study at the Middle Temple. Henry had two wives: the first was a daughter of Arthur Middleton, one of the Middle Temple signers of the Declaration of Independence, the second was a cousin, the daughter of Smith and his wife, Charlotte Izard. Ralph Izard's daughter Margaret married Gabriel (Gay) Manigault, who was a member of Lincoln's Inn, but whose brother Joseph, as we have seen, joined the Inn where their father Peter had been in chambers, the Middle Temple.

After Izard was appointed a commissioner to the Court of Tuscany (which declined to receive him), John Julius Pringle, from South Carolina, who had been attending the Inn as a student, joined him in Paris as his secretary. After the war Pringle became Speaker of the Assembly and Attorney General of their home State, but turned down Jefferson's offer of the post of Attorney General of the United States.

History has a habit of playing a dirty trick on some people. We have mentioned already that Elbridge Gerry is not remembered for his good deeds, but for the term "gerrymandering". Similarly, although Izard could claim to have worked for his country at home and abroad for many years, and to have been a member of the first Senate of the United States, he is remembered nowadays, if at all, for debunking John Adams, when he was suggesting a pompous title for the President of the new country. It was Izard who awarded Adams the grand title of "His Rotundity".

CONCLUSION

The patient reader who has lasted the course may well be saying to himself or herself: I accept that some of the Americans who contributed significantly to the success of the Revolution were lawyers who had received a part of their overall education at the Middle Temple. However, there were many more contributors, including lawyers such as John Adams, Thomas Jefferson and John Jay, who had no direct link whatsoever with the Inn. Such links as those three lawyers had were only tenuous ones: they will have learned their law from judgments and commentaries written in England by a number of first class lawyers, of whom perhaps a quarter were members of the Middle Temple, rather than one of the other three Inns of Court. It is possible that, say, John Dickinson and John Rutledge, would have been equally as effective *without* their years at the Inn. After all, roughly half the delegates attending the Constitutional Convention with them in 1787 were lawyers, but only seven were members of the Middle Temple—and one of those had never attended it because of the outbreak of hostilities. The Constitution, it may be argued, would surely have read exactly the same if none of those seven men had ever been to London.

It must be conceded by the writers that those are fair points. Dickinson might have written his Farmer's Letters in identical wording even if he had not attended the Inn in London, but had given over the same years to further study of law and history in Pennsylvania. However, when one reads the observations of Dickinson himself, coupled with the comments of others on his work, it seems likely that his London years added an extra dimension to his legal, historical and political education—one that could not have been added had he remained at home. Even if he could have bought or borrowed all the books to which he had access in London, in the Middle Temple Library and elsewhere, he would have missed the opportunity of hearing a wide range of advocates arguing cases in Westminster Hall and of listening to debates in the adjoining Houses of Parliament in the same Palace.

The mere fact that John Rutledge was prepared to finance his brothers so that they could follow him to the Middle Temple, does not prove that he regarded the experience as a crucial one. He may merely have felt that they were entitled to the same chances that he had been given, even if the trip was scarcely worth the effort and the money. On the other hand, when one reads the letter of advice his sent to his brother Edward, it is clear that John appreciated that a period of time at the Inn could be extremely beneficial. Edward might have contributed significantly to the Continental Congress even without his London "polish", but it seems likely that he was able to make some of his contributions because he had more than a legal training confined to a Charleston office and the local courts.

Chief Justice Allen sent two of his four sons to follow him to the Inn. He seems to have wasted much of his own time there as a young man, but he saw enough during his long stay to impress him with the fact that more was to be obtained there than in Philadelphia. In that city he may well have thought that the lawyers who had attended the Middle Temple, such as

Benjamin Chew, were better equipped than some of their colleagues who had not done so. In any event, although Allen was a very rich man, he did not like spending money, and is unlikely to have sent those two sons to London merely so that they could enjoy the city's theaters. He was apparently satisfied that even a good legal education with a leading lawyer at home, could be usefully supplemented in London. Chew, his successor as Chief Justice, who was an excellent lawyer, sent his own son to the Inn and encouraged a nephew, Edward Tilghman, to do so as well. If he had merely wanted them to learn to stand on their own feet, he could have advised them to go to Charleston or New York. That Chief Justice must be assumed to have had good reason for recommending an attendance at his own Inn, which could only be reached by crossing the dangerous Atlantic.

What made men like the Pinckney brothers such good contributors to the overall success of the Revolution? To start with, they were clearly lucky with their genes: their father had reached the top of the legal ladder in South Carolina and their mother was an unusually enterprising woman, who earned the respect of President Washington and others. Their education at Westminster School, followed by Oxford, will have given them the ability to tackle various problems as they arose, whether of a political or military nature. Had they not attended the Inn at all, the Pinckneys would almost certainly have been prominent figures in the tumultuous years which followed on the conclusion of their pre-law education. However, when one reads C.C.Pinckney's letter to his general, quoted earlier, about the danger to civil liberties from the projected toughening up of the local militia law, it is apparent that he saw the wider issues more clearly than the local legislators, some of whom were lawyers trained only in South Carolina.

The writers do not wish to overstate the point, but while they must concede that many of the splendid revolutionaries discussed would have behaved in an exemplary manner during the troubled years in any event, they are certain that their total contribution was the more effective because of what they had learned in London while attending the Middle Temple.

Endnotes

Chapter 1

1. Baker, 3.

2. Macassey, 11.

3. Beck, 28.

4. *The Middle Templar*: Wood, 2006, 3; Whitelaw, 2005, 45.

5. Macassey, 15, 16.

6. Billings, 155.

7. Howard, 4.

8. Beck, 25n.

9. Burnett, 34.

10. Howard, 128.

11. Tilghman was not yet a Middle Templar; he only went to London to "polish" his legal skills in 1772.

12. Weslager, 11.

13. Weslager, 127n, 128n.

14. Weslager, 135n.

15. Weslager, 140.

16. Coleman, 62-66.

17. Stockdale, chs. 1 and 2.

18. Stockdale, 163.

19. Smith, Jean E., 78, 108.

20. Burnett, 38.

21. Jensen, 74.

22. Jensen, 82, n.15; Bonwick, 98.

23. Burnett, 164.

24. Burnett, 181.

25. Kelley, 764.

26. Hamer, 11: 225; 8: 44. The reference to Westminster is of interest. Henry Laurens had lived there for a considerable time, at the house of Robert Deans in Fludyer Street, which was next to Downing Street until built over.

27. Peters, 259, 261.

28. Holland, 25, n.83.

29. Hamer, 13: 223, 413.

30. Burnett, 409.

31. Fitzpatrick, 21: 439.

32. Morgan, 267.

33. As Ramsay was acting as President, he was exempted from committee duties and so was able devote himself, with the help of the limited records, to his historical research.

34. Burnett, 213.

35. Coleman, 150.

36. Morton, 6.

37. Bethea, 23. For this Pinckney generally, see also Matthews, Marly.

38. Bethea, 26, n.23.

39. Burnett, 668.

40. Warren, 40.

41. Kirk, Russell, in his Foreword to Bradford, at xiii.

42. Barry, 335.

43. Bowen, 79.

44. Bradford, xvi.

45. Bradford, 202.

46. Bethea, 13n, 14; Morton, 149n.

47. Boyd, 12: 440.

48. There was another reason for the venue to be considered appropriate. As will be seen in ch. 3, another Middle Templar, William Allen, was largely responsible for the construction of the State House, where the Constitution was drafted.

Chapter 2

1. Holdsworth, 6: 489; 12: 78.

2. See pp. 172, 136 and 192.

3. Burd, 45.

4. George, 266.

5. Temple Bar, designed by Christopher Wren, was removed in 1878 because it obstructed the traffic in the Strand and Fleet Street, which met at that point. It was only recently returned to London from Hertfordshire. As there was still no room for it immediately outside the Temple, it was re-erected in the precincts of Wren's St. Paul's Cathedral, the work being started in 2003, when the Lord Mayor of London was a practicing barrister and Bencher of the Middle Temple, Gavyn Arthur.

6. Canady, 203.

7. Duman, 87.

8. Teignmouth, 1: 192.

9. Webber, 31: 172. Many Americans landed at western ports, such as Bristol or Falmouth, rather than sail on to London. There were two principal reasons: one was that the first dry land was very attractive after several weeks of seasickness; the other that adverse winds could make sailing to London very time-consuming.

10. Massey, 46.

11. Webber, 31: 175, 176.

12. Webber, 31: 182. The many references by students and other eighteenth-century American visitors to different theaters are interesting, especially as they are still attracting their descendants to London.

13. Webber, 31: 281.

14. SCHM, 15: 123. For their problems, see below, p. 193.

15. SCHM, 15: 121.

16. Webber, 32: 51. Gabriel Manigault also paid for Peter to have his portrait painted by Allan Ramsay, later to be one of the King's two favourite painters, the other being the American, Benjamin West. For the Chief Justice's visit, see ch.6.

17. In other words, Manigault's chambers were on the English "first floor" and American "second". The two sets of chambers on the same floor, on either side of the landing, were differentiated by the Inn by being called north, south, east or west as appropriate, but tenants rarely bothered to mention more than the floor level when giving their address. Both 2 and 3 Brick Court were demolished by a bomb in May 1941 and never rebuilt.

18. Webber, 32: 54. Mrs. Motte was the wife of Jacob Motte, who like Gabriel Manigault, was a Treasurer of the province and able to make a fortune by using the public's money to run a private banking business. Rogers, 1980, 20.

19. Pottle, 257.

20. Webber, 31: 191. Sally's shrine was probably in a little shop in Essex Court, but possibly in one at the top of Middle Temple Lane.

21. Webber, 32: 56. For Freeman, see ch. 6, note 32.

22. Webber, 31: 1.

23. Webber, 33: 276. It is not clear which Shubrick was referred to, but he was clearly a member of the distinguished South Carolina family of that name, which included the brothers Richard and Thomas Shubrick, admitted to the Inn in October 1768 and June 1773 respectively.

24. Webber, 33: 277. The guinea was £1 (or 20 shillings) plus one extra shilling, that is, 21 shillings in all. The professions generally charged in guineas rather than pounds, and so managed to wrest an extra five per cent from each client. Each shilling was made up of 12 pence, so Manigault earned £2.12.6. on his first case. (Strange to relate, some Englishmen still bemoan the introduction of the simple decimal pound.)

25. Webber, 33: 59.

26. Webber, 33: 148. Each set of chambers had two front doors. The outer one was normally shut at night and when nobody was in. It could also be closed if one wanted to keep out acquaintances such as Drayton: that practice was sometimes known as "sporting one's oak". Manigault's allowance was enough for him to keep a servant, so he did not need to resort to it.

27. Tyler, 1:427. The coif was the white cap worn by the senior lawyers known as serjeants-at-law.

28. Pinckney, Elise, 78.

29. Hancock, 128. Oswald later initiated the peace negotiations with Franklin in Paris, when he brought him letters from Henry Laurens and Lord Shelburne.

30. Canady, 190.

31. Hamer, 9: 117, 146, 151.

32. Boyd, 8: 636.

33. SCHM, 64: 5.

34. SCHM, 64: 11.

35. See generally, Jacobson.

36. Colbourn, 249.

37. Colbourn, 273.

38. Colbourn, 254.

39. Colbourn, 257.

40. Colbourn, 261, 264.

41. Colbourn, 267, emphasis provided, as those words, while summing up a basic obligation of the experienced practitioner in any profession, are still particularly apt for lawyers.

42. Colbourn, 269.

43. Colbourn, 273. For Randolph's mission to London, see below, p.158.

44. Colbourn, 280.

45. Colbourn, 420.

46. One of the authors can empathize with Dickinson, as he suffered from back and shoulder ache after serving as a judge for some time, writing a full note in each case. His judicial colleagues at one court center maintained that they been helped by the same osteopath, so he made an appointment to see him. The osteopath's speedy diagnosis was alarming: "You're crooked, twisted and bent, just like the rest of them."

47. Scull, 32.

48. Stillé, 81; Tyler, 1: 234.

49. Labaree, 37: 472.

50. Kelley, 610.

51. Klein, 59, 73.

52. Stahr, 29.

53. Tyler, 2: 18.

Chapter 3

1. Botein, 141.

2. Entry for Allen in *ANB* by Norman S. Cohen. Somewhat surprisingly, there has to date been no biography of Allen, save Cohen's useful unpublished Ph.D. thesis.

3. Harper, 168. Lafayette was taken there by Henry Laurens, whose son John had left the Middle Temple at the beginning of the year, and had just joined Washington's staff, together with the French volunteer.

4. Labaree, 3: 221.

5. Cohen , 1968, 306.

6. Cohen, Ph.D. thesis, 161.

7. Jones, 65.

8. Jones, 108

9. Franklin, 134.

10. Burd, 14.

11. Labaree, 6: 23n.

12. Burd, 23.

13. Wright, 84.

14. Burd, 24, 26.

15. Wright, 102.

16. Wright, 140.

17. Middlekauf, 102.

18. Isaacson, 49.

19. Bridenbaugh, 179.

20. Alberts, 78.

21. Burd, 41.

22. Alberts, 40.

23. Burd, 45.

24. Burd, 48.

25. Burd, 52, 55.

26. Kimball and Quinn, 207. Jefferson was to stay in Golden Square when visiting John Adams in 1786.

27. Kimball and Quinn, 210.

28. Alberts, 61.

29. Burd, 56

30. Kimball and Quinn, 216.

31. Konkle, 127n.
32. Kimball and Quinn, 225.
33. Burd, 59
34. Isaacson, 216.
35. Labaree, 12: 301, spelling drastically edited. It may have been young William Allen rather than James who was involved. Cohen, Ph.D. thesis, 293.
36. Labaree, 12: 373. Galloway was an excellent lawyer, but must have been wrong about Allen's oath. Neither author can recall his own judicial oath prohibiting "sneaking to see".
37. Labaree, 13: 295, 499.
38. Kelley, 611.
39. Reed, William B., 1853, 179.
40. Allen, James. Dates of diary entries given instead of page numbers.
41. Graydon, 107.
42. Deas, 1: 25.
43. Reed, William B., 1847, 1: 243; Graydon, 127.
44. Young, 292.
45. Smith, Billy, 255.
46. Graydon, 146.
47. Cohen , Ph.D. thesis, 171.
48. For Chew's House during the battle of Germantown, see p. 107.
49. Van Doren, 718.
50. Boyd, 15: 615; Stockdale, 162. The letter is of further interest as it led ultimately to Stockdale publishing Jefferson's only book, *Notes on the State of Virginia*, in 1787.
51. Skemp, 110.
52. Einstein, 372, 380. Trumbull's series of historical paintings show many of the men we mention. Another American painter to study with West during the war was John Singleton Copley, whose son, born in Massachusetts, had the same name. He served as Lord Chancellor three times, as Lord Lyndhurst.
53. Priestley, 77.

Chapter 4

1. Konkle, Burton A., *Benjamin Chew 1722-1810*, Philadelphia: U. of Pennsylvania P., 1932, 36. We have relied heavily on this work, as it has no rival.
2. Entry for Chew in *ANB* by Wroth, L. Kinvin.
3. Labaree, 3: 13
4. Konkle, 81.

5. Kelley, 420.

6. Konkle, 39.

7. Konkle, 118.

8. Konkle, 129.

9. Middlekauff, 101.

10. Rowe, 121.

11. Kelley, 753

12. Coleman, 219.

13. Kimball and Quinn, 220.

14. Reed, Henry, 384. The English Cliveden was known in the twentieth century as the Astor House, and notorious as the meeting place of John Profumo (then Secretary of State for War), the Soviet naval attaché, and call-girl Christine Keeler. That meeting led to the kind of scandal with which the sons of George III were very familiar.

15. Ellis, 104. We have made no attempt to make a list of the names of Middle Templars and the battles in which they participated, but perhaps a legal/military historian may do so one day.

16. Hamer, 12: 244, 272.

17. Whiteley, 60.

18. Smith, Paul H., 9: 672.

19. Coleman, 234.

20. Konkle, 217.

21. Roche, 11.

22. This Garden Court should not be confused with the present one of that name, opposite the other end of the Hall.

23. Reed, William B., 1853, 42.

24. Reed, William B., 1853, 45, 29.

25. Reed, William B., 1847, 1: 30.

26. Reed, Henry, 224, 226.

27. Reed, William B., 1847, 1: 32.

28. Reed, William B., 1853, 69.

29. Reed, William B., 1853, 76, 100; Roche, 25.

30. Reed, William B., 1853, 103, 115.

31. Reed, Henry, 230.

32. Reed, William B., 1853, 1: 85. For Quincy's mission, see, *Mass. Hist. Society Procs.*, 1916-17, 50: 433.

33. Reed, William B., 1847, 1: 43; Sosin, 149.

34. Reed, William B., 1853, 170, 172.

35. Reed, William B., 1847, 1: 57.

36. Reed, Henry, 248; Stillé, 107.

37. Reed, William B., 1847, 1: 78.

38. Oliver, 1: 7.

39. Jones, 96.

40. Reed, William B. 1853, 239.

41. Ellis, 79.

42. Reed, William B., 1847, 1: 130, 145.

43. Butterfield, *Diary*, 2: 131.

44. Reed, Henry, 343.

45. Whiteley, 34.

46. Ellis, 79.

47. Reed, Henry, 349, emphasis provided.

48. Reed, Henry, 357.

49. Boatner, 1007.

50. Goodman, 123.

51. By a strange coincidence, within hours of writing this passage exactly as printed, the writer of this section found that Reed had been criticized in the press in 1782, not for his ambition but for his military conduct. That latter-day critic, thought by Reed to be General John Cadwalader, but probably Benjamin Rush, chose to sign himself "Brutus". Boatner, 926.

52. Reed, William B., 1847, 1: 348.

53. Shreve, 94.

54. Reed, William B., 1847, 1: 48; Nash, 96.

55. For the Lee incident and John Laurens generally, see Massey. For an account blaming Washington for the debacle, see, Ferling, 195.

56. Reed, William B., 1847, 2: 39; Bradford, 86.

57. Coleman, in his excellent biography (p.34), concludes that McKean qualified at the Middle Temple in an unconventional manner, without attendance, but this would seem to be an error - possibly caused by a confusion of admission to mere student membership, with later admission to the Bar and to practice.

58. Coleman, 33, 42.

59. Graydon, 117.

60. Coleman, 157, 176.

61. Stillé, 173.

62. Morton, 262.

63. Ryerson, 265.

64. Jacobson, 122. The lengthy *Vindication*, which Dickinson wrote to explain his actions, is to be found as an appendix in Stillé, 365-414.

65. Bradford, 88.

66. Rowe, 119, 132.

67. Rowe, 232.

68. Jones, 195. The New Inn exercises were probably concerned with Chancery problems.

69. Walker, 31.

70. Rowe, 254.

71. Tilghman, 17.

Chapter 5

1. We should like to express our indebtedness to two works: Nagel, Paul C., *The Lees of Virginia – Seven Generations of an American Family*, Oxford U.P., 1990; and Reardon, John J., *Peyton Randolph 1721-1755*, Durham: Carolina Academic Press, 1982.

2. Nagel, 1990, chap.5.

3. Nagel, 1990, 114.

4. Potts, 15-22.

5. Lee, 1: 265.

6. Ballagh, 1: 10.

7. Lee, 1: 17.

8. Lee, 1: 244; Ballagh, 1: 29.

9. Lee, 1: 12.

10. Nagel, 1990, 86.

11. Lee, 1: 245.

12. Lee, 1: 199.

13. Call, 234.

14. Lee, 2: 298.

15. Lee, 1: 157.

16. Middle Temple, 3/BAL/2; BOX 27, Bundle 6, no.5. Incidentally, the Inn does not have plaques to commemorate famous earlier tenants, as its buildings would be smothered by them.

17. Riggs, 2. "On the Thames" was a correct description of the location before the river was narrowed by embankments.

18. Boatner, 698.

19. Massey, 1.

20. Judah Benjamin, the Confederate Attorney General, settled in London after the war and practiced for seventeen years from chambers in the Middle Temple's Lamb Building, which adjoined the Temple Church until destroyed by a bomb in 1941.

21. Higginbotham, 297.

22. Tyler, 245.
23. Ballagh, 1: 151. For a sound appraisal of the actual support in England, see Sainsbury.
24. Lee, 1: 211.
25. Deas, 1: 117.
26. Stockdale, 80.
27. Hamer, 8: xiii; Potts, 122. William Wragge, a Middle Templar in the legislature, opposed the gift, while Peter Manigault supported it.
28. Hamer, 9: 291.
29. Moreton and Spinelli, 50n.
30. Moreton and Spinelli, 34.
31. Lee, 1: 52.
32. Lee, 1: 54.
33. Ballagh, 1: 218, 222.
34. Lee, 1: 62.
35. Riggs, title.
36. Nagel, 1990, 97.
37. Reardon, 5, 11.
38. Campbell, 1868, 6: 308. Tradition has it that one judge, who liked his port and brandy, attributed his own gout to having "a sedimentary occupation".
39. Reardon, 17.
40. Reardon, 30.
41. Selby, xi.
42. Eckenrode, 99.
43. Peterson, 15.
44. Eckenrode, 86.
45. Selby, 47.
46. Boyd, 1:241.
47. Randolph, 218.
48. Jones, 89.

Chapter 6

1. We must acknowledge the assistance derived from Haw, James, *John and Edward Rutledge of South Carolina*, Athens: U. of Georgia P., 1997 and Zahniser, Marvin R.,1967; *Charles Cotesworth Pinckney: Founding Father*, Chapel Hill: U. of North Carolina P., 1967.
2. Adams, Revd. J., 50.
3. Butterfield, *Diary*, 2: 121.
4. Middle Temple, 7/BUB/2.

5. *ANB.* Thomas Heyward's name, and that of his father, is in the Middle Temple admission record for 10 January 1765 with the alternative spelling of Hayward. When his younger brother William was admitted to the Inn in 1772, the name was spelled Heyward. Despite the fact his father's name was Daniel, Thomas was often referred to as Thomas Heyward, Jr., as he had an uncle named Thomas.

6. Hamer, 9: 111, 586n.

7. Haw, 20.

8. Bicheno, 158.

9. Wallace, 215; Hamer, 10: 460; Rogers, 1962, 113.

10. Bonwick, 128.

11. Deas, 1: 166.

12. Haw, 77.

13. Kelley, 758.

14. Isaacson, 299.

15. Reed, William B., 1847, 1: 203

16. McCullough, 2001, 154.

17. Van Doren, 558-562.

18. *DAB.*

19. Haw, 87.

20. Moultrie, 1: 168.

21. Barry, 221.

22. Bonwick, 142.

23. Hamer, 12: 223.

24. Moultrie, 1: 404.

25. Moultrie, 1: 435.

26. Ferling, 219. Lord George Gordon was committed as a prisoner in the Tower of London, but was eventually acquitted of any responsibility for the acts of his supporters. While in the Tower he was joined by another State prisoner, Henry Laurens.

27. Wallace, 429.

28. Haw, 176

29. Bradford, 191.

30. Elizabeth Pinckney earned herself an entry in both the *Dictionary of American Biography* and the *American National Biography*.

31. Inoculation, which preceded vaccination, had been used in England for some thirty years.

32. William George Freeman was a friend of Thomas Corbett. He had been the deputy secretary of South Carolina from 1742 until he left for England with

Corbett and Peter Manigault in 1750. Hamer, 1: 95n.

33. Pinckney, Elise, 85.

34. Webber, 32: 119, 176-8.

35. Pinckney, Elise, 80, 81. Eliza Pinckney, a great experimenter with crops, would have appreciated the presence in present-day Ripley of the Royal Horticultural Society's Wisley Gardens. The Franklin house is now a museum dedicated to him.

36. Pinckney, Elise, 93.

37. Pinckney, Elise, 97, 160. As her surname is rare, Mrs. Evance may have been related to Thomas Evance, Treasurer of the Middle Temple in 1811.

38. Middle Temple, BOX 27, Bundle 6, no. 5; Elm Court was across the Lane from the Hall.

39. Middle Temple, BOX 28, Bundle 6, nos. 42 and 26. The other four exercises are nos. 16, 17, 27 and 43.

40. Rogers, 1962, 69.

41. Ravenal, 251.

42. Ravenal, 252.

43. Williams, 63.

44. Ravenal, 260.

45. Deas, 1: 99.

46. Zahniser, 39, 51. In 1779 Thomas Lynch set sail for the West Indies with his wife, en route to the South of France, where he hoped to recover his health. Unfortunately, their ship was lost with all on board. His widowed mother, who had lost her husband and son in less than three years, later married General Moultrie.

47. Moultrie, 1: 300.

48. Ravenal, 276, 277.

49. Cross, 1957, 238.

50. Jones, 199.

51. Higginbotham, 296.

52. Rogers, 1962, 114.

53. Cross, 1957, 240.

54. Ravenal, 297.The remark may have been made by C.C. rather than Thomas Pinckney: Rogers, 1980, 124; Williams, 175. The sentiments expressed were certainly those of both brothers.

55. Williams, 160, 186.

56. McDonnell, 343.

57. Bradford, 197.

58. In 2004 Thomas Ashe Lockhart, a direct descendant of that Laurens-Rutledge union and a member of the North Carolina Bar, presented a portrait of his kinsman John Laurens to the Middle Temple. It hangs by the American collection of the Inn's Library.

59. Steiner, 20; Flexner, chap.27.

60. Fitzpatrick, 21: 100; Whiteley, 189; Ellis, 80.

61. Stockdale, 67.

62. Cannon, 2: 515.

63. Stockdale, generally.

Chapter 7

1. Jones, 95.

2. Smith, Ellen Hart, 11, 22.

3. Smith, Ellen Hart, 46.

4. Hoffman, 2000, 163.

5. Bonwick, 54.

6. Barker, 351.

7. Hoffman, 1973, 105.

8. Land, 332.

9. Land, 297.

10. Land, 328.

11. Hoffman, 1973, 112.

12. Hoffman, 1973, 133, 135.

13. Bonwick, 142.

14. Smith, Ellen Hart, 163.

15. Hill, 10.

16. Morton, 53.

17. Hoffman, 1973, 114.

18. Shreve, 18, 23; Land, 313.

19. Shreve, 31.

20. Nagel, 1997, 111. Adams also found an appointment for his equally reprehensible son-in-law, William Stephens Smith, another former Washington aide, who had been his official secretary in London.

Chapter 8

1. See, DeConde.

2. Butterfield, *Adams Family Correspondence*, 5: 329. Laurens was staying over Stockdale's bookshop for a fourth and last time; John Adams and John Quincy had stayed there six months earlier. Stockdale, ch.7.

3. Matthews, Marly, 75.

4. Labaree, 37:415.

5. McCullough, 2001, 384.

6. Bonwick, 123.

7. Adams, William Howard, 100-113.

8. Adams, William Howard, chap.11.

9. Bemis, 1923, *The London Mission*, 228.

10. Zahniser, 127.

11. Pinckney, Revd. C.C., 99.

12. Bemis, 1923, *The London Mission*, 229.

13. For Jefferson's long flirtation with France, see the aptly titled book by O'Brien, Conor Cruise, *The Long Affair*.

14. Williams, 445n.

15. Pinckney, Revd. C.C., 109.

16. Pinckney, Revd. C.C., 102, 158.

17. Neel, 11.

18. Neel, 20.

19. Neel, 49, 86. Bond later also had consular responsibility for the Southern states.

20. Labaree, 37: 175n.

21. Jones, 23; Middle Temple, BOX 2, Bundle 6, p.61.

22. Williamson, 203.

23. Pinckney, Revd, C.C., 123.

24. Rogers, 1962, 264.

25. Cross, 1968, 103. Pinckney later married his deceased wife's widowed sister, Frances Middleton.

26. Nagel, 1997, 85.

27. Bemis, 1923, *Jay's Treaty*, 248n.

28. Fourteen years earlier John Jay had described Carmichael to Gouverneur Morris as "the most faithless and dangerous man that I have ever met with, in all my life". Stahr, 137.

29. Bemis, 1960, viii, 244, 251.

30. Pinckney, Revd. C.C., 146.

31. Cross, 1968,123. Deas married Anne, the daughter of Ralph Izard, whose edition of her father's letters has been quoted earlier.

32. Smith, Page, 1: 59, 70.

33. Williams, 309. C.C. Pinckney twice turned down the offer of the post of Secretary of War and once the more important post of Secretary of State.

34. SCHM, 1963, 64: 69.

35. Zahniser, 129.

36. Bicheno, 256.

37. Hecht, 115.

38. McCullough, 2001, 477.

39. Stinchcombe, 3: 73, 127.

40. Ellis, 253; Stinchcombe, 3: 530n.

41. Hill, 4.

42. Ford, 347.

43. Hill, 37.

44. DeConde, 151, 154, 172.

45. McCullough, 2001, 523.

46. Rutledge sat as Chief Justice for a short while before the Senate's refusal to ratify. His total service as an Associate and as Chief designate combined only added up to just over one year. Blair, the other Middle Templar on the Supreme Court managed more than five years, before being driven off by serious tinnitus.

47. O'Brien, 251.

48. Ford, 703. The meeting place was Falmouth, Cornwall, often used for trans-Atlantic sailings, and not the American Falmouth, now Portland, Maine (as suggested by one author).

49. William Smith added the middle name Loughton only in 1804 – and who can blame him? However, he will be referred to throughout by the longer name.

50. Rogers, 1962, chap. 5. We should like to express our indebtedness for the help received from the biography of Smith by the late George C.Rogers, a foremost historian of South Carolina.

51. Rogers, 1962, 81.

52. Rogers, 1962 ,91.

53. Campbell, 1849, 2: 531. Erskine, who was led by in the case by Lloyd Kenyon, made the important final speech as he was the better jury advocate. Kenyon succeeded Lord Mansfield as Chief Justice, and Erskine later became Lord Chancellor.

54. Matthews, Albert, 22.

55. Rogers, 1962, 208. Butler's seat was taken over in 1802 by John Gaillard, who together with his brother Theodore had been admitted to the Middle Temple in July 1782. Gaillard was to preside over the U.S. Senate for fourteen years in all, after the deaths of Vice-Presidents George Clinton and Elbridge Gerry.

56. Humphreys, 2: 22, 33; Stockdale, chs. 7 and 8. It is interesting to see that in 1807, some twenty years after his first visit, Humphreys once more called in at the bookshop for information. He reported to President Jefferson on 25 September 1807: "You may perhaps be surprised to learn that such independent characters as your old friend John Stockdale, and many others, look forward to a war with us as an almost inevitable event not very much to be deprecated, at least much less so than the loss of the smallest of their naval rights." Humphreys, 2: 362.

57. Rogers, 1962, 278, 304.
58. Matthews, Marly, 108.
59. Bradford, 202.

BIBLIOGRAPHY

Abbreviations used:
PMBH *Pennsylvania Magazine of Biography and History.*
SCHM *South Carolina Historical Magazine.*

Adams, (Revd.) John., *Laws of Success and Failure in Life,* Charlestown: A.E.Miller.

Adams, William Howard, *Gouverneur Morris—An Independent Life,* New Haven: Yale U.P., 2003.

Alberts, Robert C., *Benjamin West,* Boston: Houghton Mifflin, 1978.

Allen, James, "Diary of James Allen, Esq., of Philadelphia", PMBH, 1885, vol.9.

Baker, J.H., *The Inner Temple,* London: Inner Temple, 1991.

Dallagh, James Curtis, *The Letters of Richard Henry Lee,* New York: Macmillan, 1829.

Barker, Charles Albro, *The Background to the Revolution in Maryland,* New Haven: Yale U.P., 1940.

Barry, Richard, *Mr. Rutledge of South Carolina,* New York: Duell, Sloan and Pearce, 1942.

Beck, James M., *The Constitution of the United States,* New York: George H. Doran, 1924.

Bemis, Samuel Flagg, *Jay's Treaty,* New York, Macmillan, 1923.

Bemis, Samuel Flagg, "The London Mission of Thomas Pinckney, 1792-1796", American Historical   Review, 1923, vol.28.

Bemis, Samuel Flagg, *Pinckney's Treaty—America's Advantage from Europe's Distress,* 1783-1800, Westport: Greenwood Press, 1960.

Bethea, Andrew J., *The Contribution of Charles Pinckney to the Formation of the American Union,* Richmond: Garrett & Massie, 1937.

Bicheno, Hugh, *Rebels and Redcoats,* London: HarperCollins, 2003.

Billings, Warren M., *A Little Parliament—The Virginia Assembly in the Seventeenth Century,* Richmond: Library of Virginia and Jamestown-Yorktown Foundation, 2004.

Boatner, Mark Mayo, *Cassell's Biographical Dictionary of the American War of Independence 1763-1783,* London: Cassell, 1973.

Bonwick, Colin, *The American Revolution*, New York: Palgrave Macmillan, 2005.

Botein, Stephen, "The Legal Profession in Colonial North America", in Prest, 141.

Bowen, Catherine Drinker, *Miracle at Philadelphia, The Story of the Constitutional Convention May to September 1787*, American Past/B.O.M.C., 1986.

Boyd, Julian P. and others, *The Papers of Thomas Jefferson*, Princeton U.P., 1950-.

Bradford, M.E., *Founding Fathers*, Lawrence: U. of Kansas P., 1994.

Burd, Walker Lewis, *Extracts from Chief Justice Allen's Letter Book*, 1897.

Burnett, Edmund Cody, *The Continental Congress*, New York: Macmillan, 1941.

Butterfield, L.H., *Adams Family Correspondence*, Cambridge: Harvard U.P., 1961.

Butterfield, L.H., *Diary and Autobiography of John Adams*, Cambridge: Harvard U.P., 1961.

Call, Arthur H., *John Wilkes—The Scandalous Father of Civil Liberty*, New Haven: Yale U.P., 2005.

Campbell, Lord (John), *Lives of the Chief Justices of England*, London: John Murray, 1849.

Campbell, Lord (John), *Lives of the Lord Chancellors*, London: John Murray, 1868.

Canady, Hoyt P., *Gentlemen of the Bar—Lawyers in Colonial South Carolina*, New York: Garland, 1987.

Cannon, Garland, *The Letters of Sir William Jones*, Oxford U.P., 1970.

Cohen, Norman S., "William Allen, Chief Justice of Pennsylvania, 1704-1780", unpubl. Ph.D., Univ. of Calif.: Berkeley, 1966

Cohen, Norman S., "The Philadelphia Election Riot of 1742", PMBH, 1968, vol. 92.

Colbourn, H.Trevor (ed.), "A Pennsylvania Farmer at the Court of King George", PMBH, 1962, vol. 86.

Coleman, John M., *Thomas McKean—Forgotten Leader of the Revolution*, Rockaway: American Faculty Press, 1975.

Cross, Jack L., "Letters of Thomas Pinckney 1775-1780", SCHM, 1957, vol.

58.

Cross, Jack L., *London Mission: The First Critical Years*, Michigan State U.P., 1968.

Deas, Anne Izard, *Correspondence of Ralph Izard of South Carolina 1774-1804*, New York: Francis, 1844, vol. 1 only published.

DeConde, Alexander, *The Quasi-War—The Politics and Diplomacy of the Undeclared War with France 1797-1801*, New York: Charles Scribner's Sons, 1966

Duman, Daniel, "The English Bar in the Georgian Era", in Prest, 87.

Eckenrode, H.J., *The Randolphs—The Story of a Virginia Family*, New York: Bobbs Merrill, 1946.

Einstein, Lewis, *Divided Loyalties—Americans in England during the War of Independence*, Boston: Houghton Mifflin, 1933.

Ellis, Joseph J., *His Excellency George Washington*, London: Faber and Faber, 2004.

Ferling, John, *Setting the World Ablaze—Washington, Adams, Jefferson, and the American Revolution*, Oxford U.P. 2000.

Fitzpatrick, John C., *Writings of George Washington*, Washington: Government Printing Office, 1939.

Flexner, James Thomas, *The Young Hamilton*, London: Collins, 1978.

Ford, Worthington Chauncey, "Letters of William Vans Murray to John Quincy Adams", 63d Congress, 2b Session, vol. 148, Washington: Government Printing Office, 1914.

Franklin, Benjamin, *The Autobiography and Other Writings*, New York: Penguin, 1986.

George, M.Dorothy, *London Life in the Eighteenth Century*, London: Penguin, 1966.

Goodman, Nathan G., *Benjamin Rush—Physician and Citizen 1746-1813*, Philadelphia: U. of Pennsylvania P. 1934.

Graydon, Alexander, *Memoirs of a Life Chiefly Passed in Pennsylvania*, Edinburgh: Blackwood, 1822.

Greene, Jack P. and Pole, J.R., *A Companion to the American Revolution*, Oxford: Blackwell, 2004.

Hamer, Philip M. and others, *The Papers of Henry Laurens*, Columbia: U. of South Carolina P., 1968-2003, 16 vols.

Hancock, David, *Citizens of the World*, Cambridge U.P., 1995.

Harper, Steven C., "Delawares and Pennsylvanians after the Walking Purchase", in Pencak, William A. and Richter, Daniel K., Friends and Enemies in Penn's Woods, University Park: Penn State U.P., 2004.

Haw, James, *John and Edward Rutledge of South Carolina*, Athens: U. of Georgia P., 1997.

Hecht, Marie B., *John Quincy Adams—A Personal History of an Independent Man*, New York: Macmillan, 1972.

Higginbotham, Don, 'The War for Independence, to Saratoga', in Greene, Jack P. and Pole, J.R.

Hill, Peter, *William Vans Murray: Federalist Diplomat*, Syracuse U.P., 1971.

Hoffman, Ronald, *A Spirit of Dissension*, Baltimore: Johns Hopkins U.P., 1973.

Hoffman, Ronald, *Princes of Ireland, Planters of Maryland—A Carroll Saga 1500-1782*, Chapel Hill: U. of North Carolina P., 2000.

Holdsworth, W.S., *A History of English Law*, London: Methuen, 1924, 1938.

Holland, Randy J., *The Delaware Constitution, A Reference Guide*, Westport: Greenwood Press, 2002.

Howard, A.E.Dick, *The Road from Runymede: Magna Carta and Constitutionalism in America*, Charlottesville: U. of Virginia P., 1968.

Humphreys, Frank Landon, *Life and Times of David Humphreys*, New York: Putnam, 1917.

Isaacson, Walter, *Benjamin Franklin—An American Life*, New York, Simon & Schuster, 2003.

Jacobson, David L., *John Dickinson and the Revolution in Pennsylvania, 1764-1756*, U. of California P., 1965.

Jensen, Merrill, *The Articles of Confederation, An Interpretation of the Social-Constitutional History of the American Revolution 1774-1781*, Madison: U. of Wisconsin P., 1959.

Jones, E. Alfred, *American Members of the Inns of Court*, London: St.Catherine's Press, 1924.

Kelley, Joseph J., *Pennsylvania—The Colonial Years 1681-1776*, Garden City: Doubleday, 1980.

Kimball, David A., and Quinn, Miriam, "William Allen—Benjamin Chew Correspondence 1763-64", PMBH, 1966, vol.90.

Klein, Milton M., *The American Whig—William Livingston of New York*, New York: Garland, 1993.

Konkle, Burton A., *Benjamin Chew 1722-1810*, Philadelphia: U. of Pennsylvania P., 1932.

Labaree, Leonard W. and others, *The Papers of Benjamin Franklin*, New Haven: Yale U.P., 1959-.

Land, Aubrey C., *The Dulanys of Maryland*, Baltimore: Johns Hopkins U.P., 1968.

Lee, Richard Henry, *Life of Arthur Lee LL.D.*, Boston: Wells and Lilly, 1829.

Macassey, Lynden, *Middle Templars' Associations with America*, London: Middle Temple, 2d. ed., 1998.

McCullough, David, *John Adams*, New York: Simon & Schuster, 2001.

McDonnell, Michael A., "Resistance to the American Revolution", in Greene, Jack P. and Pole, J.R.

Massey, Gregory D., *John Laurens and the American Revolution*, Columbia: U. of South Carolina P., 2000.

Matthews, Albert, *Journal of William Loughton Smith 1790-1791*, Cambridge U.P., 1917.

Matthews, Marly D., *Forgotten Founder—The Life and Times of Charles Pinckney*, Columbia: U. of South Carolina P., 2004.

Middlekauf, Robert, *Benjamin Franklin and his Enemies,* Berkeley: U. of California P., 1998.

Moreton, Brian N. and Spinelli, Donald C., *Beaumarchais and the American Revolution*, New York: Lexington Books, 2003.

Morgan, Edmund S., *Benjamin Franklin*, New Have: Yale U.P., 2002.

Morton, John C., *Shapers of the Great Debate at the Constitutional Convention of 1787*, Westport: Greenwood Press, 2006.

Moultrie, William, *Memoirs of the American Revolution*, 1802.

Nagel, Paul C., *The Lees of Virginia—Seven Generations of an American Family*, Oxford U.P. 1990.

Nagel, Paul C., *John Quincy Adams: A Public Life, a Private Life,* New York: Knopf, 1997.

Nash, Gary B., *First City: Philadelphia in the Forging of Historical Memory*, Philadelphia: U. of Pennsylvania P., 2002.

Neel, Joanne Loewe, *Phineas Bond*, Philadelphia: U. of Pennsylvania P., 1968.

O'Brien, Conor Cruise, *The Long Affair - Thomas Jefferson and the French Revolution, 1785-1800*, London: Sinclair-Stevenson, 1966.

Oliver, Andrew, *The Journal of Samuel Curwen*, Cambridge: Harvard U.P., 1972.

Peters, Ellen A., 'Common Law Antecedents of Constitutional Law in Connecticut', 53 Alabama L.R 1989.

Peterson, Merrill D., *Thomas Jefferson and the New Nation*, Oxford U.P., 1970.

Pinckney, (Revd.) Charles Cotesworth, *Life and Times of General Thomas Pinckney*, Boston: Houghton, Mifflin, 1895.

Pinckney, Elise, *The Letter Book of Eliza Pinckney 1739-1762*, Chapel Hill: U. of North Carolina P., 1972.

Pottle, Frederick A. (ed.), *Boswell's London Journal 1762-1763*, Harmondsworth: Penguin, 1966.

Potts, Louis W., *Arthur Lee—A Virtuous Revolutionary*, Baton Rouge: Louisiana State U.P., 1981.

Prest, Wilfrid (ed.), *Lawyers in Early Modern England and America*, London: Croom Helm, 1981.

Priestley, J.B., *The Prince of Pleasure and his Regency 1811-1820*, London: Sphere Books, 1971.

Randolph, Edmund, *History of Virginia*, Charlottesville: U. of Virginia P., 1970.

Ravenal, Harriott Horry, *Eliza Pinckney*, London: Murray, 1896.

Reardon, John J., *Peyton Randolph 1721-1775*, Durham: Carolina Academic Press, 1982.

Reed, Henry, "Life of Joseph Reed", in Sparks, Jared, The Library of American Biography, Boston: Little, Brown, 1846, vol. 18.

Reed, William B., *Life and Correspondence of Joseph Reed*, Philadelphia: Lindsay and Blakiston, 1847.

Reed, William B., *Life of Esther Reed*, Philadelphia: C. Sherman, 1853.

Riggs, A.R., *The Nine Lives of Arthur Lee—Virginia Patriot*, Williamsburg:

Virginia Independence Bicentennial Comm., 1976.

Roche, John F., *Joseph Reed*, New York: Columbia U.P., 1957, No. 595 of the Columbia Studies in the Social Sciences.

Rogers, George C., *The Evolution of a Federalist: William Loughton Smith of Charleston (1758-1812)*, Columbia: U. of South Carolina P., 1962.

Rogers, George C., *Charleston in the Age of the Pinckneys*, Columbia: U. of South Carolina P., 1980.

Rowe, G.S., *Embattled Bench—The Pennsylvania Supreme Court and the Forging of a Democratic Society 1684-1809*, U. of Delaware P., 1994.

Ryerson, Richard Alan, *The Revolution is now Begun—The Radical Committees of Philadelphia, 1765-1776*, U. of Pennsylvania P., 1978.

Sainsbury, John, *Disaffected Patriots. London Supporters of Revolutionary America, 1769-1782*, Kingston: McGill-Queen's U.P., 1987.

Scull, Florence Doughty, *John Dickinson Sounds the Alarm*, Philadelphia: Auerbach, 1972.

Selby, John E., *The Revolution in Virginia 1775-1783*, Williamsburg: Colonial Williamsburg Foundation, 1988.

Shreve, L.G., *Tench Tilghman—The Life and Times of Washington's Aide-de-Camp*, Centreville: Tidewater, 1982.

Skemp, Sheila L., *William Franklin*, Oxford U.P., 1990.

Smith, Billy (ed.), *Life in Early Philadelphia*, University Park: Penn State U.P., 1995.

Smith, Ellen Hart, *Charles Carroll of Carrollton*, Cambridge: Harvard U.P., 1945.

Smith, Jean E., *John Marshall, Definer of a Nation*, New York: Henry Holt, 1996.

Smith, Page, "Election of 1796", in Schlesinger, Jr., Arthur M., History of American Presidential Elections 1789-1986, New York: Chelsea House, 1985, vol.1.

Smith, Paul H., *Letters of Delegates to Congress 1774-1789*, Washington: Library of Congress, 1982, vol.9.

Sosin, Jack M., *Agents and Merchants*, Lincoln: U. of Nebraska P., 1965.

Stahr, Walter, *John Jay—Founding Father*, New York, Hambledon and London, 2005.

Steiner, Bernard C., *The Life and Correspondence of James McHenry*, Cleveland: Burrows Brothers, 1907.

Stinchcombe, William C. and others, *The Papers of John Marshall*, Chapel Hill: U. of North Carolina P. 1979.

Stillé, Charles J., *The Life and Times of John Dickinson 1732-1808*, Philadelphia: Historical Society of Pennsylvania, 1891.

Stockdale, Eric, *'Tis Treason, My Good Man! Four Revolutionary Presidents and a Piccadilly Bookshop*, New Castle: Oak Knoll Press; London: British Library, 2005.

Teignmouth, Lord, (John Shore), *Memoirs of the Letters, Writings and Correspondence of Sir William Jones*, London: John Parker, 1835.

[Tilghman, Tench], *Memoir of Lt. Col. Tench Tilghman*, Albany: Munsell, 1876.

Tyler, Moses Coit, *The Literary History of the American Revolution 1763-1783*, New York: C.P.Putnam's Sons, 1897.

Van Doren, Carl, *Benjamin Franklin*, New York: Viking, 1938.

Walker, Lewis Burd, *The Burd Papers, Selections from the Letters Written by Edward Burd 1763-1828*, n.p., 1899.

Wallace, David Duncan, *The Life of Henry Laurens*, New York: C.P.Putnam's Sons, 1915.

Warren, Charles, *The Making of the Constitution*, New York: Barnes & Noble, 1937.

Webber, Mabel L., (ed.) "Letters of Peter Manigault", SCHM, vols. 31-33.

Weslager, C.C., *Stamp Act Congress*, Cranbury: Associated University Presses, 1976.

Whiteley, Emily Stone, *Washington and his Aides-de-Camp*, New York: Macmillan, 1936.

Williams, Frances Leigh, *A Founding Family—The Pinckneys of South Carolina*, New York: Harcourt Brace Jovanovich, 1978.

Williamson, J.Bruce, *The Middle Temple Bench Book*, London: Middle Temple, 1937.

Wright, Esmond, *Franklin of Philadelphia*, Cambridge: Harvard U.P., 1986.

Young, Henry J., "Treason and its Punishment in Revolutionary Pennsylvania", PMBH, 1966 vol.90.

Zahniser, Marvin R., *Charles Cotesworth Pinckney—Founding Father*, Chapel Hill, U. of North Carolina Press, 1962.

TABLE 1
AMERICAN COLONIST MEMBERS
OF THE MIDDLE TEMPLE
ALPHABETICAL LIST

Name	State
Walter Aitchison	Virginia
Robert Alexander	Virginia
Andrew Allen	Pennsylvania
James Allen	Pennsylvania
William Allen	Pennsylvania
John Ambler	Virginia
Robert Auchmuty	Massachusetts
Henry Lee Ball	Virginia
John Banister	Virginia
Jonathan Belcher	Massachusetts
Richard Beresford	South Carolina
William Berkeley	Virginia
Francis Bernard	New Jersey/Massachusetts
Robert Beverley	Virginia
Robert Beverley	Virginia
John Blair	Virginia
Robert Bolling	Virginia
Phineas Bond	Pennsylvania
Thomas Bordley	Maryland
William Boyd	New Hampshire
John Leeds Bozman	Maryland
John Brice	Maryland
John Bridges	New York
Sampson Broughton	New York
Sampson Shelton Broughton	New York
William Burnet	New York/Massachusetts

William Burnet	New York/Massachusetts
William Ward Burrows	South Carolina
William Byrd	Virginia
Colonel William Byrd	Virginia
Charles Carroll	Maryland
George Carter	Virginia
John Carter	Virginia
Wilson Cary	Virginia
Gabriel Cathcart	North Carolina
John Chambers	New York
Benjamin Chew	Pennsylvania
Benjamin Chew	Pennsylvania
Thomas Child	North Carolina
Edward Chilton	Virginia
Henry Churchill	Virginia
Jonathan Perrie Coffin	Massachusetts
John Colleton	South Carolina
Gawen Corbin	Virginia
Alexander Cumming	South Carolina
William Allen Deas	South Carolina
John Dickinson	Pennsylvania/ Delaware
Joseph Ball Downman	Virginia
William Drayton	South Carolina
Paul Dudley	Massachusetts
William Dudley	Massachusetts
Daniel Dulany	Maryland
Daniel Dulany	Maryland
Lloyd Dulany	Maryland
William Dunbar	New York
Thomas Elde	New York
George Evelyn	Maryland

William Fauntleroy	Virginia
William Ferrar (or Farrar)	Virginia
Henry Fitzhugh	Virginia
William Franklin	Pennsylvania
Moses Franks	Pennsylvania
John Gaillard	South Carolina
John Gaillard	South Carolina
Theodore Gaillard	South Carolina
Henry Gibbes	South Carolina
Robert Goldsborough	Maryland
Samuel Gordon	South Carolina
David Graeme	Carolina
William Gregory	South Carolina
Cyrus Griffin	Virginia
John Faucheraud Grimke	South Carolina
Andrew Hamilton	Pennsylvania
William Hamilton	Pennsylvania
John Hammond	Maryland
Benjamin Harrison	Virginia
Carter Henry Harrison	Virginia
Alexander Harvey	South Carolina
Philemon Hemsley	Maryland
Thomas Heyward	South Carolina
William Heyward	South Carolina
William Hicks	Pennsylvania
James Hollyday	Maryland
Charles Lucas Pinckney Horry (formerly Daniel Horry)	South Carolina
Daniel Horsemanden	New York
James Edmund Houston	Georgia
Rev. Isaac Hunt	Pennsylvania

Thomas Hutchinson	Massachusetts
Jared Ingersoll	Pennsylvania
Henry Izard	South Carolina
Joseph Jekyll	Massachusetts
James Johnston	South Carolina
Robert Johnston (assumed the name of Ketelby)	South Carolina
Joseph Jones	Virginia
Nathaniel Jones	New Jersey
Henry Justice	Virginia
William Keith	Pennsylvania
William Kempe	New York
Abel Ketelby (or Kettelby)	South Carolina
Edmund Key	Maryland
Philip Barton Key	Maryland
Thomas Kimberley	South Carolina
John Laurens	South Carolina
Thomas Lawrence	Maryland
Alexander Lawson	Maryland
Arthur Lee	Virginia
Henry Lee ("Light Horse Harry")	Virginia
Philip Thomas Lee	Virginia
Richard Lee	Virginia/Maryland
Robert Lightfoot	Virginia/ Rhode Island
Robert Livingston	New York
Robert Livingston	New York
Walter Livingston	New York
William Livingston	New York
Peter Livius	New Hampshire
Cornelius Low	New Jersey
Thomas Lynch	South Carolina

Benjamin Lynde	Massachusetts
George Frankley	South Carolina
Hext McCall	South Carolina
Nicholas Maccubbin	Maryland
Henry Eustace McCulloh	North Carolina
Thomas McKean	Delaware/ Pennsylvania
John Mackenzie	South Carolina
Robert Mackenzie	Virginia
Joseph Manigault	South Carolina
Thompson Mason	Virginia
John Matthews	South Carolina
William Mazyck	South Carolina
James Michie	South Carolina
Arthur Middleton	South Carolina
Robert Milligan	Maryland
John Morris	Pennsylvania
Alexander Moultrie	South Carolina
Joseph Murray	New York
William Vans Murray	Maryland
Philip Neyle	South Carolina
Henry Nicholes	South Carolina
William Oliphant	South Carolina
Peter Oliver	Massachusetts
Anthony Palmer	Pennsylvania
John Parker	South Carolina
George Percy	Virginia
James Peronneau	South Carolina
Ralph Peters	Pennsylvania
Samuel Phepoe	South Carolina
Charles Pinckney	South Carolina
Charles Cotesworth Pinckney	South Carolina

Miles Brewton Pinckney	South Carolina
Roger Pinckney	South Carolina
Thomas Pinckney	South Carolina
Peter Porcher	South Carolina
William Dummer Powell	Massachusetts
John Julius Pringle	South Carolina
Charles Pryce	Georgia
Walter Ralegh	Virginia
John Randolph	Virginia
Peyton Randolph	Virginia
Ryland Randolph	Virginia
William Rawle	Pennsylvania
Joseph Reed	New Jersey
William Roberts	Virginia
Christopher Robinson	Virginia
George Boone Roupell	South Carolina
Edward Rutledge	South Carolina
Hugh Rutledge	South Carolina
John Rutledge	South Carolina
George Sandys	Virginia
John Saunders	Virginia
Gustavus Scott	Maryland
Edward Shippen	Pennsylvania
Richard Shubrick	South Carolina
Thomas Shubrick	South Carolina
Thomas Simons	South Carolina
Clement Simpson	Georgia
James Simpson	South Carolina
William Simpson	South Carolina
Benjamin Smith	North Carolina
James Smith	South Carolina

William Loughton Smith	South Carolina
William Stephens	Georgia
Stevens Thompson	Virginia
Edward Tilghman	Pennsylvania
Richard Tilghman	Maryland
Paul Trapier	South Carolina
James Trent	New Jersey
Jacob Shoemaker Waln	Pennsylvania
Nicholas Waln	Pennsylvania
Joshua Ward	South Carolina
William Wharton	Massachusetts
Beverley Whiting	Virginia
John Wilcox	Virginia
William Wragg	South Carolina
James Wright	South Carolina / Georgia
John Izard Wright	South Carolina
Elias Wrixon	Pennsylvania
Jasper Yeates	Pennsylvania
Henry Yonge	Georgia
Archibald Young	South Carolina

TABLE 2
AMERICAN COLONIST MEMBERS
OF THE MIDDLE TEMPLE
STATE LIST

Name	State
Thomas McKean	Delaware/ Pennsylvania
James Edmund Houston	Georgia
Charles Pryce	Georgia
Clement Simpson	Georgia
William Stephens	Georgia
Henry Yonge	Georgia
Thomas Bordley	Maryland
John Leeds Bozman	Maryland
John Brice	Maryland
Charles Carroll	Maryland
Daniel Dulany	Maryland
Daniel Dulany	Maryland
Lloyd Dulany	Maryland
George Evelyn	Maryland
Robert Goldsborough	Maryland
John Hammond	Maryland
Philemon Hemsley	Maryland
James Hollyday	Maryland
Edmund Key	Maryland
Philip Barton Key	Maryland
Thomas Lawrence	Maryland
Alexander Lawson	Maryland
Nicholas Maccubbin	Maryland
Robert Milligan	Maryland
William Vans Murray	Maryland
Gustavus Scott	Maryland

Richard Tilghman	Maryland
Robert Auchmuty	Massachusetts
Jonathan Belcher	Massachusetts
Jonathan Perrie Coffin	Massachusetts
Paul Dudley	Massachusetts
William Dudley	Massachusetts
Thomas Hutchinson	Massachusetts
Joseph Jekyll	Massachusetts
Benjamin Lynde	Massachusetts
Peter Oliver	Massachusetts
William Dummer Powell	Massachusetts
William Wharton	Massachusetts
William Boyd	New Hampshire
Peter Livius	New Hampshire
Francis Bernard	New Jersey/Massachusetts
Nathaniel Jones	New Jersey
Cornelius Low	New Jersey
Joseph Reed	New Jersey
James Trent	New Jersey
John Bridges	New York
Sampson Broughton	New York
Sampson Shelton Broughton	New York
William Burnet	New York/Massachusetts
William Burnet	New York/Massachusetts
John Chambers	New York
Thomas Elde	New York
Daniel Horsemanden	New York
William Kempe	New York
Robert Livingston	New York
Robert Livingston	New York
Walter Livingston	New York
William Livingston	New York

Joseph Murray	New York
William Dunbar	New York
Gabriel Cathcart	North Carolina
Thomas Child	North Carolina
Henry Eustace McCulloh	North Carolina
Benjamin Smith	North Carolina
Andrew Allen	Pennsylvania
James Allen	Pennsylvania
William Allen	Pennsylvania
Phineas Bond	Pennsylvania
Benjamin Chew	Pennsylvania
Benjamin Chew	Pennsylvania
John Dickinson	Pennsylvania/ Delaware
William Franklin	Pennsylvania
Moses Franks	Pennsylvania
Andrew Hamilton	Pennsylvania
William Hamilton	Pennsylvania
William Hicks	Pennsylvania
Rev. Isaac Hunt	Pennsylvania
Jared Ingersoll	Pennsylvania
William Keith	Pennsylvania
John Morris	Pennsylvania
Anthony Palmer	Pennsylvania
Ralph Peters	Pennsylvania
William Rawle	Pennsylvania
Edward Shippen	Pennsylvania
Edward Tilghman	Pennsylvania
Jacob Shoemaker Waln	Pennsylvania
Nicholas Waln	Pennsylvania
Elias Wrixon	Pennsylvania
Jasper Yeates	Pennsylvania
Richard Beresford	South Carolina

William Ward Burrows	South Carolina
John Colleton	South Carolina
Alexander Cumming	South Carolina
William Allen Deas	South Carolina
William Drayton	South Carolina
John Gaillard	South Carolina
John Gaillard	South Carolina
Theodore Gaillard	South Carolina
Henry Gibbes	South Carolina
Samuel Gordon	South Carolina
David Graeme	South Carolina
William Gregory	South Carolina
John Faucheraud Grimke	South Carolina
Alexander Harvey	South Carolina
Thomas Heyward	South Carolina
William Heyward	South Carolina
Charles Lucas Pinckney Horry	South Carolina
(formerly Daniel Horry)	
Henry Izard	South Carolina
James Johnston	South Carolina
Robert Johnston (assumed the	South Carolina
name of Ketelby)	
Abel Ketelby (or Kettelby)	South Carolina
Thomas Kimberley	South Carolina
John Laurens	South Carolina
Thomas Lynch	South Carolina
George Lyttelton	South Carolina
Hext McCall	South Carolina
John Mackenzie	South Carolina
Joseph Manigault	South Carolina
John Matthews	South Carolina
William Mazyck	South Carolina

James Michie	South Carolina
Arthur Middleton	South Carolina
Alexander Moultrie	South Carolina
Philip Neyle	South Carolina
Henry Nicholes	South Carolina
William Oliphant	South Carolina
John Parker	South Carolina
James Peronneau	South Carolina
Samuel Phepoe	South Carolina
Charles Pinckney	South Carolina
Charles Cotesworth Pinckney	South Carolina
Miles Brewton Pinckney	South Carolina
Roger Pinckney	South Carolina
Thomas Pinckney	South Carolina
Peter Porcher	South Carolina
John Julius Pringle	South Carolina
George Boone Roupell	South Carolina
Edward Rutledge	South Carolina
Hugh Rutledge	South Carolina
John Rutledge	South Carolina
Richard Shubrick	South Carolina
Thomas Shubrick	South Carolina
Thomas Simons	South Carolina
James Simpson	South Carolina
William Simpson	South Carolina
James Smith	South Carolina
William Loughton Smith	South Carolina
Paul Trapier	South Carolina
Joshua Ward	South Carolina
William Wragg	South Carolina
John Izard Wright	South Carolina
James Wright	South Carolina / Georgia

Archibald Young	South Carolina
Walter Aitchison	Virginia
Robert Alexander	Virginia
John Ambler	Virginia
Henry Lee Ball	Virginia
John Banister	Virginia
William Berkeley	Virginia
Robert Beverley	Virginia
Robert Beverley	Virginia
John Blair	Virginia
Robert Bolling	Virginia
William Byrd	Virginia
William Byrd	Virginia
George Carter	Virginia
John Carter	Virginia
Wilson Cary	Virginia
Edward Chilton	Virginia
Henry Churchill	Virginia
Gawen Corbin	Virginia
Joseph Ball Downman	Virginia
William Fauntleroy	Virginia
William Ferrar (or Farrar)	Virginia
Henry Fitzhugh	Virginia
Cyrus Griffin	Virginia
Benjamin Harrison	Virginia
Carter Henry Harrison	Virginia
Joseph Jones	Virginia
Henry Justice	Virginia
Arthur Lee	Virginia
Henry Lee ("Light Horse Harry")	Virginia
Philip Thomas Lee	Virginia
Richard Lee	Virginia

Robert Lightfoot	Virginia/ Rhode Island
Robert Mackenzie	Virginia
Thompson Mason	Virginia
George Percy	Virginia
Walter Ralegh	Virginia
John Randolph	Virginia
Peyton Randolph	Virginia
Ryland Randolph	Virginia
William Roberts	Virginia
Christopher Robinson	Virginia
George Sandys	Virginia
John Saunders	Virginia
Stevens Thompson	Virginia
Beverley Whiting	Virginia
John Wilcox	Virginia

Index